BLOG MARKETING

THE REVOLUTIONARY NEW WAY TO INCREASE SALES, BUILD YOUR BRAND, AND GET EXCEPTIONAL RESULTS

Jeremy Wright

McGraw-Hill

New York   Chicago   San Francisco   Lisbon   London   Madrid   Mexico City
Milan   New Delhi   San Juan   Seoul   Singapore   Sydney   Toronto

1 2 3 4 5 6 7 8 9 0   DOC/DOC   0 1 9 8 7 6 5

ISBN 0-07-226251-6

McGraw-Hill books are available at special quantity discounts to use as premiums and sales promotions, or for use in corporate training programs. For more information, please write to the Director of Special Sales, Professional Publishing, McGraw-Hill, Two Penn Plaza, New York, NY 10121-2298. Or contact your local bookstore.

Blog Marketing: The Revolutionary New Way to Increase Sales, Build Your Brand, and Get Exceptional Results

The sponsoring editor for this book was Marjorie McAneny and the project editor was Janet Walden. The copy editor was Lisa Theobald, the proofreader was Pam Vevea, and the indexer was Valerie Robbins. Composition and illustration by International Typesetting & Composition. Cover design by Jeff Weeks.

This book was composed with Adobe® InDesign®.

Library of Congress Cataloging-in-Publication Data

Wright, Jeremy.
    Blog marketing : the revolutionary new way to increase sales, build your
    brand, and get exceptional results / by Jeremy Wright.
        p.   cm.
    ISBN 0-07-226251-6
    1. Marketing — Weblogs.   2. Weblogs — Economic aspects.   I. Title.
    HF5415.W82 2006
    658.8'72 — dc22
                                                        2005026118

CONTENTS

FOREWORD

When a bandwagon is this large and this loud, it's just about impossible to resist jumping on, and blogging—in particular, blogging for business—definitely falls into that category. Whether you read *Business Week, Fortune, Smart Company, Wired,* or even *People* and *Entertainment Weekly,* you've encountered lots of buzz about a reinvention of web pages called *weblogs,* or *blogs* for short.

But while many people still think of blogs as online diaries or journals, a small handful of forward-thinkers, leaders in the march to tomorrow, have recognized the more profound impact on the world of digital communications. Jeremy Wright is in this group, and you're lucky to have a copy of his book in your hands: without being cliquish or presenting the information as a holy writ or battle cry, Wright explores what blogging is and how it can help you better and more effectively market your business in the increasingly important online world.

I should know, too. By following the advice of Wright and many other bloggers, I now market my own management innovation and communications strategy consulting business a thousand times more effectively than I did in the past, and without spending a dime on adverts, sponsorships, or any other traditional marketing. You can see for yourself at my business and management blog, http://blog.intuitive.com/, which produces consulting clients and speaking engagements worldwide, and at my Q&A weblog, http://www.askdavetaylor.com/, which produces a significant revenue stream for my company.

Also, keep in mind that it's really not about blog marketing, per se—that's just the channel through which you need to reinvent how you communicate with both your customers and your marketplace. After all, it's the *potential* customers that you *can't* reach that are your best target for future growth, and dynamic, engaging, and informative business blogs are an amazing avenue for reaching them in a way that has never been possible with other channels.

But even if you don't want to blog, don't want to embrace this new, better, and easier way of maintaining a topical and engaging dialog with your customers and market, it's still imperative that you keep track of the discussion happening in what we call the *blogosphere*, the world of weblogs. Thousands of active weblogs have one characteristic that might surprise you: information disseminates with incredible speed. With blogs, ideas and news really do travel like the proverbial wildfire!

A quick example: Awhile back I wrote an analysis of how an online firm had mismanaged its transition from a free service to a paid service, a discussion of how the announcement could have been handled more smartly and with less of a furious reaction from the customer community. Within *90 minutes*, the CEO of the company had added his own response and commentary—all in less time than it would take a traditional news article to be printed and proofread. If I'd written about your company, would you have known about it promptly enough to respond and catch the fast-traveling buzz, or would you be surprised weeks later when a general community consensus came to your attention through the traditional (read *slow*) media outlet reports?

The world of business is changing profoundly, redefining marketing, public relations, and customer communication, among other things. If you aren't inviting this change into your own business, if you aren't jumping on the bandwagon, your competitors are, and I guarantee they'll leave you in the dust wondering where your sales have gone and why your customers are deserting in droves.

Wright talks extensively about "transmitting versus engaging" and "creating positive experiences with your customers" in *Blog Marketing.* Pay attention! They're vital to your very survival as a business; I can offer you no greater advice than to read and study this book as if your corporate life depends upon it. Because it does.

Dave Taylor
Publisher, The Intuitive Life Business Blog
blog.intuitive.com
Boulder, Colorado

For Shannon, for being everything that's beautiful in the world.
For Evan and Alex, for giving me reasons to smile, to be proud, and
to be humble every day. For every blogger. You are a community of
inspiration to me. And for Will and Jacob, both of whom believed
in me, no matter what.

ACKNOWLEDGMENTS

Thank you to my wife, Shannon, for being my refuge, encouragement, the love of my life, and every reason I want to get up in the morning. When I'm not with you it feels like someone turned the sun off. Neil Salkind, my agent, for making me believe I could do a book, and for helping me live up to my potential. Will Elder, for being an inspiration in life and in death. I miss you, Will. Mitch Tulloch, for hooking me up with Studio B, the rockingest agency ever. Suw Charman, Neville Hobson, Darren Barefoot, Boris Mann, Roland Tanglao, Kris Krug, Lee Lefever, and any other blogger who ever believed in me, laughed with me, listened to me, or linked to me. Sean Walberg, for opening my mind to writing a book. Neville Hobson, for helping out on the GM blogs bit. Nick Wreden, for lending me his insight into PR and marketing. Michael Pusateri, for giving me all of his knowledge into the Disney blog situation. Shel and Robert, for motivating me to get this done on time! Arieanna Foley, for rocking it harder than anyone I've ever seen. Without you, this book wouldn't be alive.

Yvonne DiVita, for being a great technical editor, debater, and supporter. Margie McAneny, for being the reason I chose McGraw-Hill as the publisher, and for never giving me a reason to doubt that decision. Lisa Theobald, for not only being a great copy editor, but for also being a fantastic sounding board as ideas evolved (even late in the editing process). Jon Watson, for helping with research. Steven Streight, for being a "straight shooter," in spite of everything and everyone. Robert Scoble and Jeremy Zawodny, for inspiring me to start blogging all those years ago. Marc Orchant, for keeping me going in the middle of the night in a strange city with only two weeks to go until the book was due. Jacob Murphy, for never being surprised at anything I do. Evan and Alex, for being the best sons any dad could ever ask for. And, finally, to Joe Flood (www .joeflood.com), for writing a killer little narrative to go along with this little blogging book. Thanks for helping to make my dream a reality, Joe! And, finally, to Dave Taylor for not only writing a fantastic foreword, but for always looking for new ways to challenge old-school bloggers into new and creative thinking.

Reviewers

Last but not least, thank you to all of the book reviewers, midpoint reviewers, community editors, business leaders, and bloggers who helped in making this book the labor of community that it is. Arieanna Foley, Dave Taylor, Devin Reams, Duncan Riley, Eric Coleman, Jake McKee, James Kendrick, Kevin Hamilton, Kevin Humphrey, Kynan Dent, Mack D. Male, Marc Orchant, Melissa Reinke, Michael Still, Neil Salkind, Patrick O'Keefe, Richard Murray, Tris Hussey, Lee Lefever, Neville Hobson, Jacob Murphy, Rick Turoczy, Rob Hyndman, Robert Jackson, Sarah Worsham, Scott Priestley, Shane Birley, Tim Slavin, Tyme White, Victoria Martin, Wayne Hurlbert, and anyone else who participated in this book in any way.

INTRODUCTION

News outlets today are abuzz with stories about blogs. In January 2005, *Fortune* magazine featured a story called "Why There's No Escaping the Blog." In May of the same year, "Blogs Will Change Your Business" screamed from the cover of *Business-Week*. Blogs have become so hot that some mainstream TV news reporters are quoting from the more popular blogs on the air. Unfortunately, despite all the press coverage, little is being published about how blogs can benefit you and your business. Blogs are not only here to stay, but they *will* have an effect on your business. The question is, will you use blogs to benefit your business, or will you ignore them and perhaps experience a negative consequence that takes you completely by surprise?

The power of blogging has certainly taken some by surprise. A major bike lock company was shocked when news surfaced in blogs that a pen could be used to open one of its world-famous locks. It resulted in a huge financial hit for the company, which offered to exchange potentially faulty locks with different models. Thankfully, plenty of positive stories resulting from blogs have also surfaced—stories of companies embracing the world of blogging and seeing massive expansion, goodwill, and visibility as a result.

Blogging is a communication tool, a marketing technique, a listening device, and a way to interact directly with customers one-to-one on a global scale. A business can learn a lot by reading blogs to determine what customers and non-customers alike are saying about the business. Your business can benefit by using blogs to spread the word about what your company has to offer its customers and to gain immediate feedback from customers.

Perhaps you've seen blogging featured on the covers of major business magazines, or you've started seeing notices about blogging conferences around the world. Perhaps you are simply curious about this tool that could revolutionize the way you think about your customers and conduct business. No matter where you're at in the spectrum, this book is for you. If you are interested in the future of your company, you need to understand blogging.

A Reader's Guide to *Blog Marketing*

Throughout this book, I'll explore why and how companies of all types blog and explain how you can get the most out of blogging for your own business. Initially, I'll cover the basics, such as getting into the mindset of blogging. The concept of open communication with customers is a foreign idea to many companies, but the ability to understand the value of blogging as a medium will help you understand how it fits into the business world and how it fits into your business plans.

A central concept of the book will be *transmitting* versus *engaging*. Most corporate communications are simply one-way missives—transmitting information *to* customers—whereas with blogs, the company can engage, or have a two-way dialogue, *with* customers. It can take a while for companies to make the leap from the transmitting to the engaging mindset, so I'll be revisiting this concept throughout the book. Blogging is a strong engagement medium, and the people who read blogs expect to be engaged, which is one of the reasons this book is so important—few businesses are comfortable with the concept of engaging, and many don't know *how* to engage with customers.

Another central theme will be how blogging allows you to create *positive experiences* with your customers—positive experiences can completely change the way your customers view you and your business. The more you value your customers, the more these positive experiences will occur, and the more successful your business will be. A happy customer sends other happy customers your way.

I'll also look at how successful companies are using blogs to extend their brands, interact directly with customers, and get real feedback on their company and products—and how you can do the same. You'll find that direct customer feedback is one of your most valuable assets. Customers know your business better than you ever will, and they're usually happy to share their ideas with you if you ask for them.

Later in the book, we'll explore how your company can use blogs both externally and internally, and we'll look at examples from numerous companies (including General Motors, Disney, and Stonyfield Farm) to see what lessons they have learned.

Tracking the world of blogs can be a challenge, which is why I'll spend a significant amount of time discussing how to track blogs, what information can be gleaned from that tracking, and how to put the information to good use. I'll also talk about how to respond to comments on your blogs, how to respect your readers, and how to deal with the gold mine of blogging: negative feedback.

Finally, I'll look at how blogging will change your business, how it will impact the bottom line, and how you can develop a successful blogging strategy so that you will enter the market with the fewest mistakes possible. I'll close with input from business and blogging leaders on where blogging is going—because it's difficult to prepare for the future if you don't know what that future could be.

Although thousands of new business blogs are being created each month, until now, no solid guidebook has shown you exactly what blogs are doing and how businesses can take advantage of them. *Blog Marketing* is the guidebook that will help you with your blogging endeavors. It provides the framework, but only you can provide the desire, drive, and creativity necessary to make blogs a reality at your company.

The Book Blog

I've created a blog for this book to continue the information flow and learning, at www.blogmarketingbook.com. Check it out to see examples of businesses that are blogging successfully, and feel free to share your own stories as well.

I hope this book will challenge you to rethink the way you look at your customers, employees, and relationships, as well as your company's marketing and communication strategies. If you grasp not just the act of how to blog, but also the concepts that are central to blogging, you can revolutionize your business and attract more customers and the attention of competitors and entire industry.

1

BLOGGING BASICS

*Arnold Adams is the harried owner of Everywhere Signs. He has no
time. His typical day is a blur of action and reaction:*

7:12—checking voice mail while driving into work.

7:30—opening office and checking drop-box for orders.

8:00—getting work assignments for employees.

*9:00–12:00—managing work of employees, answering phones,
taking walk-in orders.*

12:00–1:00—lunching with Big Important Client.

1:00–5:00—overseeing sign delivery and setup.

*5:00–6:00—accounting work, including calling customers about
late payments.*

6:00–7:00—all other work, including answering e-mail.

*So, when June Marzipan, his hipper-than-thou web guru, said
that he needed a blog, his second reaction was, of course, "I have
no time."*

His first reaction was, "What the hell's a blog?"

*After five years with a website, thanks to June, he was just
starting to understand how the online world worked. He loved his
website—it was colorful, well-organized, and, more importantly,
brought in business. It was up there 24/7, 365 days a year, taking
orders from customers who loved the idea of not having to come
into the shop to order a sign. And he loved the idea of taking their
money for something so easy.*

*But June was staring at him, with her disconcertingly pink hair
(when did that happen?). He had to say something.*

"Is a blog a noun? A verb? Why do you Internet people have to make up words?"
"Both and because," June said.

—Part 1 of "Blog," a short story by Joe Flood,
written for this book

I MAGINE THAT YOU COULD LISTEN, like a fly on the wall, to millions of people—your customers, employees, competitors, partners, and the media—as they talk about your business, your marketing process, your advertising, and your products. Now imagine that you could use this up-to-the-minute information to determine what your customers want, how they want it, what they will ultimately buy, and what they're willing to pay for it. This is the power of the blog.

Basing your business decisions on customer feedback and market intelligence is probably the smartest business move you could ever make. And *weblogs*, also known as *blogs*, are allowing companies to do just that. In fact, blogs have the potential not only to change the way you communicate with customers, raise your visibility, and get you direct customer feedback, but they can also transform the way your company does business internally. Using blogs can help you reduce e-mail overload, facilitate the brainstorming process to generate new ideas more quickly, and simplify a variety of project management tasks. Blogs are so powerful that to say they will revolutionize your business is an understatement—blogs have the power to create businesses, change the course of political history, and transform the way the mainstream media looks at itself.

Basing your business decisions on *actual* customer feedback and market intelligence is the smartest business move you could ever make.

Like every major communication tool, blogs expand the ability for companies to operate and ultimately to create entirely new opportunities for growth, product development, and quality control. However, blogs take this communication a step further by bringing the best aspects of mass marketing and transforming them from one-way communication into a two-way dialogue.

As I write this book in the summer of 2005, between 50 million and 100 million bloggers are actively communicating on the Internet, with the number of blog readers estimated at between 200 million and 500 million, according to *The Blog Herald*.[1] These numbers are difficult to pin down, mainly because the only conclusive studies are for North America; nevertheless, the number of blogs, bloggers, and blog readers is massive. In its May 2, 2005, issue, *BusinessWeek* magazine estimated that about 40,000 new blogs are posting information every day.[2]

Blogging grew from the ground up as a grassroots effort. What started as a few people conversing about common interests via real-time Internet postings has become a continuous conversation among millions of bloggers and readers. The most powerful thing about blogging isn't the technology; it's this massive community driving the *blogosphere*. With millions of bloggers expressing their thoughts, experiences, and information they've learned in their fields of interest, this medium has become a worldwide forum.

Part of this conversation may be about your company, which can be good news or bad. The worst news, however, would be if none of the millions of voices out there were talking about your company or its products.

IT'S ABOUT COMMUNICATION

The reality is that blogging is a medium. Blogging is also a content style. Because the earliest blogs were built on the principles of an authentic voice, honesty, and authority, most blogs are expected to have those qualities—this holds true even more so for the corporate blog. Blog readers (even brand new ones) are so conditioned to reading a personal voice on blogs that they expect it from companies, too. This presents unique challenges for business leaders who want to understand blogging, as the concepts of transparency and authenticity are not often associated with corporate communications practices.

Because they're publicly available on the Internet, blogs are wide open, ready to interact with all of your customers. Blogs let customers hear what is on your mind, and they create a space for customers to tell you exactly what they are thinking about. Blogs are the next best thing to going door-to-door to each of your customers' homes or offices; they give you and your company a way to create and sustain real relationships with real people.

Past marketing efforts were always transmissions from companies—one-way communications aimed at as wide an audience as possible, such as advertisements, popup windows on the Internet, and the like. With blogs, however, you're *engaging* with your customers, as every reader is reading your blog by choice, every reader is choosing to interact with your business, and every reader wants to hear more from you. This powerful new way of communicating creates and empowers customer evangelists in ways that were practically impossible before blogs existed.

WHAT BLOGS CAN DO

An open and honest public blog, written by an authoritative voice from within your company, allows your business to create a different type of experience between you and your customers: it allows you to create legitimate conversations that simply weren't possible before online blogging. Blogging means your company will no longer need to depend on expensive focus groups, feedback forms, e-mail, and other time-consuming and tedious methods used for gaining feedback.

If you want to know why your latest product isn't selling, you can ask your customers on your blog; they'll tell you the truth. If an executive was recently fired for a corporate scandal, you can tackle the issue on your blog in an open manner. Such honesty makes an impression with your customers, which will be more real than almost any media article on the subject. Even more important is that any person who reads your blog is doing so by choice—he or she came to your blog to see what you have to say. Blogs are just about the only marketing tool for which this holds true.

One of the biggest mistakes companies make is looking at blogs as just another way to get out the same old marketing message. Nobody wants to read that kind of thing on a blog. Blogging is really about three things:

- **Information** Telling your customers what you're doing and finding out what they are thinking.
- **Relationships** Building a solid base of positive experiences with your customers that changes them from plain-old consumers to evangelists for your company and products.
- **Knowledge management** Having the vast stores of knowledge within your company available to the right people at the right time.

Without blogs, company messages can get so filtered by public relations or the media that CEOs and other senior management have decided to talk directly with customers—whether it be in the company's stores, on the company's airplanes, or at special events set up specifically for communicating with customers. The value of direct customer feedback is obvious, and blogs provide that on a global scale.

Blogs are effectively a form of free advertising that your customers are begging for. Blogs are easy to track, provide a means to generate and measure buzz, and allow you to create positive experiences, and ultimately customer evangelists, simply by being real.

You can also use blogging for exciting internal purposes—to help employees generate and try out new ideas, involve and empower employees, and improve your ability to communicate internally. Whether you're a global Fortune 100 company or a mom-n-pop plumbing supply retailer, internal blogs can help you stay organized and external blogs can change the way people relate to your business.

BLOGS WILL CHANGE YOUR BUSINESS—WHETHER YOU LIKE IT OR NOT

One of the biggest challenges facing your company is that, like it or not, your competitors are or will be using blogs. Not only that, but by scouring the blogosphere they can get all kinds of competitive intelligence on what you're doing, what your customers think about you and your products, and where your company and the industry are going. Of course, all the same tools could be yours as well.

The question for you, then, isn't *should* you get into blogs, but *how* will you get into blogs and how will you leverage them to maximize their return to your business? *Blog Marketing* helps you decide how to develop a blogging strategy, how to launch your blog, and how to participate not only in your own blog but in the overall culture of blogging.

WHAT'S IN A BLOG?

With so many new blogging terms in use, I could write a dictionary (in fact, I included one in the back of this book). However, if you learn the following terms, you'll look blog-savvy at your next dinner party (or corporate meeting):

- **Blog** A website comprising *blog posts*, or content written by the blogger, which are typically organized into categories and sorted in reverse chronological order. Most blogs allow readers to comment on individual blog posts.
- **Blog posts** Individual items posted to the blog (using *blogware*) by the *blogger*.
- **Blogger** The individual who maintains the blog and/or writes blog posts using the blogware.
- **Blogosphere** The community of blogs, bloggers, and blog posts.
- **Blogware** Software used to create blog posts and manage blogs.
- **The conversation** What happens when bloggers, especially millions of them, blog.
- **Permalinks** Permanent links attached to a particular blog post that remain unchanged.
- **Trackbacks** URLs that other bloggers use to cite posts or parts of posts; for example, when you, Blogger A, write about something Blogger B posted on in her blog, it's best to let Blogger B know she has been mentioned in your blog. Trackbacks send Blogger B an e-mail with a notation that her blog has been cited.

WHO'S BLOGGING TODAY

Companies are blogging at a phenomenal rate. From large companies, such as Microsoft and Boeing, to small companies, such as Thomas Mahon's tailoring business and Elisa Camahort's marketing and public relations firm, businesses of all stripes are using the revolutionary power of blogs to create positive experiences, increase influence, and provide continual dialogues. Some of these businesses will be your competitors, others will be your partners, and some blogs might even be written by your employees.

From GM's increasingly popular and respected series of blogs to the Disney Channel's use of blogs as an internal communications tool, more and more companies are turning to the diverse power of blogs to meet their current and future challenges head on. Blogs allow their customers and partners to see what companies are doing on a daily basis, which can be a powerful motivator for customers to continue doing business with blogging businesses.

GM's popular FastLane Blog (Figure 1-1) spreads news, provides information for enthusiasts, and creates a community space where thousands of aficionados can discuss what is important to them. GM has also created a special Smallblock Engine Blog to engage customers with even more specific interests. Creating a place where customers can talk about what's important to them is only one of a large number of ways your business can use blogs to increase communication, redefine your brand, and change the way you do business.

Microsoft, arguably one of the largest and most successful companies in the world, knows the power of blogs. Thousands of Microsoft product managers, developers, testers, and executives use blogs to talk directly with customers in a clear and authoritative way; to listen to customer complaints, suggestions, and ideas; and to track what customers and partners are saying. In fact, Microsoft uses blog research so thoroughly that each product development

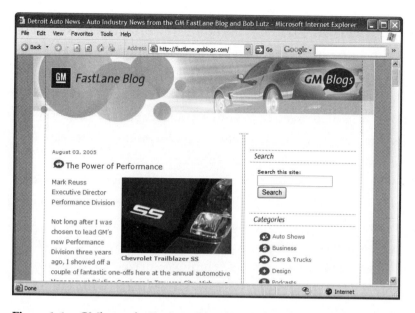

Figure 1-1 GM's popular FastLane Blog directly engages customers' passions, fueling a dynamic, feedback-driven community.

team is directed to look for blog feedback *before* making significant changes to applications. Blogs don't run Microsoft, but they do provide an unprecedented level of feedback for a company that needs to get real consumer information about products before it's too late to do anything about it.

Dallas Mavericks basketball team owner Marc Cuban started blogging because he was tired of "giving in-depth responses to a media question only to have the result be what the reporter or columnist intended to write and I was just fodder to help them make their point." He saw blogs as an ideal way to "present my position on a topic in its entirety and not have to worry about how they condense a two-hour conversation into 500 words."[3] Cuban built a blog that allowed him to express his thoughts regarding issues and interests. His blogging passion served to energize his team's fan base even further.

If having an open conversation with customers outside your company can transform your business, allowing *employees* space to share their interests and work ideas and build relationships can be even more powerful. In mid-2005, IBM turned to internal blogs to serve its employees. IBM's official blogging policy states that the primary goals of this blog network are for employees to learn and to contribute.

The Disney Channel has also made innovative use of internal blogs (Figure 1-2). While the company once used massive paper logs to keep track of engineering changes and issues, several years ago Disney began implementing blogs for these tasks. Now the blogs present an integrated, employee-driven solution to the impracticability of paper. I discuss Disney's use of blogs in more detail in Chapter 4.

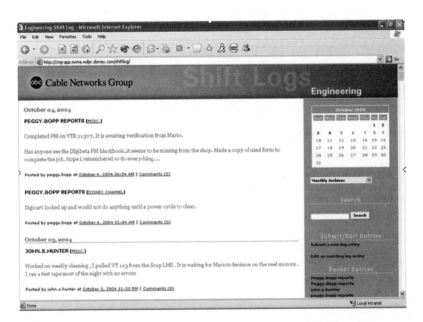

Figure 1-2   The Disney Channel uses internal blogs to manage engineering shifts as well as other tasks.

Many employers who allow blogging internally find that employees who blog change their workdays and attitudes. They enjoy their work more, they connect more with people outside their teams, and they share and receive information on a whole new scale. These companies are seeing their products, processes, and quality of service increase as a result of employees being more communicative, more involved, and more outwardly focused.

Throughout this book, we'll look at companies that use blogs to make a real difference in business. A fair number of these companies are in the technology sector, purely because this industry is where blogging got its start. However, the growth of blogs among every business is astounding—from churches to rail yards, from yogurt and ice cream companies to retail stores, and from jewelers to a major cable company; all are using blogs in innovative ways to transform their businesses.

BLOGGING HISTORY 101

The history of blogging is a long and convoluted one. Blogging has been around in some form since the earliest days of the Internet. In fact, one of the first web pages was similar to a blog in that its author, Internet creator Tim Berners-Lee, regularly updated it with a list of all websites (only a few dozen at the time).

Blogging eventually evolved into a means of sharing both personal expression and other information that individuals found valuable. Since its beginning, blogging has enjoyed a slight duality: on one hand, it serves as a great online diary, and on the other, it's a fantastic communications tool.

Until 2004, blogging was a fairly specific activity, with only about 5 million bloggers worldwide—most of them fairly secluded in their own little niches, blogging about pets, businesses, and tech-related issues. Then came the US 2004 presidential election, and blogs suddenly began getting mainstream attention. Bloggers unearthed issues about candidates, blogged about all kinds of events that journalists couldn't be bothered to attend, and even received press passes to the Democratic party's national convention.

Overall, 2004 was a huge year for blogging, as business thought-leaders such as management guru Tom Peters, author and lecturer Malcolm Gladwell, entrepreneurial expert Guy Kawasaki, and leadership authority Steven Covey woke up to the power of blogs. In fact, these days, no business author's work is complete without starting a book blog. As a result, the business magazines of the world such as *Fortune, Business 2.0,* and *Fast Company* have awakened to the power of the blog and businesses around the world are taking notice. While blog-related inquiries to marketing and PR companies were initially met with blank stares, these companies quickly caught up to the idea, and now blog consulting is a staple of consultants large and small.

The early twenty-first century has been marked by mergers and acquisitions in the blogging space as well as a number of scandals—but more than anything, it has been marked by *growth.* If 5 million bloggers were online in 2004, more than 50 million were blogging by the start of 2005, and that growth won't slow down anytime soon. In fact, the collective number of blogs has grown so rapidly that no one service has been able to keep up with it, which is one of the reasons that nobody is entirely sure how many people are actually reading blogs. Suffice it to say that a lot of people are writing them, even more are reading them, and more still are being influenced by them. These days, the question isn't "Do you know what a blog is?"; it's more likely "What's your blog?" or "What's your favorite blog?"

The growth of blogs among businesses has been astronomical. Thousands of new business blogs are being created by companies of every size, in every industry, for just about every purpose imaginable. So, what will you do with your blog?

WRAPPING IT UP

Now that you have a clearer understanding of what blogging is, where it came from, and—in broad strokes—what it can do for you, what's your next step? Get into the blogging mindset. As mentioned, hearing what customers *really* think can be intimidating, but it's an even more intimidating proposition for your business if you bury your head in the sand and choose not to listen. It takes most companies some time to get comfortable with the blogging way of thinking, so in Chapter 2, we'll discuss more about the blogging mindset and how you can learn to value your customer interactions.

2

GETTING INTO
THE BLOGGING MINDSET

For decades, businesses have tried to determine what their customers wanted by using focus groups. As the business world got more complex and markets became more competitive, the kind of information that could be gleaned from focus groups became inadequate for most businesses. Focus groups didn't provide enough information, nor was the information valuable over the life of the product.

Realizing the limitations of focus groups and similar marketing practices, companies decided that they needed to know more about who their customers were, how they interacted with the company, and how the company could reach out to customers in a meaningful way. This idea of getting a "360-degree view" of customers was a nice concept, but it was never really achievable within the limited spectrum of marketing and communication tools that were available.

Customer Relationship Management (CRM) software was designed to try to pull together information from various systems to provide an idea of not only whether a customer had interacted with your business, but what kind of interaction occurred, who was involved in the interaction, and what it meant to the company. Unfortunately, most companies could get only limited answers to these questions: whether a customer had bought a company product or ever called in with a question or comment, and whether his or her current contact information was valid.

CRM software didn't contextualize any of the information it collected. It simply created a repository of information. It didn't create any data on what the customer actually thought, nor did it allow a way for customers to provide direct feedback. To supplement this CRM data, businesses began to hire customer relationship specialists and product evangelists—individuals whose sole job was to make customers aware of the company products on a one-to-one basis—to interact with customers directly. For most businesses, this created some sense of value, but the practice simply couldn't be applied to a large number of customers. Because each individual customer relationship staffer had only so much time, the staffer typically spent most of his or her time nurturing the relationships that had the greatest return—the big spenders—and the majority of other customers were left out in the cold.

KNOW HOW TO TREAT YOUR CUSTOMERS

Every successful company uses some type of measuring stick when comparing itself to other similar companies. Businesses looking to succeed in the current interactive, customer- and conversation-driven marketplace must consider factors other than the financials. Companies need to value the knowledge made available to them through employee and customer input. One way to do this is by never confusing customers with the popular marketing term: *consumer*. A customer should never be called a *consumer*. A consumer is someone you use for profit; a customer is an asset. Customers are your best product managers, your best evangelists, and perhaps the only people in the world who will tell you the truth about your company. Listen to them. The easiest way to help customers become more involved in a positive, passionate, way about your business is to talk to them and treat them as equal partners.

Customers are your best product managers, your best evangelists, and perhaps the only people in the world who will tell you the truth about your company. Listen to them.

JetBlue CEO David Neeleman realized early on that without talking to his customers he would never be able to build a customer-centric airline. As a result of his unique approach to customer interaction, Neeleman has been featured in a variety of business magazines. When he flies, he flies just like everybody else, in coach. He even drives himself to the airport. Once there, he waits in line—just like you and me. He is, for all intents and purposes, just another customer—at least until the plane gets into the air.

TOO SCARED TO LISTEN?

For several of my clients, nothing is scarier than opening the floodgates of customer feedback—until they realize that the only thing scarier than hearing what customers have to say is *not* hearing what they have to say and suffering the consequences.

If the idea of customer feedback is frightening to you, ask yourself why you are afraid. Are you afraid your service is subpar and that you cannot fix it? You must take responsibility for your actions. It's better to have unhappy customers knocking at your door than no customers at all. Remember that an unhappy customer is a happy customer waiting to happen.

Then he walks up and down the aisles, talking to customers, hearing what they have to say.

At the end of the day, every company lives and dies by how well it serves, supports, and interacts with its customers. Every customer experience is put on the global scale of "success" or "failure." Neeleman is doing everything he can, not only to reduce the number of negative experiences with JetBlue, but to create a positive environment where he leads by example—showing that employees need to care about customers.

CUSTOMERS ARE ASSETS

Too often, businesses look at their customers as they would rows in a spreadsheet. Businesses spend time figuring out how to get more money out of them, analyzing how often they come back and how much they spend on each trip, and figuring out how much a customer will spend on a particular item. But customers can and should be much more than just an income stream.

Customers' experiences can range from completely unhappy to glowingly positive. Both types of customer can greatly influence your company's reputation.

Generally speaking, customers fall into one of five categories:

- **Evangelists**   These types of folks have had so many positive experiences with your company and/or product that whenever a subject even mildly related to your company, products, or services comes up in conversation, they just *have* to tell everyone about it. Many different companies enjoy this type of customer—for example, Apple Computer evangelists can be so passionate that they'll say Apple is a *religion*. These customer evangelists are the types of passionate people that will transform your business, and the currency they deal in is positive experiences.

- **Regular customers**   These customers enjoy your product or service. They may admit it's not the best in the world, but they buy it because it has value, it is the cheapest, or they haven't found anything better. They've had enough positive experiences that the negative ones seem paltry in comparison.

- **Reluctant customers**   These customers have had negative experiences with your company—often many negative experiences—to the point at which they simply expect a negative experience or a poor product every time. Occasionally, they'll be pleasantly surprised and will leave contented, but generally they simply accept that they have to buy from you and they move on. In many ways, these customers are living a balance of positive, negative, and blasé experiences.

- **Occasional sufferers**   These customers don't enjoy your product or service, but they buy from you when they have to, and only because they have to. Some people who eat at fast food restaurants fall under this banner—although they will never evangelize or even talk positively about what they're buying, they'll buy it when absolutely necessary.

- **Saboteurs**   These customers have had so many negative experiences (or perhaps only a handful of incredibly negative experiences) that they will go to whatever ends necessary to do whatever harm they can to your business.

Each of these personalities is created over time through a pattern of individual experiences with your company. Successful companies strive to create positive experiences for customers through positive environments, well-trained staff, great value, and quality products; whatever your customers are looking for, that you are able to provide, is a potential positive experience. Do you provide a storefront? Investing in a positive shopping space is vital. Do you provide food or hospitality services? Smiling, courteous, and energetic staff are a must. Do you provide analysis or consulting services? Knowledgeable consultants, value-added services, excellent communication, and constant follow-up will create positive experiences for your customers.

Most customers don't look for reasons to be unhappy; in fact, most are looking for positive experiences, and often it takes only one of those in a given industry to transform the way customers look at every single service provider in that industry. The influence wielded by businesses who create positive experiences is disproportionate to their size: Apple Computers isn't the largest or most popular computer manufacturer (not by a long shot), yet it is one of the most-watched tech companies on the planet. BMW and Mercedes don't sell the most cars in America, but the consumer desire to own one is palatable. Starbucks may make great coffee, but people aren't necessarily buying just the coffee—they're buying an overall positive experience.

But creating positive experiences isn't really about being a luxury supplier like Apple, BMW, and Starbucks are in their industries. You can create positive experiences no matter what business you're in by having friendly and knowledgeable staff members, offering exclusive discounts, and generally building your business by contributing to their experiences.

Positive experiences create emotional responses, and nothing is worse than a customer who feels no emotion toward your business: no emotion means no loyalty, so customers really have no reason to stay.

TALK TO YOUR CUSTOMERS

One of the reasons blogging is such a strong phenomenon is that it takes tools such as market research and product testing from a birds' eye view to the one-to-one human interaction level. If a blog about your company exists, you can simply e-mail the blogger to ask him some questions. If a blog post about your company concerns you, or even excites you, you can take the opportunity to create a positive experience that's being handed to you and respond directly and appropriately.

> **Blogs are all about having conversations—just remember to contribute in a meaningful way, and you'll be sure to create a positive experience for the person to whom you're responding *and* for all those who'll read the post in the future.**

Better than all of this, though, is that if you have your own blog, you can directly ask your customers what they think. Thinking of launching a new line of beverages? Ask your customers what types of drinks they like. Want to launch a new piece of software? Ask your customers what features they want, what features they don't want, and how much they'd be willing pay to get what they want.

Blogs are all about having conversations—just remember to contribute in a meaningful way, and you'll be sure to create a positive experience for the person to whom you're responding *and* for all those who'll read the post in the future.

FIVE STEPS OF EFFECTIVE COMMUNICATION

Your customers are talking, your employees are talking, and your partners and suppliers are talking. With blogging, the conversation is potentially limitless.

The challenge for most companies who engage in customer conversation isn't obtaining feedback; it's how best to deal with the feedback, both positive and negative. At the end of the day, you need to realize that these conversations include current customers, potential customers, employees, and partners. If you ignore these comments, you are ignoring valuable feedback, potential new marketing strategies, innovative new product ideas, and concepts that could completely transform your business. The conversation will go on either with or without you—and your competitors are most certainly listening.

MICROSOFT LISTENS

The example set by JetBlue CEO David Neeleman, while rare, isn't unique. Lots of companies talk directly with customers to get their feedback and to improve on or launch new products. Microsoft, the world's largest software company, regularly flies customers and industry experts to its campus in Washington for fantastic powwows. The company invites dozens of key customers and partners to the event, where they all spend several days brainstorming as a group. Individual product teams gain huge value from these events—they get to engage directly with customers, pitch their vision for the future, hear customer responses to that vision, and interact with customers in a way that is impossible outside the event.

Whereas, once upon a time, Microsoft's most effective customer feedback mechanism was these onsite powwows, the company is now making massive use of blogs. It's been said that Microsoft is slow to catch on to a new trend, but fast to apply it—and blogging is no exception.

Within the space of a year, more than 1000 Microsoft employee blogs featured developers and product managers talking directly to customers every day instead of just once a year. These days, many employees are reading dozens (if not hundreds) of blogs every day to see exactly how customers are responding to Microsoft products and services. Microsoft employees are also contributing to other blogs, searching for terms that are important to them that may be popping up in the blogosphere, and generally being aware of the fact that real people are talking about the company. Microsoft now is easily able to listen in and contribute to the conversation on a daily basis.

The best way to engage in a real-world conversation is to go through the following five steps for effective communication: listen, understand, value, interpret, and contribute.

Listen

Listening is like being a sponge, and the best sponges hold water indefinitely. Until you are ready to contribute—to squeeze some knowledge from your sponge—you need to be taking in a lot more that you're putting out.

Understand

By understanding what is actually being said, apart from any biases or agendas—especially your own—you begin to value feedback. You need to ensure that you keep that value. Value the conversation,

WHAT IS AUTHENTICITY?

by Aaron Brazell, blogger and social commentator (www .technosailor.com)
Authenticity is...

Passion. It is the thing that drives people to be successful in what they do. It is the drive of a successful blogger. Passion is the engine which powers the boat and keeps people coming back.

Conviction. It is the thing that causes people to relate to the blogger. Though the topic may not necessarily be agreeable, conviction demonstrates that the blogger has fully bought into his perspective.

With these ingredients, successful bloggers will secure new readers and maintain their existing readers. There is nothing worse than a flakey writer. Readers know it and the blogger knows it deep inside.

the individual, and the feedback more than you value your own opinion. If you don't do this, when it comes time to contribute, your comments will be out of context and will hold much less value than they otherwise would.

Value

Valuing *everyone's* contribution can be difficult in the best of times—some people in any large conversation don't listen, don't value others' contributions, and therefore simply don't deserve to be talking. However, when you're a business listening to feedback about your company, products, and industry, it's far too easy to discount certain contributions as unworthy of your attention. Don't fall into this trap. Before you can contribute and properly respond to what's going on in a conversation as big as the blog posting, you need to value everyone involved—after all, the one person you value one time could well be your next big customer evangelist.

Interpret

Before you take the step in becoming involved in the global conversation happening on blogs, you need to interpret and evaluate what has already been said and determine whether you actually have any valuable and unique insight to offer. After all, if the only thing you have to say in a large conversation is "Yes, I agree!", it's probably best to live by the adage, "Even a fool is thought wise if he keeps silent."

Contribute

The final step in effective communication is to contribute something of value to the group. What valuable information can you offer? When the conversation centers on your area of expertise, you can offer authority, passion, and a unique perspective. Unlike most parties, where not everyone gets a chance to talk to everyone else,

I DON'T HAVE MILLIONS OF CUSTOMERS!

You may not have millions, or even thousands, of customers, but in the world of blogging, everyone has an equal voice. No matter how big or small your business, or how many people are interested in your products, blogging provides a unique opportunity for you to talk to your potential customers—at least those who happen to be online and reading—and for them to talk to you. Big businesses are great at yelling, but small businesses are great at talking. Blogging allows for a balance: it allows for big businesses to talk one-to-one with customers, and it allows small businesses to gain visibility by using what they know to create big-business style opportunities and growth.

Blogging *can* help your business grow. For example, two of my clients are small fashion boutique businesses, who, thanks to the increased visibility and customer feedback that blogging enabled, have been able to open new locations. Increased visibility and online sales, and their ability to reach out to their ideal audience and figure out the best place to launch new stores, are responsible for this growth. Blogging gave them a unique opportunity to expose their businesses to fashion aficionados, fashion editors, and newspaper columnists from around the country—largely because these small stores love to tell stories and share the secrets of why they love fashion. Their passion was contagious, and soon articles were being written about them in all kinds of publications.

While your business may not have millions of customers right now, you never know who you might influence, who will read your blog, and where that might lead. Act like you're small by talking, but think big by not forgetting that real opportunities for growth do exist.

thousands of blog readers and writers are waiting eagerly to hear what you and your company have to say. Once you have properly prepared to contribute to the conversation, you can be sure that you will not only be heard, but that you will get feedback.

PARTICIPATION BREEDS PASSION

While listening to and participating in the conversation can seem intimidating and sometimes overwhelming, the benefits of doing this are impossible to ignore. Beyond the value of simply getting customer feedback, you can create relationships with each and every one of your customers, which was impossible before the blog.

Participating in this conversation offers several benefits:

- Creates customer evangelists.
- Builds trust among your entire customer base.
- Helps you become a thought leader in your industry.
- Lets you share and gain knowledge.
- Provides product feedback.
- Uncovers new growth opportunities and new markets.

In fact, the ways in which blogging benefits your business are limited only by the creative ways you can find to use blogging, be they through internal blogs that get your employees the information they need to know, external blogs that help you become a leader in your industry, or product-specific blogs that let your customers interact with you in a meaningful way. Whether an individual is a saboteur or an evangelist, every relationship you create and every time you step outside the boundaries of your company, you can create positive new experiences with each and every individual with whom you interact.

CREATING CUSTOMER EVANGELISTS

One of the most powerful benefits of blogging is that it helps you create evangelists. In their 2002 book, *Creating Customer Evangelists*, Ben McConnell and Jackie Huba tell us that passionate company evangelists can inform and empower your customers to carry your brand's message to others. Customer evangelists are powerful tools. When you give other customers the power to embrace your brand, they will take your brand's message with them wherever they go, telling others about their experiences with your company and thereby extending your brand in a positive way that would not have otherwise been possible.

Passionate messages can spread like wildfire; as soon as one passionate person enters a community, the dynamics of that community completely change. Most customers will become happy evangelists for your business and products if you provide enough positive experiences. They need to love your company and your products, even if your products aren't "perfect."

Creating passion isn't about making people like you; it's simply about using your passion to fuel more passion. The reality is that companies that create a stir, live on the edge, and try new ideas are going to be both loved and hated. And, just as in any relationship, sometimes you can't be sure whether a customer is a true friend unless you listen to what he or she has to say. A blog is the perfect place for that.

BUILDING TRUST WITHIN YOUR CUSTOMER BASE

The best way to build trust is to be consistently trustworthy. Doctors earn trust after years of being fair, caring, professional, and knowledgeable. Similarly, your business builds trust with your customers in the real world by delivering on your promises.

For example, if you promise to have the best prices but don't, you are betraying your customers' trust; if, however, you deliver on that promise consistently, customer trust increases as a natural result.

Blogs are a great way to build trust, because they allow you—a real person, and not some corporate marketing brochure—to communicate with your customers, users, and community more regularly than any other medium allows. Ideally, your blog should attract at least one posting per day—as a result, you have an opportunity to build trust by delivering on your promises daily.

BECOMING A THOUGHT-LEADER

Thought-leadership isn't a new concept; it was proposed in the 1960s and finally given a name in the 1990s. The term refers to the ability to lead by proposing new and innovative ideas. The modern-day application of thought-leadership with regard to business has been applied to companies that publish respected industry newsletters, participate in conferences (or host their own), and generally disseminate information in the hopes that more people will be exposed to the company and willing to invest in its products.

The strong appeal of thought-leadership–based marketing makes a lot of sense, as becoming more visible relative to respected information ultimately means more interaction with customers and potential customers. The challenge for most companies engaging in a thought-leadership campaign is that it can be expensive. Maintaining newsletters, attending and speaking at conferences, and remaining publicly visible isn't easy or cheap.

Blogs provide a unique opportunity for thought-leadership in that they allow businesses to publish information people want in the way they want it. Add to that the ease of finding, subscribing, and contributing to blogs, and it's obvious that blogs are one of

WHY BLOG?

This question is an important one. Paul Chaney, a prominent blog consultant from Radiant Marketing Group, compiled this list (http://radiantmarketinggroup.com/2005/05/26/blogs-beyond-the-hype/) of reasons why a business should blog:

- **Search Engine Marketing**   Blogs give you an increased presence on major search engines like Google and Yahoo!.
- **Direct Communications**   Blogs provide a way for you to speak directly and honestly with your customer.
- **Brand Building**   Blogs serve as another channel to put your brand in front of the customer.
- **Competitive Differentiation**   Because blogs give you the opportunity to tell your story over and over, they help set you apart from the competition.
- **Relational Marketing**   Blogs allow you to build personal, long-lasting relationships with your customer that foster trust.
- **Exploit the Niches**   Blogs help you fill your particular industry niche.
- **Media & Public Relations**   Blogs are excellent PR tools. The media calls you, not your competition.
- **Reputation Management**   Blogs enable you to manage your online reputation.
- **Position You as Expert**   Blogs enable you to articulate your viewpoints, knowledge, and expertise on matters pertaining to your industry.
- **Intranet & Project Management**   Blogs make great, easy-to-use applications for internal communications within an organization. This may be one of the least well-known and underutilized areas of blogs.

the easiest ways to engage in a thought-leadership campaign. The challenge, of course, is that you still need to create material, research and comment on news, and generally discover and impart information of value—as you would via any other medium. Most companies that are highly attuned to their industry are aware of these challenges and are already addressing them.

TRANSMITTING VS. ENGAGING

Most businesses and companies function in a "transmission" mindset. When they have a new product, they exhibit some kind of advertisement—be it a sign in the window out front or a national television ad. They try and create buzz by displaying *SALE!* in advertisements and in the window, in great big letters that are impossible to miss. The reality is that people don't want to be talked *at*, they want to be talked *with*.

Companies around the world are beginning to realize that while transmission-based communication is an important part of getting out your message, far more effective tools are at their disposal. Dialogue is a powerful way to broadcast your message while simultaneously getting customer feedback.

Before blogs, press releases were one of the best ways to communicate news about your company. You'd send the press release to a local paper or wire service, hope that some fraction of journalists would pick up on it, and then you'd gain some exposure for a fairly low cost. The problem with press releases and similar transmission-style endeavors, though, is that after the press release leaves your company, you rarely see any return. Traditional response rates for transmission-based advertisements, such as television ads, radio campaigns, and press releases, is reported to be a measly 1 percent. At best, you might see an article or two in the news, though most likely it will just be a regurgitated piece from your press release. Or worse, you hear nothing at all.

Tools such as blogs allow you to go beyond the press release and traditional media coverage. They help you engage with your customers and create a real dialogue. These dialogue-based initiatives don't replace press releases, advertising, or focus groups—they compliment them.

Consider Boeing, a leading aircraft and aerospace manufacturer, which began ramping up the production and marketing of its new plane, the 787 Dreamliner. The company used the traditional transmission-style marketing: press releases, launch parties, media tours, interviews with engineers, and the like. However, Boeing also allowed Randy Baseler, vice president of marketing, to blog (www.boeing.com/randy). Through his blog, Baseler was able to extend the message into a dialogue that included information about a Boeing competitor's offering, the Airbus A380.

Baseler responds to posts on other blogs, discusses what other blogs are talking about, and reads a vast cross-section of flight and aviation blogs. This blog allows Boeing to use a transmission-style message, which is great for getting the cold hard facts out to the world, as well as a personal dialogue, which is great for communicating passion, having a conversation, and listening to what customers and aviation enthusiasts think.

HOW TO START BLOGGING

When I talk to executives, business owners, marketers, or consultants, I invariably get asked one of two questions: "What is a blog?" or "How do I start my own blog?" Hopefully, by now I've answered the first question, but the second deserves an in-depth look.

The process for contributing to any conversation goes something like this:

1. Listen to the conversation.
2. Understand what's being said in the conversation.
3. Value the audience and the conversation itself.
4. Interpret what is being said, and evaluate what you have to say.
5. Contribute to the conversation.
6. Listen some more.

Every successful blog follows this pattern. The first step is to find some blogs in your area of interest and read and study them. Suppose you own a construction company. If you're going to start successfully blogging in the construction industry, you should begin by looking for other blogs dealing with the construction industry. The best way to find blogs dealing in this area is to do an Internet search using Google or your favorite search engine. The goal here isn't necessarily to find the most popular site, but to find blogs that give you value by reading them. Figure 2-1 shows Google search results for *construction blogs*. As you can see in the figure, a vast number of construction-related blogs are out there—in fact, Google found more than 3 million of them.

Many blogs contain *blogrolls*, a list of blogs that the blogger reads, admires, and respects. If you find a blog you like (or don't like) and the blogger adds links to other blogs in the industry, you may be able to find more hidden gems or more of what you're looking for. Once you have found two or three blogs of interest, start reading them on a daily basis. If you see a post in which you are interested or one about which you have an opinion, consider leaving a comment.

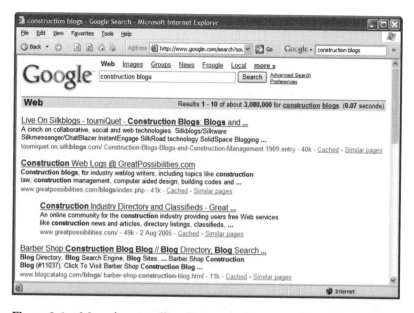

Figure 2-1   More than 3 million hits resulted from a search for *construction blogs* on Google.

Do this for at least two weeks. During this period, you may locate other blogs you like to read, or you may decide to use a feed reader to follow posts (see the next section). A blogroll is a quick and easy way for similar blogs in the same community or industry to build each others' traffic, and it's something you shouldn't ignore for your own blog. Without including a blogroll, your company's blog may fade into obscurity. If nothing else, a list of "Blogs We Read" can show other bloggers that you know the important blogs in the industry, and that you aren't afraid to read them.

FEEDS: THE SECRET TO EFFECTIVE BLOG READING

As you've undoubtedly realized by now, checking more than a small group of blogs for updates on a daily basis can be a time-consuming process. To avoid having to search the vast Internet blog by blog to find what you're looking for, you can use a *feed* to subscribe to information so that it comes to you, rather than you having to find it. Using feeds on your blog can also help readers and customers find what they're looking for quickly and easily.

A feed is actually not intended for human usage, but is used for interpretation by various types of applications, most commonly referred to as *feed readers, news readers,* or *aggregators* (all essentially the same thing). Feed readers allow a user to subscribe to a feed, much the same way a person subscribes to the daily newspaper—thus, the user is automatically informed when a particular blog has been updated and something new has been posted.

Two kinds of feed readers are available: desktop feed readers, which are applications that live on your computer, and web-based feed readers, which are online applications that you can access from anywhere with any computer. A list of feed readers and a comparison of each can be found online at Weblogs Compendium, at www.lights.com/weblogs/rss.html. The most popular desktop feed reader is NewsGator (www.newsgator.com), which is a plug-in for Microsoft Outlook that allows you to read your blogs as if they were e-mail messages. The most popular web-based feed reader is Bloglines (www.bloglines.com).

After you have downloaded a feed reader, you subscribe to the feeds for the blogs you want to read. Most blogs and feed readers allow you to type the address of the blog into the feed reader, and the feed reader will do the rest. Once you have subscribed to the feeds for the blogs you read, you no longer need to check the blogs on a daily basis. When a blog is updated, your feed reader will automatically download the update and let you know that new content is ready to read.

Not only will using a feed reader save you the trouble of going to a number of blogs, but it will also allow you to search past blog posts written by your favorite authors for valuable content.

Feed readers are designed to save you time and put you in control of the information you receive: since you no longer need to visit blogs just to see if new content has been added, you are free to use your time more effectively. And because you sign up for the feed, you are in control of what kind of information you receive. If you don't like the material, you can simply unsubscribe to a particular blog.

After you've read your choice blogs for at least two weeks and made the occasional comment, you can consider starting your own blog, where you can effectively respond to the posts from your favorite bloggers and float some of your own ideas.

Read "Choosing the Ideal Blog Platform," by blog consultant Paul Chaney, for information on what tool or platform to use.

START BLOGGING

After you've chosen a platform, your next step is to start blogging—but don't tell anyone about it just yet. If your blogging tool of choice allows you to password-protect your blog, I highly recommend that you do so. As with any new venture, the first couple of weeks can be the most difficult time, since during those weeks you will be learning how to accomplish your goals. During the first two weeks of writing your blog, you will learn how to use the software, how to link and track blogging, how to make use of comments, and how to perform all kinds of other blog-related activities. In addition, because blogging is a lot like creative writing, you may struggle to find your voice. All this is usual, though: blogging is a new medium for many, and the process of finding your voice is important, as it's possible that your voice as a blogger will stay consistent throughout your blogging career.

Try to spend no more than 15 to 20 minutes each day reading blogs, commenting on blogs, and writing your own posts. In my experience, 15 minutes each day is the ideal period for most new

CHOOSING THE IDEAL BLOG PLATFORM

by Paul Chaney, blog consultant (www.radiantmarketing group.com)

The first thing you need to know is that there is no one "ideal" blog platform. What may be useful in one situation would not suffice in another. Which platform is right for you is dependent on your needs.

While there are many platforms available, I want to mention the three most popular and outline a few of their features.

TypePad

Though postured more for personal use, this platform (www .typepad.com) provides enough versatility to make it useful for business applications as well. It contains all the standard blog platform components such as comments, categories, and trackbacks. Its WYSIWYG editing interface makes it very easy to use and requires no knowledge of HTML, although there is an HTML editing option if you need access to the source code. In addition, one of TypePad's most attractive features is its ability to set up photo albums and incorporate them into the blog.

The TypePad platform requires a monthly fee, ranging from $5.00 to $15.00. The fee can be paid a year in advance for an additional savings.

TypePad offers a number of standard templates, but allows for a great degree of customization using its wizards. However, because it is what is known as a *hosted solution*, fully customizing the platform to the look and feel of your existing website can be challenging except for the most experienced designer. If that is what you desire, the last two options are for you.

Movable Type

TypePad's elder sibling, Movable Type (www.movabletype.org) is particularly designed for business use. The platform sits on your server and can be completely customized to fit the look of your site. In fact, it essentially becomes another directory of your site.

The interface is not as user friendly as TypePad and does require some knowledge of HTML. There is a one-time license fee for use of the platform, which varies depending on the type of use and the number of users.

WordPress

This platform (www.wordpress.org) requires perhaps the most sophisticated level of technical knowledge for implementation. However, because it is open source software, WordPress is free to use. That doesn't mean it is lacking in features. Many professional bloggers swear by the platform and use it exclusively. Its administrative interface is remarkably simple to use, and it is perhaps one of the most versatile platforms available. Like Movable Type, it resides on your server and requires the use of a MySQL database.

bloggers, as it offers a few minutes for reading, a few minutes for commenting, and a few minutes for blogging.

Many new bloggers feel a compulsion to write dozens of pieces a day, read hundreds of blogs, and comment on nearly every one of them at least once. These well-intentioned individuals quickly burn out and abandon blogging. Instead, as a new blogger, start slowly. Don't take on too much at once. Try not to get overwhelmed by how much you could be doing. Stay focused on why you started blogging and what values you and your business find in blogging.

After you have blogged privately for two weeks, consider launching your business blog site. Launching a blog is a fairly simple process: you simply make it public and tell a few customers and friends about it. At this point, you may be tempted to build up traffic. But traffic isn't what's important at first; instead, finding your voice, making sure blogging meets with your strategic objectives, and listening and responding to posts are most important.

As discussed in Chapter 1, blogging started as a community of like-minded people who linked together through the Internet. In addition to linking to others, leaving comments and sending occasional e-mail correspondence can have a profound effect on your network of readers. In blogging, you build your trust, reputation, and authority on your own merits. If you consistently post opinions founded on accurate information, the number of bloggers who link to your site will steadily grow, as will your influence.

TRACKING BLOG ACTIVITY

You can hire a million data entry specialists to transcribe all the information you gather from blogs, or you can use one of the many blog tracking services available today. I'll get into these in more detail in Chapters 7 and 8. For now, let's take a look at a few of the ways you can track what is happening on your blog:

- Blog tracking systems
- Feed tracking systems
- Trending systems

Blog tracking systems, such as Technorati (Figure 2-2), typically monitor how often blogs link to each other. This gives both the

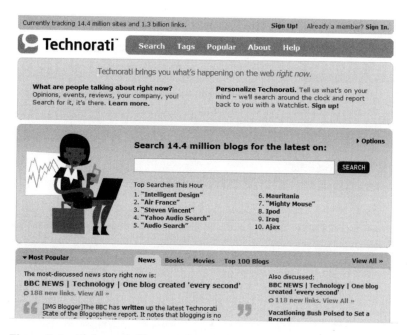

Figure 2-2   Technorati allows you to search blogs in real time and to track how many people are linking to you and your competitors.

blogger and the blog reader a clearer sense of their blog traffic. More links mean not only more readers, but more credibility.

Feed tracking systems are similar but rely on the feeds that most blogs publish. Computer programs, like feed tracking systems and feed readers, use feeds to determine what's new on a blog; feed tracking systems can therefore tell you all the blogs who have linked to you on a daily basis or return a list of blogs that mention specific terms. The largest of these are PubSub (www.pubsub .com), shown in Figure 2-3, which allows you to have search results returned to you as feeds on a daily basis so that you don't need to search for new results every day, and Feedster (www.feedster .com), which allows you to search the millions of feeds available in a Google-like manner.

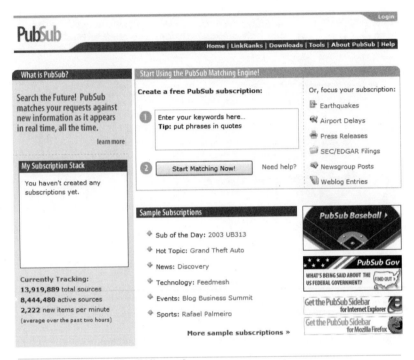

Figure 2-3 PubSub allows you to get new links and mentions sent directly to you, instead of needing to search for them on a daily basis.

Thanks to tools such as Technorati (www.technorati.com) and PubSub (www.pubsub.com), bloggers can see who links to their sites within minutes of the link being created, as shown for the Tinbasher blog in Figure 2-4.

Trending systems, such as BlogPulse (www.blogpulse.com), shown in Figure 2-5, track conversations from their origins to their endpoints, so you can see how a conversation grows; they also track specific terms across a period of time, allowing you to compare that graph to other important terms. You could use a trending system to monitor how many times your company is mentioned versus how many times your competitors are mentioned, track

Figure 2-4　The Tinbasher blog's Technorati results show the number of posts linked to the site.

Figure 2-5　BlogPulse tracks what blogs are saying, and then graphs those results over time.

how specific company news spreads across blogs, and track how bloggers respond to that news.

The great thing about these services is that they are all *free*. That isn't to say that you can't pay for higher end services or pay consulting companies to produce daily, weekly, or monthly reports.

BRANDING AND CUSTOMER EXPERIENCE

Far too many companies think of their brands in terms of the concrete: a product, a logo, a trademark. But your brand is larger than that. Your brand is the impression you leave on your customers. Sure, your logo and corporate imagery, as well as advertising, are a part of that. But they don't leave the most lasting impression of your brand.

Experiences, relationships, and trust—all intangible assets—are the single largest source of value for your business brand. Your brand lives in the experiences your customers have with your company, your products, and your frontline teams. Your brand lies in the minds of your customers, and like a wildfire, each of your customers can spread your brand message (the way they perceive it) to others—and they often will, either because of a positive or, more important, a negative experience.

In fact, as described in various marketing books, such as 2002's *The Tipping Point* by Malcolm Gladwell, even very small changes in the way customers perceive your company can have radical effects on your bottom line.

Treat your customers with the respect they deserve, and they'll respect your brand, too.

WRAPPING IT UP

In this chapter, we have looked at the ways that you can get into the blogging mindset, some of the benefits of blogging, as well as how to start participating in the conversation. In Chapter 3, we'll explore the power of blogs for your business, including how blogs can be used to generate new ideas, build teams, and bring in customers and affect mindshare.

3

THE POWER OF BLOGS FOR BUSINESS

Now that you are familiar with how blogs have added a new dimension to corporate communications and how engaging in the conversation is absolutely essential for your business's success in the blogosphere, you are ready to begin looking at the powerful possibilities blogging offers your business. You've likely been asking yourself such questions as "How can blogging benefit my company?" and "What would my successful blog look like?" since you started reading this book.

This chapter covers the practicalities of business blogging and what it means for you, including how it can impact your bottom line and how it will bring in customers and affect mindshare. It also examines several companies from a variety of industries that are succeeding at blogging; these early bloggers have paved the way for later blogging luminaries—like you.

HOW BLOGS CAN HELP YOUR BUSINESS

Let's get back to business basics—not because I think you don't know your own business, but because I honestly believe that blogging can help each core fragment of what makes up a successful and viable company. The core needs for any business are as follows:

- Decent ideas
- A great product
- Visibility
- A well-trained team of people who work hard to make the company succeed

You also need good marketing, great customer relations, an awesome sales force, decent customer support, and a host of other factors. But if you have ideas, a product worth selling, a solid team behind it, and potential customers, the rest will follow naturally.

CREATING GREAT IDEAS

Every company has great ideas waiting to come to the surface. The problem with bringing those ideas to the surface is threefold: giving ideas space to develop, helping ideas get improved, and implementing the best ideas.

Often it takes only one person to come up with a great idea, but it may take 100 or more people to support and implement that idea. If the idea loses support, the company will need another great idea to keep going. Great ideas can increase a business's costs and people power, but they can also increase a business's revenue and marketing power. This is why large companies who live or die by their great ideas employ researchers who spend their time seeking epiphanies.

The challenge for companies who invest in ideas is often that the best ideas don't get to the top, don't get reviewed, or don't even get considered. This *idea barrier* could be killing your company. A truly open and internally viewable idea blog, or even individual employee blogs that allow people to float new ideas for peer review, should allow the best ideas to rise to the surface for selection and review. We'll look at the concept of idea blogs more in Chapter 6, as they are an exciting way to empower your employees and generate thought.

CREATING GREAT PRODUCTS

The next challenge is deciding which great ideas get turned into products. After all, what good is thinking up the greatest idea in the world if your business can't actually sell it?

Smart companies hire people who are able to turn a great idea into a great product. These people, often called *product specialists* or *product managers*, know customers, know the market, and know how to deliver new products on time and on budget. However, to do their jobs well, product specialists need to talk directly to customers. This is where focus groups, customer demo days, and other customer-listening techniques come into play. Some companies even employ staff evangelists to work one-on-one with individual customers to maintain a good relationship.

We all know cases in which even the most well-intentioned products underperformed. Relying on a small sample of customers to reflect what the entire world desires is risky at best, and foolhardy at worst. If you can't ask everyone in the world what they want, you're unlikely to be able to deliver what everyone truly desires. With blogging, you *can* ask—if not the entire world, then at least your entire blog readership, who are probably connected to and/or reading other blogs from all over the planet. Once you have insight into what a large community of readers wants, you can begin delivering it.

INCREASING VISIBILITY

Marketing is all about visibility—making the right people aware of the right product at the right time. Allen Weiss, founder of MarketingProfs.com, says that marketing is about customers, and he's right. The hard reality, though, is that often marketing isn't about individual customers. Often, it's about creating a global message to which individual customers will respond.

New methods of effective marketing include creating "viral" campaigns, customer-centric events, and otherwise helping customers spread the word through incentive programs and contests. Visibility is also sought through media reports, event sponsorship, and interactive websites.

However, these visibility campaigns lack effectiveness on the one-to-one level. Companies assume that millions of people will be contacted, but only a small percentage of these people will respond. This method of marketing has its upside, but it doesn't do anything to create relationships with customers, create positive experiences, or create customer evangelists.

HAVE YOU CAUGHT THE BUG?

In recent years, *viral marketing* has become the rage. The viral marketing strategy encourages customers to pass along information to others, often via e-mail. It's effective because it can be crafted once and left up to individual consumers to spread the message themselves. Halo 2, a popular video game for Microsoft's XBox console, engaged in one of the most successful viral marketing campaigns ever with the creation of the "I Love Bees" pseudo-game.

At the release of one of the final trailers for the game, shown in theaters around the world, the final XBox logo briefly faded to *www.ilovebees.com*, the website address for a heretofore unknown honey manufacturer in California's Napa Valley. Visitors were greeted with a series of disturbing and cryptic messages, including a countdown to some unknown event (though astute visitors eventually guessed that it was the game's launch).

The campaign built up an incredible buzz that was broadcast to the world via millions of curious visitors obsessed with solving the puzzle. Entire websites and communities sprang up around trying to find a solution. Why? Because everyone loves a mystery.

Campaigns such as "I Love Bees" rely on users to spread the word—something that blogs also rely on. Trusting your message to your users is one of the ways to allow them to "own your brand."

HAVING A GREAT TEAM

One of the best ways to build a great business is to create a great team. Great teams will think up great ideas, build visibility, and spot defects in products, which they will then correct. A great team can fix just about any problem, given the right resources, and is happy to take on just about any challenge.

Unfortunately, great teams can be difficult to create and keep motivated. Anyone who's built successful teams knows that more often than not some particular "X Factor" will make or break the team: often the ability to find common ground and common interests can be a make-or-break issue. A team comprising colleagues with common interests, backgrounds, or passions will be able to rely on those commonalities, even in the most adverse circumstances. The challenge is to find employees who fit together; few employee profiles include information that will help you find the common ground.

To solve this dilemma, many large corporations are turning to self-forming and self-sustaining teams. These people have found that they have things in common and they work well together. Companies post internal team opportunities that "ultra teams" can choose to tackle or ignore. Sometimes projects will be assigned based on need, but, generally, having a team own a topic is a more effective tactic.

The challenge for companies looking to enable these dynamic teams is in figuring out how to enable employees to connect based on passion. Passion is an important part of any successful team—without passion, a team will not only find itself quickly in a rut, but it will likely find its members unable to gel, have fun, or help the company in a meaningful way. You'll learn how to create dynamic internal teams in Chapter 6.

HOW BLOGS IMPACT YOUR BUSINESS

Of course, creating a successful business involves more than having great teams, great ideas, great products, and increased visibility—but if your business could do only these four things right, you'd be off to a good start. The real question is how blogging can augment or help in each of these areas.

Ideas   Good ideas are always hard to come by. Several adventurous companies have begun blogging for new product ideas, assuming that their users know what they want better than the companies do. GM's FastLane blog (http://fastlane.gmblogs .com) is a great example of this: GM runs new concepts by readers at the site, inviting them to comment. By providing a space for customers to interact, you can be assured that they *will* interact. As a company, you need to be ready for the feedback that will come as a result.

Products   Traditional product development leverages a roomful of customers to make decisions for a world full of people. The end result is a series of focus group insights that have no real-world applications. Blogging affords the opportunity to ask the world of customers about what they actually want.

Visibility   Most traditional visibility campaigns are single events that rarely go beyond the customer's first experience. Even the best viral campaigns that encourage customers to spread the word are really just single-interaction events. Blogs let your readers decide how and when to interact with you. Not only do they give customers control over the relationship, but they encourage customers to continue to engage with you over time, thus providing a multitude of experiences they can subsequently share with friends and associates. Blogs encourage customers to become participants and participants to become evangelists. And they encourage everyone to come together as a community.

Teamwork   By creating opportunities for your staff members to communicate effectively, you create a space for more meaningful interactions. Blogs come in where other types of communication fail. It's been said that e-mail is where information goes to die. When was the last time you actually looked at a message you'd archived awhile back, "just in case"? Blogs are where living information resides. People in your company can find others with similar interests by searching topics that other internal bloggers have considered. Creating ad-hoc connections based on content that is created and owned by internal bloggers is a great way to keep your teams well oiled, motivated, and in touch with people with similar passions across your organization. Think about the efficiencies that could be gained for the whole company if these experts had an easy way to exchange and archive ideas.

IDEAS TO HELP YOUR BUSINESS

Beyond the core concepts of improving your ideas, products, visibility, and team cohesiveness, blogs can improve your business dozens of other ways. Here are a few examples to wet your whistle as we get deeper into exploring blogs.

Improve Customer Loyalty   Elisa Camahort is a passionate blogger. She helps theatres in her area, such as 42nd St. Moon (http://42ndstmoon.blogspot.com) by blogging behind-the-scenes details, which dedicated theatre-goers love. She also features discounts for theatres to track how effective blogging is at driving new ticket sales. Overall, the ability to connect with their niche audience has been a huge boon for the small theatres that Camahort passionately serves.

Build an Early Buzz   Nooked (http://blog.nooked.com/) was first *envisioned* on the blog, was *built* on the blog, and has *grown* through the blog. Nooked is an RSS tracking company—RSS stands for Really Simple Syndication and refers to a format used for easily distributing news on the Internet via feeds or channels. At each step of the way, the Nooked blog has been full of inside information that is devoured with abandon by those following the project's progress. It is the perfect example of how to use blogs to build a buzz early on in a product's development cycle.

React to Negative Events   Earlier this year, General Motors engaged in some major restructuring. GM Chairman Rick Wagoner took a larger degree of control in the company by restructuring selected units so that they reported directly to him—these selected units were previously under the care of such key executives as Bob Lutz. Interestingly, Lutz is the primary author of GM's exceedingly popular FastLane blogs. Instead of being silent about the event, Lutz was able to turn what many had considered a demotion into a positive thing: he was able to focus entirely on what he loved— product development. Several hundred bloggers and commenters supported his attitude by commenting and followed his example of how to deal with negativity in a public forum.

Extend Your Influence to Your Influencers   For many companies, the key to success is knowing who influences the industry. For Microsoft, developers are first priority. To influence developers, Microsoft launched Channel 9 (http://channel9 .msdn.com), which gave a true inside look at the company through daily video profiles of important figures in each product group.

The response to this blog and its video angle took everyone at Microsoft by surprise; the blog community grew to more than 50,000 members, making it one of the largest developer communities ever.

HOW BLOGS BRING IN CUSTOMERS AND AFFECT MINDSHARE

The challenge that today's companies face is one of *mindshare*. Mindshare is all about how many people are aware of your product. Think of it like market share, except instead of having a percentage of the market in terms of dollar value, you

Create places that are meaningful to your customers; only then will your mindshare grow.

value mindshare on the percentage of people who know what the heck you do. The problem is that everyone is vying for mindshare, and customers only have a certain amount of *mindspace*.

BLOGS AS MARKETING TOOLS: THE STONYFIELD FARM STORY

Even if you are a relatively small company, your blog can have a huge effect on your company's profile, your customer relationships, and the way customers think about you and your products.

In April 2004, the Stonyfield Farm yogurt company began blogging (www.stonyfield.com/weblog/). Stonyfield runs five blogs, each targeted at a different part of their market. Some are targeted at farmers and those who remember traditional farming nostalgically; others are targeted at parenting and healthy living, as having a healthy image appeals to busy parents.

The focus on healthy living, the environment, and family values are important facets of the company's personality, something it prides itself in having maintained, despite the company's phenomenal growth.

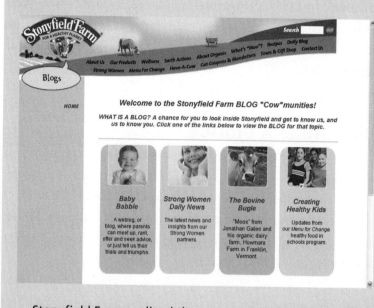

Stonyfield Farm realized that customers make buying decisions at the refrigerated food section in the grocery store. Shoppers are conditioned to choose the lowest priced item for most commodity items such as yogurt. However, Stonyfield believes that by tying its values to its customers' values, it can create a lasting impression that makes the extra cost per purchase seem completely worthwhile.

Using your blogs as a way to reflect your business's values, culture, and priorities is one of the best ways to ensure that your blog isn't simply another vehicle for spouting the same old marketing drivel to which customers are becoming desensitized. Blogs allow you to talk directly to your customers as important people, which is an opportunity you should never ignore.

The reality is that the more companies vie for mindshare through regular transmission methods, the less effective all campaigns are. The simple reason is that customers are able to dedicate less and less of their mindspace to each company or product. The answer to the challenge is simple: create spaces where your customers can consistently engage in dialogue with you. Create places that are meaningful to your customers; only then will your mindshare grow.

BLOGGING IS A CHOICE

Clearly, if you are not blogging, you are losing customers you could be gaining, you are losing customers you currently have, you are losing influence you could be wielding, and you are losing out on relationships that could redefine your company. When your customers are talking, you have a responsibility to engage with them.

The great thing about blogging is that it can have business benefits regardless of whether or not you actually have your own blog: you can still listen to your customers and engage with them even on blogs that are not your own. Obviously, having your own blog will allow greater benefits, such as customers being able to communicate directly with you, your being able to create positive experiences on your blog, and having the human voice of your blog become associated with your company.

Every business has a choice to make: either ignore blogging or embrace it. Blogging isn't going away any more than regular websites are going away. Soon enough, customers will simply take for granted that every company has a blog. Businesses will either participate and engage or ignore and distance themselves.

Increasingly, customers are looking for businesses that do more than simply provide the lowest prices—they are seeking relationships. Companies that continue to cut prices, cut corners, and take customers for granted are engaging in a race to the bottom. On the other hand, businesses that value their customers, engage with them, and make them participants in the company's future are engaging in a very different type of race—a race to the top. In which race would you rather engage? What happens to companies who win the race to the bottom? Do they survive, thrive, or take a dive? What about companies who win the race to the top of their markets? Time will certainly tell. Either way, customers are taking notice. Companies such as JetBlue and WestJet, both definitely engaging in a race for the top, are beating out competitors as large as United and Delta in the airline industry, primarily because these successful airlines pay attention to their customers though blogging.

Customers are price sensitive only when you are price sensitive. It's far more valuable to your business and your customers to focus on the unique value you create—the examples of Starbucks, Apple Computers, and BMW don't have to be unique. Price sensitivity is a creation of companies that follow what the market does; it's far better to *define* the market than to serve it.

In every industry, on every continent, companies dedicated to serving customers with an engaging customer-centric experience are facing one common challenge: managing growth. Blogging, listening to blogs, and participating in the conversation are merely extensions of having a customer-centric business. Whenever you value your customers, they will become your company's greatest evangelists and will do your marketing for you. Blogs can do more than marketing, though; they can aid your product development and public relations, and even open entirely new markets and opportunities.

COMPANIES THAT BLOG

Once you have established that listening to the blogosphere is a natural and valuable way of finding value in the ongoing conversation, the next logical step is to come up with something to say. The best way to do this is to start your own blog. Most companies must first determine what type of blog to establish, who should write the blog, and other important issues. Unfortunately, the "safest" thing that many companies choose to do is to establish the blog as a *YAMO—Yet Another Marketing Outlet.* A copy writer is hired to turn company news into glib posts, highlighting words such as *innovative* and talking only about the company's strengths.

The problem with treating your blog as another push venue is that it does nothing to respect customers. Your customers already see and hear your buzzwords in your commercials, press releases, interviews, and via all the regular channels. If they want to hear how innovative you are, they can go to your website. Instead, why not help them use your blog to read your opinions on issues in the industry, news (yours and others' news), and insights.

Your blog needs to communicate more than just a standard marketing message. It needs to communicate something authentic, passionate, and authoritative—the exact types of things that come through if you are talking face-to-face with a customer.

If you are going to create only one blog, let the passion and authority of the author shine through in an authentic way. For many companies, a CEO or executive may provide the best perspective. Sun Microsystems has hundreds of staff blogs, but the most widely read is the blog by Sun's president, Jonathan Schwartz (http://blogs.sun.com/jonathan), shown in Figure 3-1. Nobody is more passionate and authoritative on the subject of Sun than Schwartz, and he happily tackles issues head-on in an impressive manner.

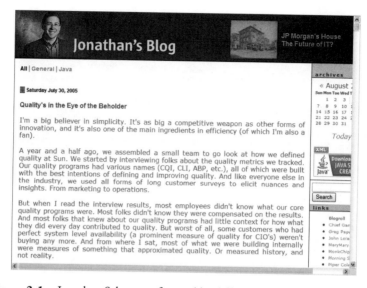

Figure 3-1 Jonathan Schwartz often tackles difficult issues in a passionate and authoritative way.

Be Real: The Scoble Story

On the flipside, sometimes the most important person to be blogging in your company may not be an executive. For Microsoft, one of Sun's direct competitors, the most important blogger is arguably Robert Scoble (http://scoble.weblogs.com), whose site is shown in Figure 3-2. Scoble started blogging before he joined Microsoft—his existing blog was actually a major force in landing him the job. In his role as a technical evangelist, Scoble has to be both authoritative and honest.

One of Scoble's rules is to tell the truth, even if it means admitting that a competitor's product is better or if it means Microsoft is doing something wrong. This can be scary for an executive to do—though Sun's Schwartz does it quite successfully. For Scoble, this comes naturally, and the net effect is that he has become one of the most influential people in a company with more than 55,000 employees. The external effect is that Microsoft now has a trusted

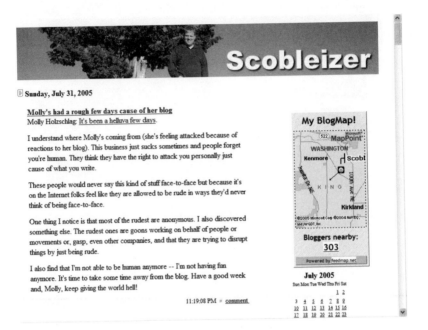

Figure 3-2   Robert Scoble, a lowly technical evangelist for Microsoft, is one of the most influential people in the company, thanks largely to his honest and open blog.

voice who will give the straight and passionate answer to even the hardest questions.

The question of who in your company should blog isn't an easy one to answer. However, if you are going to create only one blog, make sure your blogger has the following three characteristics: passion, authority, and authenticity. You can't lose.

Let Your Employees Speak for You: The Monster Story

Monster.com, a major job site, successfully illustrates the concept of empowering your employees to be your blogging voice. Its official blog (http://monster.typepad.com), shown in Figure 3-3, includes blog posts from dozens of staff members who contribute

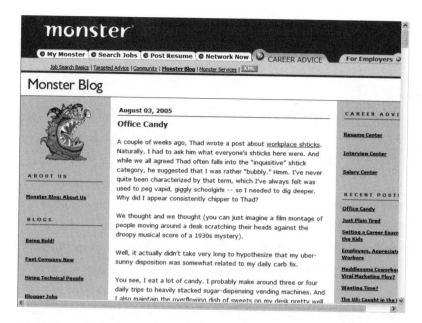

Figure 3-3 The Monster blog, written by dozens of employees, is a great example of how individual employees can express their passion while still providing value to customers.

on a variety of topics, from their first days at work, to their pet peeves (even with coworkers and managers), to their dreams and aspirations. Some of this is unique to the Monster blog—because the company helps people find jobs, letting its employees discuss issues similar to those experienced by other employees in other companies is a good way to relate to potential clients.

The great thing that Monster does, though, is let their employees be real people on the blog. There isn't a lot of marketing speak or "Rah! Rah! Monster rocks!" going on. You can tell employees are happy working at the company because of the passion and energy in their blog posts. You can tell that employees love helping other people find great jobs because it comes across readily in the text. Monster isn't *using* its employees to gain mindshare; it's *empowering* them to have a voice. This is valuable for a company whose main goal is to help others find their dream jobs.

COMPANIES THAT DON'T BLOG

Having your own blog is not a prerequisite for benefiting from what's happening in the blogosphere. Sure, having direct input, establishing yourself as a thought leader, and having an engaging location for customers to communicate on your website is all very, very good. But your business can get value from blogging while not having its own blog.

> **If all you do with blogs is listen to what is happening and respond appropriately, you have already gone a long way toward establishing a successful blogging strategy.**

Nevertheless, you must realize that a conversation is going on—and it's a conversation to which you want to listen. By acknowledging this basic fact, you can leverage and monitor what is already happening in the blogosphere—whether or not you have your own blog. We'll get into how to track the blogosphere more later in this book; for now, let's take a look at a few brief examples of ways you can listen in on bloggers' conversations: Technorati (www.technorati.com) and PubSub (www.pubsub.com).

Technorati watches blogs like a hawk. It allows you to search blogs either for specific terms (such as your company name or products) or for specific web addresses (such as your company's website) to see who is talking about you. Technorati also provides another vital piece of information: how many bloggers are linking to the person who is talking about you or linking to you. Services similar to Technorati also let you track your *competitor's* links—this could be one of the most powerful competitive intelligence services you've ever used, as it gives you real feedback and real information into your competitors and the challenges they are facing. Not only will you be able to gain wisdom based on customer input, but you'll be able to avoid your competitors' mistakes.

I would never suggest that you consider blogs with 1000 blogs linking to them more important than blogs with only 10 or 20 blogs linking to them; you should be aware of every individual blogger's reach. Treat each and every blogger as a customer, and treat the blogger with the respect that every customer deserves. However, be aware that if a blogger with a large audience is pissed off, his or her audience could be angry as well. Either way, this angry saboteur can eventually turn into a powerful evangelist, as every bad situation has the potential for even greater returns when addressed quickly, openly, and with respect.

PubSub monitors the feeds that bloggers produce. (For more information on feeds, see Chapter 2.) As PubSub monitors the feeds produced by the entire blogosphere, you can request that it produce a custom feed just for you. That feed could include the names of your products, your company name, the name of your CEO, and even the names of your competitors, allowing you to keep tabs effectively on your entire sphere of influence. Of course, you may want to split these into separate feeds; PubSub allows you to have as many feeds as you like, and you can organize them however you want.

PubSub specializes in letting you know who is saying something as soon as it has been said. Technorati, however, can tell you how important a particular issue is—who is talking about it, who is responding, and how fast is the news spreading. Using both tools together provides a powerful arsenal for understanding and participating in the flow of conversations.

Once you subscribe to the feed PubSub has produced, your aggregator or feed reader will automatically notify you whenever PubSub sees something new that meets the criteria you established. Never before have you had the power to react to a negative situation, crisis, or customer revolt as quickly as in the world of feeds. In most cases, you can be made aware of issues less than 10 minutes after a blogger blogs about it. This completely transforms your ability to work with customers quickly and, thanks to the power of your company blog, respond to it within minutes or hours instead of days or weeks. This can help stop negative word of mouth from spreading; but, even better, it creates a positive association with your company. People don't expect pristine experiences, but they do appreciate and respect honest, authentic, and open discussion about how a company is willing to improve products and experiences.

RESPOND TO YOUR AUDIENCE: THE KRYPTONITE LOCKS STORY

Companies may not effectively respond to issues happening in the world of blogging for several reasons: they may not be aware that blogs exist, or they might be aware of blogs but discount their importance. Kryptonite Locks is a bit of a unique story in that the company was aware that blogs existed, but it simply chose not to respond to bloggers for a variety of reasons.

In 2004, Kryptonite, maker of top-selling locks, suffered at the hands of a blog. A blogger discovered that it was possible to pick a Kryptonite lock with nothing more than a standard Bic pen.

After the blogger blogged about it, the issue was quickly picked up by Engadget (www.engadget.com), a popular gadget and geek blog with a reader base of more than a quarter million readers a day (see the article at www.engadget.com/

entry/7796925370303347). The conversation about the issue quickly spun out of control. Worst of all, Kryptonite had no idea what was going on until it was too late. In short order, *The New York Times* and the Associated Press had picked up the story—and there was no turning back for Kryptonite.

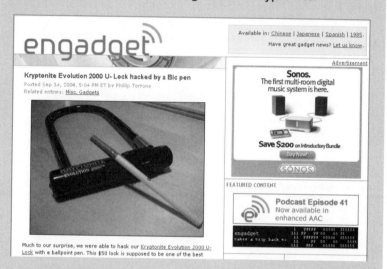

Kryptonite's business was hit with a class-action lawsuit (www.kryptonitesettlement.com/), and the company engaged in a massive lock exchange program (www.kryptonitelock .com/inetisscripts/abtinetis.exe/templateform@public?tn= product_exchange_faq), which will likely cost it an arm and a leg.

The question for us isn't whether or not Kryptonite's locks were easily compromised; instead, the question is, "How would this situation have looked if Kryptonite had responded in less than an hour, on the blogger's original blog, on Engadget, and on its own (if it had one) blog?" Kryptonite's crisis-management team was completely unprepared for the realities of the new blogosphere, where one blogger can identify an issue with the product, talk about it, and tell more than 20 million people about it in less than a week. Kryptonite's representatives said that they were more than aware of the furor happening in the blogosphere, but they were too busy responding to customer e-mails, sorting out the lock exchange program, and figuring out what exactly was wrong with the locks to respond. It's difficult to blame a company for decisions made during a time of crisis—after all, making difficult decisions is part of being in crisis mode.

While your company is, realistically, unlikely to encounter an issue of this magnitude, the ability to nip issues in the bud within minutes or hours is a powerful motivator for tracking what the blogosphere is doing or saying. If all you do with blogs is listen to what is happening and respond appropriately, you have already gone a long way toward establishing a successful blogging strategy.

WRAPPING IT UP

Leveraging the power of blogging for your company involves more than just reading blogs, tracking blogs, and writing a few posts here and there. The first part of this book covered the foundational aspects of blogging: what it is and where it came from, the conversation and why it's so important, and the power of blogs for your business.

Next, we'll cover how to get started with blogging in your business, including examples of two Fortune 500 companies who are truly innovating in the blogging space—Disney and General Motors—and we'll look at the best ways your company can use blogs both externally and internally.

This isn't to say that this book will provide a comprehensive list of every possible way you could or should use your blogs. At the end of the day, you know your company better than I ever will. However, these next chapters will provide core principles for successful blogging, the mindset required to implement blogging successfully, as well as all kinds of ideas. I encourage you to do something *different*. Yes, each of these examples has worked for companies in the past, and they may well work for you. But don't do the same thing everyone else does. Figure out what is best for your company and chase after that—even, and especially, if it's new, exciting, and scary. You won't regret it.

4

HOW YOUR COMPANY CAN USE BLOGS

"Make sense now?" June asked. She had explained everything in her typically thorough and occasionally patronizing manner, as though she were dealing with a child.

"I get it," Arnold said. "We could use a blog to engage our customers in a conversation. Plus, we could pick their brains for ideas for new business."

"Well, if you want to put it that way," June harrumphed.

Arnold leaned back in his chair. "After all, how well do we know this town? All those new developments along the interstate—who lives there?"

"Just remember, Arn, that this is a conversation—we have to give them something of value."

Arnold leaned forward in his chair. "I bet there are pizza shops, schools, gas stations, all sorts of places that need signs up there. They don't know what they're missing. That 20-foot banner we did for Bratz Daycare—they told me their business is up 30 percent."

June responded, "Yeah. Those are the kinds of stories that would be great for the blog. We could provide ideas for them on how to improve their business with some serious signage. How inexpensive signs can be and how color makes a big difference in grabbing those people driving by. We could let them know what works and what doesn't work."

"What doesn't work? Why would we want to tell them that?" Arnold asked. "And all this story-telling… wouldn't this be giving away some of our business intelligence?"

Once June stopped laughing about his "business intelligence" comment, the pair sat down to hammer out some rules for their blog.

—Part 2 of "Blog," a short story by Joe Flood

Now that you know the blogging basics, it's time you figured out exactly how your company can use blogs and what those uses will mean for your business. This part of the book provides the hands-on, rubber-meets-the-road, chicken-hits-the-skillet kind of information I'm sure you're champing at the bit to know.

As I mentioned early on, a blog is really a tool meant to achieve an end and, as such, it is meant to support you, your business, and your business's goals and assets. Having a blog without a goal is a lot like walking a penguin through Central Park—sure, it's interesting, but it probably isn't helping anybody.

And as with any brand new tool, you need to figure out how to use a blog. In the next few chapters, you'll see how you can use blogging by including some creative and innovative tactics employed by companies both large and small to leverage blogs for their own strategic well-being. The only thing limiting your use of blogs is your ability to dream up new ways to use them.

HOW DO I USE BLOGS?
LET ME COUNT THE WAYS...

I asked Arieanna Foley of Blogaholics (www.blogaholics.com) to compile a list of uses for blogs, which she happily did in Table 4-1.

External	Internal
Communication	Knowledge management and sharing
Marketing	Administrative tool
E-mail newsletter support	Internal document review
FAQ section	Collaboration
Industry news opinion	Idea archiving
Service updates	Internal dialogue
Learning	Dynamic archiving—not stale like e-mail
Interactive journalism	Corporate intelligence—knowing
Source of research	what your employees are saying and thinking and seeing the patterns
Public feedback	Loyalty—creating identification with
Custom queries/watchlists	the company through interaction
Aggregation of news sources	Status reports—what we work on,
Self-expression	and with whom—all tracked on each employee's aggregator
Storytelling	Top-down idea/goal setting
Customer service	Bottom-up idea generation and interaction
Public relations	Creation of corporate culture of
Viral marketing	expression, collectivity, knowledge sharing
Campaigning/social reform	Getting the info out faster: Have an
Community building	idea? Frustrated with the chain of
Sales mechanism	getting someone to listen? Post and it will get noticed, supported, and heard
Brand loyalty—a human face	Calendar sharing

Table 4-1   Arieanna Foley's Uses for Blogs (*continued*)

External	Internal
Knowledge management (broad scale—ourmedia.com)	Meeting announcements
	Meeting notes vs. e-mail broadcast notices
Trending	Sharing of market intelligence
CRM—Customer Relationship Management	Brain-storming about strategy, feature sets, and process
	Sharing customer notes
Buying behavior	Asking others for help
Competitive intelligence	Ability to segment blogs by individual or department for easy blog subscription
Polling	
Thought leadership	Best practices
Product changes	Thought leadership
Crisis management	Team creation—match up those passionate about an item, or match up people with differing ideas so they can work out the optimal solution
	Organized links—categorize links within the blog to most frequent info, strategy, technical manual, sales material, online learning

Table 4-1   Arieanna Foley's Uses for Blogs

Obviously, this isn't a comprehensive list, as companies are thinking up new ways to use blogs every day. Equally obvious is the fact that I can't cover all of these uses in this little book. I will, however, be taking a look at some of the top ways you can use blogs internally and externally to improve your business.

As you can see in Table 4-1, the problem isn't finding ways to use blogs, it's finding the right way to bring the most value to your business. If your goals are internal, and you're trying to increase communication, you can accomplish them in a variety of ways. If your goals are external, and you're trying to increase the trust and visibility of your company, a thought-leadership oriented blog can be ideal.

We could get pretty deep pretty fast, but for now let's look at two companies that are using blogs in innovative ways to reshape the way they do business in the areas in which the blogs are targeted.

GIVING YOUR COMPANY A VOICE: THE GENERAL MOTORS STORY

In January 2005, a milestone event happened: Bob Lutz, vice chairman of General Motors, started blogging. Lutz was the first executive leader of a non-tech Fortune 100 company to be a primary contributor to a blog. His personal style and approachable passion created an entirely new communication channel for GM, allowing customers to engage with him directly about products, services, and the future of the company. Lutz is equally passionate about car design and his blog, which is an important part of being a successful blogger at any level of a company, and he constantly affirms his belief in his audience and in blogging. "We want you to keep watching and keep talking to us, that's why I'm out here," Lutz declared in his second blog post (January 7, 2005, http://fastlane .gmblogs.com/archives/2005/01/great_comments_1.html).

In just five months, the GM FastLane blog (see Figure 4-1) became one of the most important unfiltered voices on the Internet, as the company expressed itself freely through Lutz and other executives, and as customers learned that their voices were heard. The scores of car enthusiasts who frequent the FastLane blog, as well as GM's earlier blogging endeavor, the Smallblock Engine Blog, have in Lutz a willing and able communicator whose passion for cars in general, and GM vehicles in particular, is contagious.

Figure 4-1   GM's Popular FastLane blog allows Lutz and other executives to have real conversations with real customers.

Most of the posts on the FastLane blog, as well as GM's other blogs, attract scores, if not hundreds, of comments, creating a dynamic, passionate, and vibrant community. If there were ever any doubts that blogging was all about the conversation that takes place between companies, customers, and bloggers, the FastLane blog put those doubts to rest. According to the Feedster Top 500 for August 2005 (http://top500.feedster.com/), the FastLane blog is among the top 500 blogs on the Internet, and the willingness of the team behind the blog to learn and adapt to blogging has been phenomenal.

GM became one of the first companies to create a *podcast* (an online radio show distributed directly to MP3 players), which is a hit among customers. The blogs, podcasts, and overall interaction with customers provide GM valuable and direct feedback from customers, car owners, and enthusiasts about what they think of GM as a company, as a car maker, and as an innovator. This is feedback the company would not otherwise be able to obtain in such a direct manner.

A POSTER CHILD FOR EXECUTIVE BLOGGING

Neville Hobson (www.nevon.net) wrote a case study in early 2005, which included information about GM's blogging efforts as well as the growth and lessons learned on the blogs. Hobson refers to the GM FastLane blog as "undoubtedly the current poster child for executive blogs." Since FastLane's launch, several other GM executives have become involved in the GM blog, adding a "breadth and depth of interaction developing on the blog while remaining wholly focused on the blog's key goal—developing dialogue about GM's products and services."[1]

GM's foray into blogging has been challenging as it continues to run while still learning to walk. The blog has included trackbacks, started a podcast, and interacted successfully with bloggers around the world. Each new step in reaching out to the blogging community of enthusiasts has created new and positive experiences for customers. More than that, though, the GM blogs have become a place for customers to share their passions and positive experiences, thus creating a self-sustaining community of product evangelists for GM.

GM has given its customers a voice in the company, but it has also gained so much trust with customers that it, too, has a direct and unfiltered line of communication with the marketplace that has become indispensable.

LESSONS LEARNED

General Motors—and, in particular, Lutz—has led the field in terms of using blogging, podcasting, and other emerging ways of communicating *directly* with customers. Among the lessons that can be learned from Lutz and the crew who run the GM blogs are these:

- *Don't be afraid to be honest.* Several times since the GM blog started, GM could have played dumb and stayed quiet in hopes that a negative comment or issue would simply disappear or be forgotten. Instead, Lutz and other GM blog contributors have tackled rumors, layoffs, corporate restructuring, and product line controversies head-on. They've been open and honest, and in so doing have not only got the truth out about what's going on at GM (as any true *window blogger* would do, as we'll see in Chapter 5), but they have also created a sense of trust with readers.

- *Use blogrolls.* Blogrolls show off the other blogs that you read and respect. From the first day of GM's blog launch, a blogroll was included, not only to increase their visibility (all the bloggers they linked to were aware of the links quickly, thanks to blog tracking services), but also to show that GM bloggers knew what they were talking about: the GM blog didn't link to every car blog in the world—only those that matched its passions and interests.

- *Ask people what they think.* If you ask no questions, you get no answers. GM has been openly soliciting customer feedback from the beginning and has, as a result, not only culled a huge amount of free customer feedback, but also earned a reputation among readers and car enthusiasts for caring about what people think.

- *Be passionate.* When you are speaking for your company, it is sometimes easy to fall into a mishmash of legal-cum-PR speak that uses a lot of words without saying anything at all. Most press releases use this tone. GM has shown, primarily through Lutz, that passion isn't something to be feared. This blog has shown that it's far better to passionate about the right thing than to be dispassionate about everything.

- *Be fair to competitors.* It is too easy to think of your company as the best in the business, or at least to try and convey that to readers. GM has been unafraid to praise its competitors on its blog. The result is that GM has built up great trust among its readers, so that when GM *does* say it is the best at something, readers tend to believe it.

- *Have a genuine voice.* Real people have to write your blog, so why not let them sound like real people? GM has consistently allowed the people who write the various blogs to act, sound, and respond normally, without using PR jargon. The relationships that have been built, and the buzz that has been generated as a result, have been phenomenal.

This list of lessons learned isn't a requirement for you to succeed in blogging. However, by adopting these principles, you, like GM, can not only raise your profile among bloggers and blog readers, but also build up a huge sense of trust, goodwill, and passion. Any company can produce an advertisement that says it is passionate about its product, but GM shows it through its blogs, every day. So can you.

USE BLOGS IN INNOVATIVE WAYS: THE DISNEY CHANNEL STORY

The Disney Channel is kept on the air by more than 130 technicians who work a variety of shifts. These individuals take care of the actual Disney Channel as well as operations for Toon Disney,

SOAPnet, and ABC Family. Together, they provide more than 100 hours of programming every day.

Because of the nature of the work, each shift produces a shift log that notes events that occurred during the shift as well as any outstanding issues. This allows for a consistent flow of information that is crucial to the success of the operation. In the entertainment business, change is constant, and that change must be communicated both to administration and to incoming shifts. In addition, as shifts come on, they must be able to catch up quickly and easily.

The original version of the shift logs was paper-based (as shown in Figure 4-2), which meant that the various log books had to be physically distributed and archived. Trying to read people's

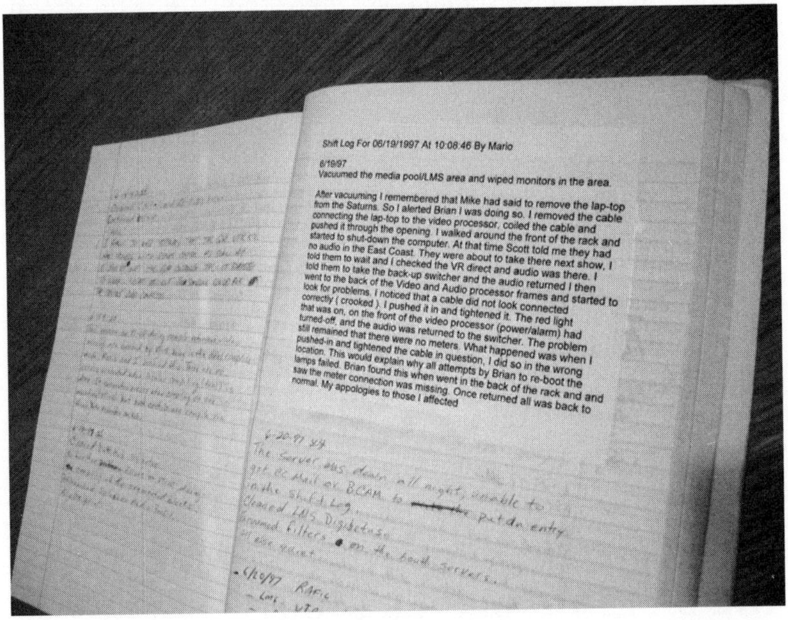

Figure 4-2   Disney's original paper-based shift logs were not only inefficient, but they could be difficult to read and were impossible to search.

handwriting and not being able to archive or search the logs in any streamlined fashion were problematic, to say the least.

As a result of these challenges to their goals, the Disney Channel has been working on a more elegant solution for several years.

WORKING ON A SOLUTION

The first solution was a basic database that was developed in-house. The feature set was minimal (no searching or editing capabilities), but it was certainly no worse than the paper system, and it meant an end to the piles of archived binders stored in a warehouse. Turning to a database-driven system truly wet Disney's whistle for something more robust and useful.

As Michael Pusateri, vice president of engineering, tells it, at some point someone got the bright idea of using blogging software for the shift log. At the time, the most popular blogging software was Movable Type by Six Apart (www.sixapart.com), which the team chose to use. They installed the software on their existing Linux servers, imported the previous 9000-plus entries into Movable Type, and began tinkering with the software. Their first adjustment was to incorporate their existing usernames and passwords into Movable Type, so that users wouldn't need to remember more than one password.

The new shift log system (Figure 4-3) was introduced gradually, by letting users choose to use it when they were ready. Within two weeks, more than 100 technicians were using the new system.

NEW SYSTEM, NEW CHALLENGES

The new blog-based system quickly became popular—so much so that users of the system started requesting new features and capabilities. In particular, users didn't like that they had to *check* the

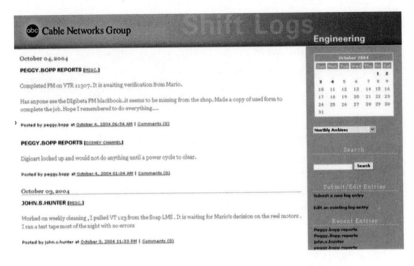

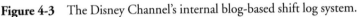

Figure 4-3   The Disney Channel's internal blog-based shift log system.

system for new entries, despite the fact that every previous system required that users check the logs manually for new entries. Users also found it difficult to forward information to others in the company or the engineering group.

As a result, Pusateri and his group made some changes to the system. Notably, they eschewed the temptation to use e-mail as the notification method, and instead decided to use RSS (Really Simple Syndication), the most popular method of producing feeds at the time.

In conjunction with the feeds, they decided to use NewsGator (www.newsgator.com) as the mechanism for staying up to date on the feeds (Figure 4-4). NewsGator is a plug-in for Microsoft Outlook that makes new RSS items arrive on the screen just like regular e-mail. The net result was that users were not only able to forward the RSS items quickly and easily, but they were in control of subscribing to the feeds—as opposed to being automatically included on an e-mail whether a user wanted it or not.

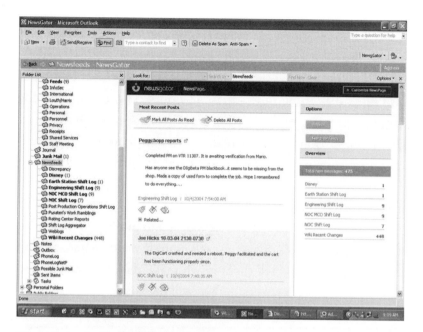

Figure 4-4   A sample of the modified version of Outlook for Disney, which includes NewsGator.

THE RESULTS

By making the system user-focused instead of software-focused (with the software making the rules), Disney had quick uptake on the system and a willing community of users. Changes had a much higher level of visibility, thanks to the combination of RSS and NewsGator, and it moved most of the conveyance of information out of e-mail and into the blog. In addition, users could make comments on a blog entry itself, which was a great help when looking up archives.

Conventional wisdom dictates that a high-end change-management system would have been best for a shift log environment. The cost would extend beyond the software, though, to consultants and implementation costs. This approach would have cost a lot of money and taken a fair amount of time to put together. The alternative was to keep it simple, see what worked, and fix what didn't. The blog software was not only low cost, but it was also up and running in less than 48 hours. The goal of the blog project was to get to the starting point (that is, to reach the point the other software had reached), and then focus on incremental improvements. The choice of blogging software also allowed Disney to modify the software as needed, something many higher end systems simply didn't allow.

Pusateri's advice for companies wanting to implement new solutions or paradigms is this: Don't tell employees it's a new solution or paradigm. Simply tell them it will make their jobs easier. Also assure them that whatever's broken will be fixed.

Disney was looking for a system that

- Was computer-based, so that employees didn't need to write information or archive it in a physical location
- Allowed for editing of past entries
- Had reasonable search capabilities
- Allowed users not only to be notified, but to be in control of those notifications
- Was easy to maintain, low cost, and easy to implement
- Was customizable

Movable Type fit the bill, thanks mainly to the innovative and outside-the-box thinking by Pusateri and his team.

LESSONS LEARNED

The Disney Channel's case study was enlightening for a number of reasons—a variety of lessons learned in this case can be applied to your company's blogging strategy and growth:

- *Start simple.* One of the reasons that the end solution works so well is that Disney didn't design massive software to solve its problem. At each step, only bare minimum problems were solved. As a result, they eventually settled on a solution that worked, at which point they were able to implement bigger features that made peoples' lives easier.

- *Think outside the box.* As you are implementing your blogging strategy, it will become easy to do what everyone else is doing. Stop and think about ways that your company can be different. Blogs are great, but they are just tools, and as more people use those tools it will become less and less remarkable when new companies join in. To get truly noticed, you'll need to do something different. Maybe you'll produce a weekly podcast, or you will invite industry analysts to comment on issues; maybe you'll include employee interviews. The way you differentiate your blog will come directly from the goals and objectives you create in your blogging strategy. Dare to be unique.

- *Give people what they want.* The first step is to meet your company's initial goals. After that, you need to be prepared to listen, so that you can continue to respond to and meet the needs and desires of your business, your industry, and your readers. Don't be afraid to re-examine your blogging strategy, and be flexible enough to try out a variety of different solutions. People like to be heard.

ESTABLISHING A HEALTHY BLOGGING ATMOSPHERE

As you begin to blog and appreciate the complexities, benefits, and potential offshoots of blogging, you will undoubtedly begin to wonder how to get your employees to blog. The first step is to

The key to a healthy blogging atmosphere is to have the company, leaders, and managers value blogging, bloggers, and blog feedback. realize that it's entirely likely that some of your employees are *already blogging*. With millions of blogs in the world, assuming that none of your employees is blogging is about as naive as assuming that none of your employees has ever downloaded music online—it could be true, but the odds definitely aren't in your favor.

Communicate with your employees about blogging. For some companies, this may mean a staff meeting about blogging; for others, it may be an e-mail asking for input. At a bare minimum, it should include a blogging policy and some information to managers about how to handle blogging-related issues. The goal of any blogging policy or guideline should be to communicate what is and isn't acceptable. Some companies actually choose to make blogging a *required* part of an employee's day.

Creating a healthy blogging atmosphere goes beyond the policy you create, however. Having executives who blog and who encourage blogging is a great way to introduce blogging, though it isn't a requirement. The key to a healthy blogging atmosphere is to have the company, leaders, and managers value blogging, bloggers, and blog feedback.

This is why having a corporate blog, product-specific blogs (if you make products such as cars or software), or market-specific blogs (if you create a wide variety of products) is important: it allows your customers to provide feedback in a variety of locations and therefore allows you to use that feedback in a variety of ways. Far too many companies who blog have only one official blog, which is so focused it seems like just another marketing vehicle. This approach is problematic, with the biggest problem being that it allows customers to communicate with you via only one blog venue instead of many.

Building a culture that values blogs requires that you create foundational value statements such as these:

- We value blogs.
- We value bloggers.
- We value blog-based input.
- We value employees who blog.
- We value customers who blog.

Each of these value statements is important.

Valuing blogs means realizing that while a fair amount of noise is being made out there, finding and reading actual customer feedback can be more valuable than any other form of customer communication. Valuing bloggers involves more than just saying "yes, they're out there"; it means reaching out to bloggers and customers for feedback on your company and your products. Creating passionate customers is effective, but reaching out to existing influencers and creating relationships with them will not only revolutionize your business, it will also pave the way for the third value statement: valuing blog-based input.

The challenge with blog-based input isn't getting feedback; it's knowing what to do with both the positive and negative feedback, as well as having a place where you can respond to feedback in an open and timely manner.

THE VALUE OF CONVERSATION: THE iUPLOAD STORY

One company that values blog-based input is iUpload, which creates content management and blogging software for enterprises such as Adobe and CTV, one of Canada's largest television networks. iUpload is a fairly small company, with about 20 employees, though the company is growing quickly. In early 2005, blogger Mark Vandermaas approached the company looking for information on services, pricing, and other features. During the conversation, wires were crossed and people got confused (as sometimes happens in real-world communication).

Mark posted information about his experiences with iUpload to his blog (at http://voiceoflondon.iuplog.com/default .asp?item=99350), which was, ironically, powered by iUpload:

> As of today, April 11th, nearly one month after my initial request, I still do not know the price of the Community Publisher software, and no one from iUpload has contacted me. My wife summed it up best when she asked, What's the big secret? – Mark Vandermaas

iUpload had dropped the ball and he, justifiably, wanted to know why!

Within days of Mark's post, Robin Hopper, iUpload's CEO, responded (http://hopper.iuplog.com/default.asp?item=85308). Hopper succinctly explained where and how things went wrong, apologized, and promised to make things better. He cleared up, in public, the question about pricing and promised to take a number of concrete steps to avoid this kind of confusion in the future.

The net result was that Mark updated his post with the following:

> I have to admit that after notifying iUpload's CEO, Robin Hopper of this post I was half-expecting that my blog's switch would be flipped to the off position.
>
> Since my intent was to help rather than offend I offered to take the post down once he had a chance to review it. This is where it gets good: not only did he not want me to delete this post; Robin told me that he appreciated the

feedback, and that he wanted to post something on his blog with a trackback to it! You can read his post by clicking on the link in his comment below.

Today, I heard from iUpload. Turns out they weren't trying to brush me off; I just got lost in the middle of a frenetic growth stage and misread their actions. We all make mistakes. If you're good, you fix them. [emphasis mine] **If you're really good you fix the mistakes and then fix the procedures that didn't work. But if you're destined for greatness, you have the guts to let someone like me tell the world what you learned from it. Well done, iUpload!** – Mark Vandermaas

This story illustrates a number of core concepts for successful business blogging. First, Mark complained in public about what had happened. When you drop the ball, customers *will* complain. Second, iUpload wasn't afraid to respond honestly to Mark's commentary. Not only did iUpload leave his post on the site, but the CEO responded to Mark's concerns in public on his own blog. The net result? Hopper's response and effort transformed Mark from a mistreated customer into a customer evangelist. And all it took was a little bit of blog love.

Imagine the situation if Hopper hadn't responded, or if he'd responded by dismissing Mark's claims. It's entirely likely that not only would Mark not have bought software from iUpload, but he would have told a fair number of people in his circle of influence about the experience.

The lesson? Creating a blog-friendly culture requires moving past your fears. Fears paralyze us in everything from skydiving (in my case) to spiders (ditto) to responding effectively to customers. There is nothing wrong with being afraid of something new, but taking that first step and actually going skydiving—or blogging—is an incredible experience. Trust me!

WHY YOU WANT YOUR EMPLOYEES TO BLOG

Listening to customers' blogs is obviously an important part of growing your business, because it gives you a window into what they think about your company. It creates real passion and understanding. Employee blogs are similar. In "Why Internal Blogging Rocks," Suw Charman, a renowned British expert on internal blogging, lays out some of the main reasons that internal blogs are critical to your company's success.

WHY INTERNAL BLOGGING ROCKS!

by Suw Charman

The best software bends to your will. It fits in with the way you work, rather than making you change your behavior to suit it. This is where so many big, lumbering knowledge management (KM) and content management systems (CMS) fall over: they force the user to behave in a way that is unnatural and uncomfortable, and anyone who's coerced into using them will stop just as soon as they think they can get away with it.

Blogs, on the other hand, are inherently flexible. You can have one blog with one author and open access, or multiple blogs with multiple authors and a complex access permissions system. Whatever you want, you will find software that either just works or that you can hack into exactly as you want.

Fast and simple to implement, blogs don't require a huge IT budget. Even the most expensive of blogging solutions is a fraction of the cost of traditional KM and CMS platforms, so you can toy with them and if they don't work you can just toss them out. They're easy to use, too: there's no 300-page user manual or three-day residential course to go on. If you can surf the Web, you can use a blog.

Blogs are suitable for almost any purpose—for example, event logging, cross-shift communications, team building, project management, knowledge sharing, and business conversations. Any scenario in which individuals need to share what they know, discuss problems, and make new connections with other individuals can benefit from a blog. Flexibility. Simplicity. Ease of implementation. Cost effectiveness. Just a few reasons why internal blogging rocks.

As with any large project, launching internal blogs in a company can be a challenge—and getting people to adopt, read, and communicate using them can be even more challenging. Following is a series of rules, guidelines, and advice on how to create a successful internal blogging platform, as well as how to get it properly adopted. The first step is to reach out to your employees: the more they own the concept of blogging, the better.

You don't even need to call this *blogging*. Unless your organization is already pro-blog, you can just as easily use a more organization-specific name. Several of the companies I've worked with in the past have simply called their blogging platform my*Company* (where *Company* is the company name). This has given the employees ownership over the blog and has also allowed the company to build the features of the blogging platform around individual employees.

GETTING EMPLOYEES INVOLVED

After you reach out to your employees for feedback, you will likely want to bring on a select group of employees as part of the planning process. These people will go back to their groups or departments and evangelize for the new offering, as well as ensuring that the new internal blogging platform addresses their needs as employees. The goal here is to provide value to the individual employees, to empower the individual employees, and to make finding other similarly minded employees easy.

The most successful internal blogging platforms have the following three properties in common:

- *They bring value to the individual.* If there is no value for the individual employee, there will be no blog posts. And no blog posts means no value for anyone.
- *They make finding other similar-minded individuals easy.* Some companies facilitate this via a unified category system or by asking employees to create a list of interests (much like today's social networking services such as LinkedIn, www .linkedin.com). Others do this via an internal blog-focused search engine. The easier it is for employees to find each other, the more connections will be made.
- *They make it easy to read, browse, and subscribe to the blogs.* "Find similar blogs" and "Find comments by this author" are great features to allow people to find others with whom they agree. As in the wider world of blogging, connections that are made are often more abstract than just "I'm an engineer, and that guy's an engineer so we should connect." People will connect based on personality more often than career.

Ensure that as you roll out your internal blogging system, you don't make it restrictive. The more control the individual employee has, the better. While some managers will fear that employees will use the blogs for frivolous things, if you've hired smart people, they will use the technology wisely and efficiently—especially if everyone in the company can read it. Much as in the real-world blogging community, the price for being a fool is having everyone laugh at you—and not in a good way!

Some companies have set up project-specific and process-specific blogs, and anyone can contribute to these blogs, as opposed to having individual blogs. The more relevant to employees' jobs and interests the non-individual blogs are, the more they will be read and therefore the more valuable they will be.

If you encourage employees to blog, you need to give them time to blog. The last thing employees want is to feel like they are stealing time away from other projects while blogging. Ensure that employees—and managers—know that blogging is part of the job and that it is highly encouraged. This doesn't mean that employees can blog for eight hours a day, but it does mean that it needs to become part of their daily workload. Encourage employees to be responsible in their blogging, and that their blog and the other company blogs are an extension of their responsibilities, not a replacement. Be as open as possible, and talk about it with employees or employee advocates.

TIPS FOR BLOGGING SUCCESS

Encourage employees to comment. Comments create communities and trust and spread knowledge even more freely than blog posts. The more employees believe that they own their blog, their ideas, and their micro-community, the better.

Be aware that blogging may involve or be a catalyst for cultural change, and know that some people will be threatened by that idea. Ensure you have a process in place not only to address people's concerns, but also to improve the blogging offering. It's unlikely you'll get it right the first time.

Start simple. As illustrated in the examples of Disney and GM, large success doesn't require large plans. The simpler the solution, the more easily employees can see how it benefits them and their jobs. Organic growth is the best kind for any type of community or knowledge-based initiative.

Finally, have a purpose. Don't start blogging because blogging is cool, hip, or makes you more stylish. Have specific goals attached to the internal project, such as "to help employees connect more easily," or "to create an online knowledge repository for the future," or even "to generate new ideas." You can then revisit the new platform every few months and see how well it is succeeding at these goals and learn what you can do to help it along. Your internal blogging needs to grow organically, but it also needs to be ready to change organically.

WRAPPING IT UP

In this chapter, we looked briefly at how to use blogs and a few examples of prominent companies making innovative use of blogs. Ultimately, the options for how to use blogs are limitless. The key is to decide where your business is going and then figure out whether blogs are the right tool to get you there.

In the next two chapters, we'll look at the top ways blogs can be used internally and externally and more examples of companies that are using each of the techniques. Hopefully, these will stir up some thought for how your business could make use of blogs, and even for how you could push the envelope of what is possible in the world of blogging.

5

WHAT TYPE OF BLOGS ARE BEST FOR YOUR COMPANY

This chapter provides a framework to help you understand and remember the top seven ways you can use blogs to market your business, create relationships, and create positive experiences for your customers. Some blogs will require that you use a mixture of these methodologies, while others will employ only one of these seven basic blog types. No matter; as long as your business is getting value from your blog, you're succeeding.

EXTERNAL BLOGGING PERSONALITY TYPES

Instead of providing a dry list of the top ways you can use blogs, I've decided to look at blogging in a different way. I have taken the top seven types of business blogs and personified them as different characters, or locations, within a city. Let's take a tour of this virtual city and visit some people and places your business may want to work with as it discovers, experiments with, and eventually embraces blogging:

- **The Barber** Barbers can prove to be prominent citizens— they know the right people, have lots of wisdom from years of listening to customers, and have no problem sharing that wisdom. In some ways, a barber serves as a pundit or analyst, or perhaps an adviser. The barber deserves to be heard not only because she sees things differently, but often because she's *right*.

- **The Blacksmith** The blacksmith is like the barber in that he knows the industry, except he is typically *inside* a company and is thus hammering industry and opinion through the company forge. Software developers at IBM, Sun, and other large technology companies fulfill this role as they bring their experience to bear on a problem.

- **The Bridge** A bridge blogger is a person who makes connections, influences, and helps bring people together. She is obsessed with relationships and connecting people, and as a result she can often function as a peacekeeper. In a corporate setting, the public relations professional may be a natural bridge blogger—or it could just as easily be the company secretary.

- **The Window** A window blogger is similar to a blacksmith blogger in that he typically works inside a company and uses his experience to frame his opinions. The difference between the two types, though, is that a blacksmith blogger typically talks about things *inside* the company, while a window blogger typically talks about things *inside and outside* the company.

- **The Signpost** A signpost blogger in unusual in that she typically doesn't share her opinions—at least that isn't the primary reason for her blog's existence. A signpost blogger points out cool things of interest in her industry. She may not have much to say in each post (maybe only a few words describing a topic of interest), but she may post dozens of short notes per day as she comes across interesting tidbits, perhaps pointing readers to information at other sites.

- **The Pub**   Pub bloggers create discussions designed to bring in people from all spectrums of a particular issue to talk something through and have a laugh at themselves or others in the process. Peter Davidson's blog is a solid pub blog example; "Thinking by Peter Davidson" (http://peterthink .blogs.com/thinking), shown in Figure 5-1, allows a group of likeminded thinkers to explore a variety of issues.

- **The Newspaper**   A newspaper blogger functions in many ways like a journalist—attempting to do more reporting than opining, she does her best to stick to the facts. Many political blogs are newspaper-ish in nature, as are a few technical blogs, such as Engadget (www.engadget.com), shown in Figure 5-2, which focuses on the latest "gadgety" news.

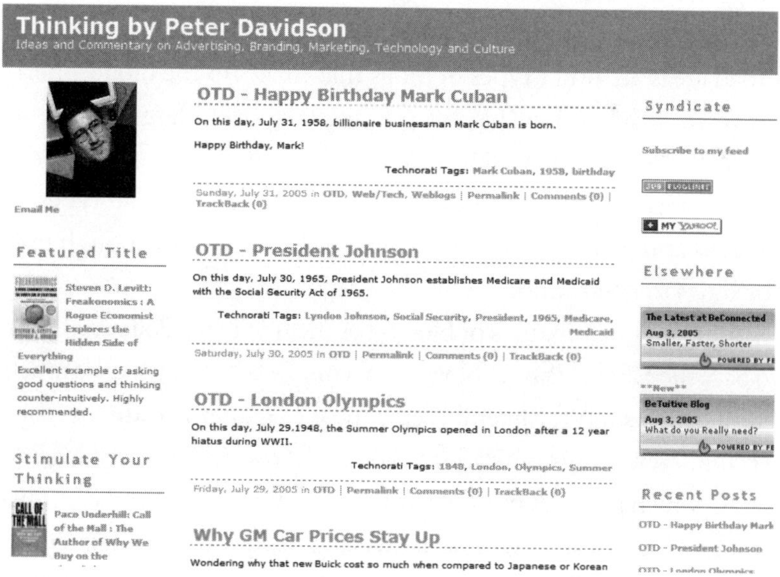

Figure 5-1   Peter Davidson's blog is a popular pub blog.

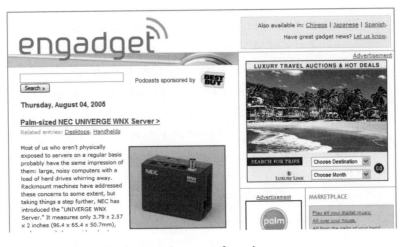

Figure 5-2 Engadget is a popular source for gadget news.

A single blog may often include characteristics of several of these types; however, because blogs are generally written by one blogger or a small group of bloggers, you can often see an overriding trend as to what type of blogger is at work. Mixed in with these broad areas are other types of blogs that make up the blogospherical town—the post office, where people go for a large variety of information; the town hall, where important decisions are made; and all sorts of other oddities. A healthy town needs all types of citizens and places, and there are certainly more than enough uses for blogs to go around.

Some unique mixtures of blog types include Dave Pollard's "How to Save the World" (http://blogs.salon.com/0002007), which is much like a coffee shop for likeminded people to gather and discuss topics; the "New Communications Blogzine" (www.newcommblogzine.com), which provides monthly insights from marketing and communications leaders; and "Doc Searls Weblog" (http://doc.weblogs.com), where Doc not only shares his opinions, but frames them with dozens of other opinions from the blogosphere.

THE BARBER

Growing up, I was afraid of barbers. I guess I couldn't really imagine getting any girls to like me if I was missing an ear. Even at a young age, though, I knew that the barber was important. I knew that great barbers weren't the same as great haircutters or hairstylists. Great barbers engaged me, advised me, and helped me grow into a man. Each visit to the barber was a time of potential growth and change.

In the world of blogging, barbers are few and far between. This is largely because a barber isn't born; he is made. You don't wake up one morning with the wisdom to become a barber; it's something you learn over years of listening, advising, and leading.

For a business, establishing a barber blog will often mean rising above company issues and even company policies. A barber will be honest about his company and his industry's faults, as well as their potential. He won't pick sides, but he'll trumpet every success. For being impartial, he will gain both respect and derision. Companies don't often intend to hire barber bloggers, but having a barber who is both accountable and honest, while still being open and authentic, writing one of your external blogs is like finding a Tiffany lamp at a garage sale—a true find.

A variety of bloggers have walked the line between wise and available, proficient and humble. In fact, such bloggers are found in every industry. Most barber blogs are centered around one industry or a section of an industry. These bloggers don't hide the fact that they are employed by certain companies, but they are so open and honest that this fact generally doesn't seem to taint their perceptions. The value of having a barber blogger for your business is massive but hard to quantify. How do you put a dollar figure on not only having an expert in the field blogging for your company, but also having him being regarded as one of the thought-leaders in the industry? How much is it worth to have him, and therefore your company, be found whenever someone is looking for information on what you provide?

When you think of the world of PR and marketing, names such as Steve Rubel and Andy Lark quickly surface. Their respective businesses, CooperKatz and (until early 2005) Sun Microsystems, benefit from the blogging generated by these men. The reason? Any company smart enough and brave enough to let someone like Rubel or Lark be open and successful, without feeling jealous, must be a great company to work with.

Overall, a barber blogger brings three key benefits to a company:

- **Visibility** Especially for small or boutique companies, such as CooperKatz, having an industry-defining blogger on your staff can transform your company.
- **New ideas** The great thing about bloggers who are leading their industries is that typically they interact with lots of people. As such, they are able to create new relationships, identify new opportunities, and generate new ideas effectively.
- **A human perspective** It's difficult to put a value on having a blogger who makes your company seem human, approachable, and caring. While you may not want to seem weak, it's hard to argue the value of seeming real.

Prominent barber bloggers can also bring in side benefits, such as getting you and your company invited to participate at industry conferences and contribute to trade publications, and otherwise raising your profile for success within your industry.

One thing that can be said about barbers is that people trust them. Regular people, like your customers, suppliers, and employees, trust barbers because they tell the truth, have wisdom, and aren't afraid to share it.

HAVING A BARBER ON YOUR SIDE

Back in mid-2004, nobody knew who Thomas Mahon was. The youngest tailor of custom-made suits on London's famous Savile Row, Mahon allied himself with Hugh Macleod, a popular and respected barber blogger. Through this relationship, Mahon secured lots of interviews and incredible blog exposure; today, as a result, he is growing his business faster than he could have ever imagined. (For more on Mahon and his blog, see "An Authentic Marketing Voice" later in the chapter.)

While having a barber as one of your bloggers can provide a strong voice for your company, he shouldn't be the only voice for your company. You also need people who can convey information effectively, people who can build relationships, people who can point out valuable information, and a whole suite of other people, personalities, and places to provide input and support. An effective city isn't built up of only barbers, and neither should be your company's external blogging presence.

THE BLACKSMITH

The barber may cut a wise figure, but the blacksmith can be an imposing one. He works craftily with his hands, and it shows. Nobody doubts a blacksmith's ability, as his handiwork is displayed all over town. Similarly, blogging blacksmiths are visible in a way that differs from barbers. A blacksmith is visible because his craft, and therefore his talent and knowledge, are always visible. A blacksmith blogger will dive into a deeper level of knowledge of his craft and expertise than any other blogger; as a result, most of his readers are also blacksmiths. Software developers usually fall into this camp.

A blacksmith blogger is essential to any company looking to gain trust in the industry, because blacksmiths talk to other black-smiths, creating an exchange of knowledge directly between the people who have it, which makes everyone's life easier. A black-smith can also help to solve customer issues effectively, because he knows the issue better than anyone else in your organization.

In many ways, the typical blacksmith blogger is a "ground floor" worker. He isn't typically in management and likely doesn't get much credit from within the company. But he knows his stuff, and others who know their stuff respect him for it. While barber bloggers are usually popular, the sheer number of blacksmith blogs in a company will often mean they are far more effective at com-municating than most people realize.

Don't be fooled into thinking this is only a high-tech phenom-enon. Individuals in law, finance, healthcare, and other industries ruled by small to medium-sized businesses are gaining increasing exposure for themselves and their companies solely through their knowledge and their willingness to help.

A blacksmith blogger can help a company in a number of ways, including these:

- **By helping customers**   Blacksmith bloggers, because their work is so visible, are often asked by distraught customers how to solve simple issues. For lawyer blogs, this might be in the form of basic law advice; for home improvement blog-gers, it might be information about where to find a certain kind of building material, for example. Blacksmiths are shar-ing people, and the goodwill they generate with your cus-tomers is valuable.

- **By spreading news** Because of their knowledge of their craft, when blacksmith bloggers breaks news, people listen. Successful blacksmiths won't just break news, though, they'll also tell people what it really means. When Microsoft was beta testing its new search engine, for example, the MSN search team blacksmiths used the blog to announce the launch, to admit what areas needed work, and to inform the public about where the product was heading. This helped develop trust and expectations of the product to come.
- **By establishing relationships** While barbers establish top-heavy relationships with visible people in the industry, blacksmiths establish relationships with other blacksmiths, generally fostered around mutual respect and admiration. Some of these "underground" relationships are often the most valuable ones for a company, as they are privy to wisdom and knowledge to which your company otherwise wouldn't have access.

Some businesses will not be comfortable with allowing blacksmith bloggers in, largely because of a fear of openness or of sharing information. These companies think that every bit of information that leaks out is value they are losing, because knowledge is power. However, they often don't see that every piece of information they provide via a blacksmith blogger is also returned several times over in valued customer support.

As your secretiveness decreases, the community's trust in your company increases. This is a foundational part of employing and encouraging blacksmith bloggers. While you obviously don't want them to give away anything truly secret (like upcoming product designs or financial issues), blacksmiths can do common sense things to increase your customers' trust in you, to build relationships, and to help customers.

A PERFECT JEWEL

Rebecca Thomas owns a jewelry store and decided to start a blacksmith blog (www.rebeccathomasdesigns.com/blog) to increase the size of her business and to share stories, patterns, techniques, and other things of interest to her customers. This is her blogging story.

Rebecca Thomas Designs
Handcrafted silver jewelry

Search

Browse archives

« August 2005

Su	Mo	Tu	We	Th	Fr	Sa
	1	2	3	4	5	6
7	8	9	10	11	12	13
14	15	16	17	18	19	20
21	22	23	24	25	26	27
28	29	30	31			

The stars of the site

Jewelry Gallery
Bethany Collection
Giselle Collection
Linnea Collection
Sofia Collection
Personal Wardrobe
Experiments in Design

Syndicate

XML

Navigation

· albums
· recent posts

Popular content

Today's:

· A little story

blogs

More pictures up!

I've added nine more pictures to the galleries over the weekend, including one of my very first pieces! Check out the galleries to see the new pieces!

It's also come to my attention that in the rather haphazard design of this website, there really is never a place that explains how to order a design or even contact me, so I'm working on a page to change that. I expect it to go live in the next day or two.

I may also try to move some of my pattern and technique sheets from my wiki over here soon.

For now, however, camp calls!

⊞ **kirylin** – Sun, 07/31/2005 – 10:41am
⊞ **add new comment** – 2 reads

Designing for a friend

I've decided to give the story   ☒ Aventurine flat mail ring

Recent blog posts

· More pictures up!
· Designing for a friend
· The pictures are back!
· New auctions up at eBay
· The albums are missing!
· The joys of technology
· You don't have to crazy to work here...
· Time goes so quickly sometimes
· Camp begins!
· Advice for using U-Pins

more

Shopping places

eBay
Olde Garage

Press

Interview with Free From 9 to 5:
Part One
Part Two

"As I started thinking about the presence I wanted my jewelry business to have on the Internet, I knew I wanted to include a blog. I was already writing other topic blogs. I figured another one wouldn't be too difficult.

"Where my other blogs had been born on impulse and nurtured haphazardly, I wanted this new one to be more thoughtful. After all, it was going to be my best way to develop a relationship with potential customers. I could have taken the 'build it and they will come' approach, but based on my blogging experiences I knew that I wanted something that would engage visitors, that would encourage them to take a chance on me and my work.

"More importantly, I wanted the jewelry pieces themselves to engage visitors. Every single one of my designs has its own story, and those stories can reach people far better than just the pictures. At our core, we are a society of storytellers. We weave them around us every day in our lives, and we respond to them because they often reflect something in our own lives.

"I blog to share the stories of my designs. I blog to share patterns, techniques and stone lore. I blog to share the stories of my business as it struggles to become established. I blog to bring a human touch to my business."

A blacksmith is key to building that trust, building relationships, and creating positive customer experiences. They aren't a replacement for a customer support system, but they can definitely help customers with issues that may be more or less common. Employing or being a blacksmith takes a lot of work, but once you see your craftsmanship displayed across town and people's lives made better thanks to your efforts, it's worth the hard work.

THE BRIDGE

While a bridge may not necessarily be the most important location in all towns, for those who need to cross it, it is absolutely essential. In riverside cities, the presence of bridges unites one side of town with the other. So it is with bridge bloggers. They read blogrolls so they can find new blogs to read, and then they read hundreds, or even thousands, of blogs. They devour these blogs so that they can build relationships, expand their world, and make connections.

For your business, bridge blogging can have unexpected results. Some bridge bloggers have facilitated conversations with people who wouldn't otherwise have spoken to each other, while others have introduced people who have gone on to found incredibly successful companies. A bridge blogger has two primary areas in which she finds value: relationships and making connections that wouldn't otherwise be possible.

Bridges create relationships with people around the world, across industries, and across disciplines. Sometimes, these relationships didn't exist before.

Having a bridge blogger in your business can have some interesting effects:

- **Create new business opportunities**   Because bridge bloggers are relationship oriented and passionate about who they know, they are incredibly good at finding unusual opportunities that either your business or your customers may not have considered. The number of new opportunities a bridge blogger is able to create is proportionate to the number of relationships she is able to build in distinct industries. The more relationships she has, the more your business will benefit.
- **Create new customers**   Because a bridge blogger knows so many people and is so passionate, she is a natural salesperson. But because she rarely comes across as trying to sell, largely due to her passion and honesty, most people don't realize they are being sold.

In addition to building external relationships, a bridge blogger also builds relationships within your company. Much like the blacksmith, the bridge cares about people and in many ways will function as an advocate for customers, ensuring that the right

FROM A YAHOO TO A YAHOOLIGAN

Jeremy Zawodny is a search evangelist at Yahoo!, and his popular blog (http://jeremy.zawodny.com/blog) is a perfect example of a bridge blog. Not only do his discussions pull in people from all walks of life, but he also seeks out relationships with people inside and outside his industry. In fact, Zawodny is such a natural "un-salesperson" that he has helped get people hired at Yahoo! because he believes in the company so much.

things are done for the right people. Bridge bloggers create positive experiences for customers, something all businesses need.

Allowing a bridge blogger to do her thing should be a natural extension of any corporate endeavor. Relationships are basically give-and-take, and any relationship that costs more than it provides generally isn't worth having. Relationships take work. Bridge bloggers are happy to do some of that work, as long as their work is rewarded and good things happen for both parties as a result. A bridge blogger doesn't want to enable a one-sided relationship anymore than you want to be part of one, which is why you need to make sure that you are valuing both your bridge blogger and the good relationships she's building.

THE WINDOW

A window allows people inside to see out and people outside to see in. A window blogger is someone who gives a distinct perspective on the workings of your company to the outside world and, thanks to her honesty, relays what's happening in the outside world back to the inside.

Jonathan Schwartz (http://blogs.sun.com/jonathan) is perhaps the most well-known window blogger, as he often gives insight into his company's (Sun Microsystems) ways and means. And he's well positioned to do so, considering he's the company president. However, you don't need to be well-positioned to be a window blogger; you need only insight into the life of the company, which is something most employees should be able to pull off.

Window bloggers are often seen as an odd, though respected, bunch. They, like barbers, don't pull any punches. They tell it like it is, good or bad. But they also go beyond that by citing reasons for decisions made and why mistakes happened, or by announcing the launch of new products. Window bloggers thrive on *context* and *communication.*

A window blogger in your company can best be used by encouraging her to do the following:

- **Share background**   Whether a mistake has been made or a great piece of news has been announced, a window blogger is much like a back-channel into an organization. She can provide the inside scoop on what's going on and why, without it sounding like a marketing pitch. Her honest opinions, which build trust over time, and her frank assessments of company developments and the industry are valuable for people wanting to know what something *means.*

- **Deal with complaints**   While she shouldn't serve as the only customer service department, because a window blogger knows the company, she is able to share why something in particular happened. Did the phone system disconnect a caller? Maybe a power outage occurred, which is something people can relate to. The intent of a window blogger is never to spin, because most people relate to the truth.

ALL GOD'S CREATURES SHOULD BLOG

Brian Bailey is the web director at Fellowship Church in Dallas, Texas. He has been blogging for more than a year at his personal blog (www.leaveitbehind.com/home); however, his church recently began embracing blogging as a business decision. Bailey's blog has long been a view into a sophisticated web technologies group, as he grappled with choices of programming languages and platforms, chose to use Microsoft's .NET Framework, and then moved to an open-source alternative. Thanks largely to Robert Scoble (http://scoble.weblogs.com), Bailey's blog has become one of the more popular Christian blogs out there.

The Fellowship Church's blog (http://blog.fellowshipchurch .com) is a window blog, as it covers recent happenings in the church and offers a unique view into the organization's inner workings. The blog also regularly interviews staff and church members, providing a unique place for people to share experiences. In this way, the blog goes beyond being just a window.

Successful window blogs don't always need to be written by individuals. Many companies are starting window blogs, where they interview executives and staff, post video interviews, and otherwise try and give people on the outside a look inside the company.

While the use of a window to see in is an obvious benefit, successful window blogs also allow companies to see out. As people learn about your company, they learn to trust you and will often open up and give you permission to enter their lives in ways that they wouldn't have considered before. Being bold and establishing a window blog or encouraging window bloggers in your company can help build a two-way trust in unique and encouraging ways.

THE SIGNPOST

As you might imagine, a signpost points the way to useful and important places. Today's real-world signposts point us to major sporting locations, restaurants, and other items of a tourist nature; others provide signs to ensure civil order, such as speed limits and parking boundaries. A signpost is designed to do two things: inform and point the way. Similarly, a signpost blogger does two things: informs readers about useful information and points the way to other useful information.

While signpost bloggers may not give you the direct benefits of other, more personally visible types of bloggers, they do provide two important benefits:

- **Provide a source of information**   A signpost blogger is someone people learn to trust and visit on a daily basis, either through feeds or by accessing the blog itself. As such, the blogger is seen as a knowledge- and thought-leader, someone people seek out for a distinct point of view.
- **Filter information**   Because people learn to trust the signpost blogger, they learn to see into his personality and values. In fact, many signpost bloggers are incredibly influential because they've demonstrated their ability not just to find good information, but also to filter out the garbage.

A signpost blogger is a valuable asset. Many companies have set up signpost-style blogs as their official company blogs (mixing in some company news, of course), because they work so well as

YEARS OF TRUST

Roland Tanglao is a major signpost blogger from Vancouver, Canada. He writes a variety of blogs, but his personal blog (www.rolandtanglao.com/) is an eclectic mix of tech news, advocacy, life, and pointers to other interesting things.

Tanglao's posts typically comprise one or two sentences about why he believes something is worth his attention, a quote, and a link to the site where the quote came from. Tanglao rarely delves into his deep convictions or thoughts on a topic (at least not on his blog), and he is well respected for his ability not only to be fair, but to find things that are worth looking at—whether you're in business, a techie, or just curious.

It's taken years for Tanglao to develop a sense of trust and respect, as both a blogger and a person, and it's something he isn't willing to give up. Many expect Tanglao to keep up his blogging style for many years to come.

information outlets. You can tell folks what's going on, include a tidbit of opinion, and get feedback not only on your opinion, but also on issues that people care about.

Signpost bloggers do need to ensure that they have meat in their overall blogging strategy, rather than just pointing out interesting things. Signpost blogs can help your company gain trust and a decent amount of visibility, but they won't likely help your product development, overall image, or customer knowledge—at least not directly. That doesn't mean you should shy away from having, or being, a signpost blogger, however. The choice of what you include on your blog is up to you as an individual, your time, and your business priorities. A signpost blogger requires a variety of sources, a solid eye for what's valuable, and the ability to devote a bit of time to write short posts on subjects that are worth blogging about.

THE PUB

Pubs and bars have always been an essential part of any town. While some are raucous places ruled by bad beer and loose conduct, the best pubs have always been a place of social unity, where ideas (and laughs) are exchanged in a more open and honest way than in any town hall.

Pubs are gathering places where communities go to share ideas and have some laughs. The alcohol is a secondary concern in the greatest pubs—music may draw people in, or interesting people may be the ticket. For others, such as authors C.S. Lewis and J.R.R. Tolkien, pubs provided the atmosphere and the mutual respect among creative types who frequented the venue.

Like great pubs, a pub blog can be an incredible addition to any community. The pub blogger welcomes people, creates community, enjoys discussion, and loves laughing at and with friends old and new. Everyone feels at home on a pub blogger's blog, and everyone wants to have a say, largely because everyone actually gets heard. While a pub blogger, much like any bartender I suspect, *has* an opinion, she values the exchange of ideas and personalities too much to quell any discussion by forcing her opinion onto others.

A pub blogger can be boon to a business by providing the following:

- **A sense of equality**   When any individual's voice is heard, everyone's voice is stronger; this is an important principle in blogging. Equally important is that anytime you don't provide a place for your customers to be heard, they'll go elsewhere to sound off, even though they would probably rather be communicating directly with you. Having a place where all voices are equal means that all voices get heard.

- **A sense of community** It's easy to know when you have a true community behind you, but it's incredibly difficult to get one going. Communities are invaluable, though, as they help information spread, they help create customer evangelists, and they create positive experiences for your company, without you doing very much at all.

- **A sense of fairness** One of the fundamental challenges facing companies today is ensuring not only that everyone has a place to have his say and has people to relate to, but also making sure that something gets accomplished in response to people's comments. Most people value fairness. Customers expect companies to do the right thing, and customers want to be heard, especially when things aren't right. A successful pub blogger allows people to be heard but can also assure people that the right thing is being done—assuming, of course, that the right thing *is* being done.

In a true pub blog, everyone is equal and everyone has a voice. Some larger pub sites, such as MetaFilter (www.metafilter.com) and Slashdot (www.slashdot.org), get around the potential cacophony by allowing anyone to submit a posting and then having a select group of editors approve the best ones for publication. This allows anyone to submit information and ensures that a large pool of participants create an equalizing force that motivates the community not only to read the best stuff but also to seek out their own stories as well.

Creating a pub blog takes the strong community aspect of blogs and amplifies it. For this reason, many companies looking to start pub-style blogs are establishing forum or bulletin board systems, and then having blogs run on top of those, balancing authors with the community. Microsoft's Channel 9 (http://channel9.msdn .com) is a pub blog, and a variety of other companies, such as Citrix and Novell, enjoy such blogs.

THE NEWSPAPER

A newspaper is meant to be an impartial source of information. While modern newspapers do have editorial and opinion sections, they generally provide information presented as objectively as possible. Newspapers are, by nature, heavily transmission based. Little interactivity is going on—unless you count the crossword puzzle or the letters to the editor section.

The point of a newspaper is to tell people what is going on in the world and their community. This is also the purpose a newspaper blogger fulfills. She isn't necessarily looking for feedback, nor is she trying to build relationships, trust, and other personal commitments. Newspaper bloggers are transmitting news, and as long as they do it effectively, it's not exactly a bad idea. Yes, engaging your audience and building trust, community, and all that stuff is good. However, sometimes you simply have something to say, and a blog is a great way to say it.

Thanks to the power of feeds, you can know when and what people are reading. Feeds brings a special dynamic to news type information, because not only can you determine who is reading, you also know that the people who actually want the information you are providing are getting it. One of the reasons many information-based sites are starting blogs that provide value in bite-sized chunks is that regular information allows readers to interact with the company, without any commitment on the reader's part. With feeds, readers are in control. Companies can still get readers' attention, and they still create positive experiences for the readers—never a bad thing, especially if you provide information on a daily basis.

A newspaper style blog is also a great opportunity to serve as a central hub for information in your industry and community. You don't necessarily get the community together on your site like a bridge or pub, but by keeping the community informed, you stay visible, relevant, and in the center of it all.

The challenge with a newspaper blogging, as with a real newspaper, is content creation. Producing a newspaper style blog requires a lot of time and effort. A true information source requires planning, resources, and time. Therefore, ensure that your company will actually benefit before beginning such a blog. Yes, it's a great way to get information out to readers—and in a much more reliable manner than e-mail—but it's also a *lot of work*. Some companies, unfortunately, jump into blogging quickly; post interesting, lengthy entries with all kinds of insight; and then eventually stop blogging because it's too much effort. Before you start a newspaper blog, ask yourself if it's what you really want.

Another way to launch a successful newspaper blog is by building traffic with another type of blog and then letting readers or the connected community provide the content. This not only empowers the community, but it means that the blog writers don't bear the full responsibility for creating all the content.

No matter what kind of blog you eventually start, the first question you should ask yourself should not be "What kind of blog should I start?" Instead, it should be "What am I trying to accomplish?" Determine your goals first and work toward them using blogs. If you decide to share information with customers in a transmission format, a newspaper blog may be the way to go. That said, if you can produce a successful newspaper blog, you can reap some great rewards.

WHAT KIND OF BLOGGER ARE YOU?

Each of these profiles has positives and negatives and can be some-what abstract—largely because you'll likely use bits of all of these types in your blogs. Sometimes you'll want to inform, sometimes you'll want to discuss, and sometimes you'll want to point out interesting things that are going on. A healthy blog is a balanced blog.

Let's take a look at some popular types of blogs and how they match up to these profiles. You can learn some interesting things by looking at examples of blogs to see where they're strong and not so strong. In the following sections, we'll look at the following types of blogs:

- CEO blog
- Marketing blog
- Aggregation blog
- Staff blog
- Specialized blog (marketing, business development, and so on)

THE CEO SAYS...

The *CEO blog* is a common type and refers to a blog created by anyone in a senior position of leadership within a company. When the first CEO blogs appeared, they were regarded with a lot of cynicism. After all, bloggers and readers reasoned, since when did a CEO talk authentically or honestly? But thanks to solid examples by CEOs and senior executives such as Bob Lutz (http://fastlane .gmblogs.com/), Jonathan Schwartz (http://blogs.sun.com/ jonathan), and Mark Cuban (www.blogmaverick.com), company leaders now have solid examples of not just how to blog success-fully, but also *why* to blog. Each of these leaders has embraced the chance to shape public opinion, talk directly with customers, and tackle industry and company issues head-on, instead of going through marketing folks and journalists.

CEO, executive, and business owner blogs are powerful because they present the mostly unfiltered views of a single blogger who is an important part of a company. They are real people, and they are human—at least the successful ones are.

Most successful CEO blogs are a combination of blacksmith (written by someone who knows the company well), bridge (they make connections with people), and window (they allow people to see into the company, while letting the company see out). By drawing on the strengths of all three types, successful CEOs, executives, and business owners can build rapport and trust, convey important company news, provide feedback on the industry, and inform people about what's going on within the company.

It's important that CEO bloggers resist the urge to stand on a soap box and preach to the masses. Successful CEO bloggers have learned, through example, that the best blogs are written more from an "on the couch" perspective than an "on the soap box" one. Customers would much rather interact with leaders as people than as company mouthpieces.

AN AUTHENTIC MARKETING VOICE

The concept of the *authentic marketing voice* isn't new; however, it is still catching on. While some popular marketing professionals write blogs, such as Steve Rubel (www.micropersuasion.com) and Johnnie Moore (www.johnniemoore.com/blog), here we are interested in blogs created specifically for marketing purposes. Some companies use blogs as one of their *only* means of marketing.

One company that uses blogs for marketing is English Cut (www.englishcut.com), shown in Figure 5-3, which was helped along its way by popular marketing thinker and blogger Hugh

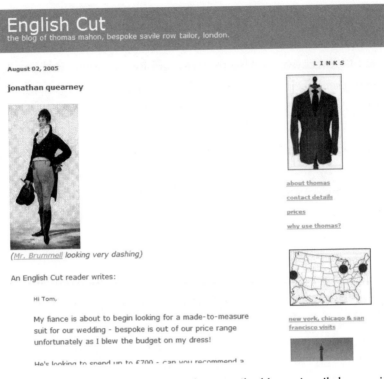

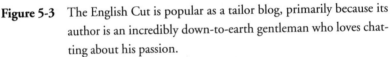

Figure 5-3   The English Cut is popular as a tailor blog, primarily because its author is an incredibly down-to-earth gentleman who loves chatting about his passion.

Macleod (www.gapingvoid.com). London tailor Thomas Mahon has created quite a stir; in fact, largely thanks to his blog, he is one of the most well publicized tailors in Savile Row history, having been featured in dozens of magazines and newspapers.

The power of this blog is simple: it talks about that which is often considered unattainable, $5000 custom-made suits, as if such things are perfectly normal and totally necessary. Mahon and Macleod don't pull any punches: the suits are expensive. What keeps readers' interest is that they can tell that Mahon and Macleod sincerely love the tailor's craft as well as that simplest of joys: putting a smile on a customer's face.

The English Cut is chock-full of talk about how suits are made and marketed and lessons learned. As such, this young blog is a great mixture of the barber (offering his wisdom on his industry), the blacksmith (publicly talking about the secrets of his trade), and the pub (providing a place for people to talk about, and relate experiences with, custom-made suits).

They key to producing successful marketing blogs is to learn to give. The English Cut not only gives away precious information, but it even gives away suits (on occasion). While it is an anomaly in the tailoring industry, this blog is used to create relationships and to make Mahon's company seem very human and down-to-earth. Having marketers run similar projects is great—as long as those marketers understand the medium of blogging.

PULLING IT TOGETHER

Aggregation is the act of pulling multiple sources into a single destination, and an aggregation blog, which pulls multiple blogs together into one, can be a powerful, if simple, way for companies to become an information source in their industry. You can become a thought-leader in your industry in a variety of ways, and although the most effective way is to lead with your own thoughts, many companies have begun turning to aggregation blogs as a means of at least providing leading thoughts to their customers.

A successful aggregation blog takes information from a variety of feeds (official mainstream media, prominent blogs, and company blogs) to provide an overview of what is happening in the industry. You might call this the "Industry News" section of your website.

While it isn't as powerful or trust-creating as having a barber or blacksmith blog, this newspaper/signpost style of blogging can have value for a company. It shows that you know your industry, know the players, and value feedback, which is especially good if you actually do know the industry, know the players, and value feedback.

Here are some tips on creating a successful aggregation blog:

- *Choose your sources well.* In this style of blog, the only real control you have over the content is whether you choose to publish individual posts from your sources. So the higher quality (and more aligned with your values) those sources are, the better.
- *Do other blogs.* Having an aggregation blog is a good start, but it doesn't really allow you to interact with your particular audience. It's a good way to test the waters and make sure the software works, but you can use many more powerful ways to embrace blogging than simply being an information source.
- *Provide a personal viewpoint.* If you are going to use blogs to provide information for your customers, you should be providing your own point of view as well. As such, CEO blogs and staff blogs are powerful tools to augment your aggregation blog—and the best posts from these fantastic company-owned sources can be included in the aggregation blog.

STAFF BLOGS: FROM THE HORSE'S MOUTH

Staff blogs can be among the sharpest tools in your company's toolbox. Good staff blogs can influence your industry, improve your customers' experiences, and empower your staff to help people. While a CEO, executive, and business owner often look at the big picture, a staff

Encouraging staff blogging means ceding control and empowering your staff to communicate directly with the public, which is one of the reasons clear blogging policies are so important.

blogger can blog about day-to-day challenges and victories. If the blogger is a software developer, as many of the earliest staff bloggers were and still are, she'll often blog about code snippets, the status of new technology, and new and innovative things she is learning. If he's a chef, he'll talk about new recipes, tips for success, and what he'll put on the menu when he opens his own restaurant. If she's in marketing, she'll talk about new marketing techniques, ways to encourage real conversations, and the value of transparency.

Staff bloggers love to blog because it *empowers* them to help themselves, their companies, and their customers. Staff bloggers are the quintessential blacksmith bloggers—they share information and experience and encourage others to do the same, and together everyone learns more than they would on their own. It's a little bit like any successful team endeavor: everyone works hard, and everyone eventually gets out more than they put in.

Encouraging staff blogging means ceding control and empowering your staff to communicate directly with the public, which is one of the reasons clear blogging policies are so important. This book's appendix includes an example of a blogging policy. Employers have also tailored their policies to their employees. IBM, for example, allowed employees to write their own blogging policy. The result was a fair and balanced dictum for empowerment that laid out the ground rules but also encouraged employees to take risks.

Your company's blogging policy should be unique. If you are in a highly competitive industry, you may not want your staff blogging about what is happening on a day-to-day basis. You may not want your staff to deal directly with client issues, so your policy may strongly recommend that they route those issues to a customer service or technical support team. The reality is that for most businesses, staff blogs will exist whether or not they are approved. Encouraging them means leveraging their strengths.

Discouraging them may mean losing good employees over a simple matter of communication and trust.

IN THE HANDS OF A SPECIALIST

Specialist blogs cross a number of lines. In many ways, they are staff blogs with the inside scoop. They are also like CEO blogs in that they don't typically deal with day-to-day things, but are often in big picture mode. As such, specialist bloggers such as PR and marketing people, managers in areas such as IT and customer service, business development professionals, and consultants overall tend to mix the approachable style of staff bloggers with the influential status of CEO, executive, and business owner blogs.

For example, hundreds (if not thousands) of successful PR and marketing bloggers are publishing their work every day. These folks have started their own knowledge repository at TheNewPR/ Wiki (www.thenewpr.com), which includes interviews and essays. It also hosts the annual New PR Blog Week, in which the world's leading PR and marketing professionals contribute valuable essays on topics that matter to them.

Not to be outdone, business professionals host a variety of events on their blogs. The Carnival of the Capitalists (www .elhide.com/solo/cotc.htm) is a weekly event with contributions by the top business minds who happen to blog on the Business Blog Book Tour (www.apennyfor.com/bbbt/), which is a monthly event in which leading business authors contribute to important business blogs.

Every industry has leading blogs, and having your bloggers among the more high-profile members of the blogging industry is never a bad thing. These specialist bloggers are one part barber, one part blacksmith, two parts bridge, with just a pinch of signpost and newspaper thrown in for good measure. They are personable, knowledgeable, relationship-driven people who are full of valuable information that they are more than willing to share. Encouraging successful specialist bloggers is as easy as saying, "Hey, have you thought of starting a blog?" Most individuals in these professions are already aware of blogging and its influence, and they just need a gentle nudge to get involved.

That isn't to say that being a specialist blogger is easy. In an ever-growing pool of experts, only the remarkable get noticed—which is one of the reasons having company support is so valuable. Very few specialist bloggers actually blog from within a company; most are independent and own their time. Supporting and encouraging existing professionals in these areas will not only set them apart, but will provide a unique perspective that will make them better bloggers.

WRAPPING IT UP

In many ways, this chapter has been unusual. Instead of examining many of the ways you could use blogs practically, I've chosen to look at external blogs from a "mindset" or "personality" perspective. It's entirely likely that you see the benefit of nearly all of these profiles, and that you can even identify with a handful of them.

The realty is that bloggers aren't some predefined list of personalities any more than regular people are. Blogs are a reflection of the people who write them, and bloggers are people who have a place to express their voice, thoughts, opinions, and knowledge. Using blogs as marketing tools for your business is really all about letting people be themselves in a public space. It can be scary, exciting, and challenging. One of the biggest challenges is knowing what to expect, and hopefully the personalities and examples in this chapter have provided food for thought in terms of how you believe your company can blog for success.

The best way to find out how people think isn't to observe them—you must ask them. The best way to engage someone isn't through a survey—it's through a question. And the best way to establish real communications—the two-way variety, which is where you will find the most value—is through a two-way medium.

In the next chapter, we'll take a look at internal blogging—why companies do it, what types of internal blogs exist, and how you go about launching a successful internal blog. Later chapters cover how to start blogging, how to track what bloggers are saying, and the future of blogging.

6

USING BLOGS TO INCREASE INTERNAL COMMUNICATION

The concept of internal blogging poses a number of challenges to companies that are willing to embrace it. You can use blogs in a number of fantastic ways, some of which were discussed in Chapter 4. We looked at the example of the Disney Channel, which uses internal blogs in an innovative way to save money, make people's jobs easier, and make information easier to access. In this chapter we go deeper into the uses of internal blogs and provide a brief overview of how to get blogging kick-started at your company. We look at the benefits of blogging and at how to develop an internal blogging strategy.

HOW INTERNAL BLOGGING STARTS

Blogging will begin internally at your company either by executive decision or by grassroots support. Both ways pose unique challenges.

As with any new idea, decreeing the use of blogs from on high can create a challenging scenario. The tried-and-true method is to show your employees the benefits of the new tool while getting buy-in and ownership at both the middle-management and grassroots levels. Getting buy-in early from key figures at these levels of the company means that blogging isn't being pushed on people, but is being made available by company leaders as well as being championed by the grassroots and encouraged by managers.

Employees typically won't begin blogging simply because you tell them to. That said, smart employees who recognize the value and time-savings that blogging can provide, when properly used, will often take up the idea quickly. When you are deciding to encourage blogging, it's important to note that not every employee will opt to use the blog.

Many employees are already busy with other work, may not trust management's intentions, or may not be aware of blogging's value or blogging at all. While each of these problems has a solution, often the easiest way to combat these feelings is not to combat them at all—let employees make a choice. The best bloggers, whether internal or external, are those who make the choice to start blogging because they see the benefits of doing so, not because you tell them it's in their best interest.

The second way blogging can start is more common: employees want to start blogging. The idea comes as a grassroots level request, with employees seeing the benefit for their team or for the company as a whole and asking to start a blog. Some teams will simply start using blogs on their own because they see the benefits, and nothing stops them from using blogs. Others will request a new server or space on existing servers to create blogs.

Regardless of how blogging starts, you should encourage employees to use blogs internally (assuming that it fits with your blogging strategy). Suggest new and innovative uses for blogging, such as using blogs for document sharing or for brainstorming new ideas. Implement official blogs. A grassroots movement means you can honestly say that you are supporting your employees' new ideas and that you are allowing them to take ownership of this exciting new tool. If you need a blogging policy, let employees draft it. If you are aware of external employee blogs, encourage them to blog about things they care about internally as well.

No matter how you plan to start, you eventually need to create a plan and a strategy for your internal blogs—with external blogs, the audience is the world; the audience for internal blogs is your company, which means that the people you are able to please are your staff members, executives, and managers. Although there isn't really such a thing as a "popular" internal blogger, typically a CEO blog will be more often read than an engineer's blog (except, of course, by other engineers).

A properly implemented blogging strategy will increase communication both from the company to staff members and among like-minded individuals; reduce e-mail by allowing chronological public discussion to occur; generate new ideas; make your company more fluid and dynamic; and empower your staff. The end result of a properly implemented blogging strategy is happier, more motivated, and ultimately more efficient employees, which is never a bad thing.

HOW TO USE BLOGS INTERNALLY

You can use blogs internally in a variety of ways. Instead of simply listing all of them, I'll show the top eight ways your company can use internal blogs. This list should stir up some thoughts about ways that you can leverage the low-cost, high-adoption technology that blogging can be.

You can blog internally for

- Project management communication
- Internal communication and marketing
- Idea generation and vetting

- Employee involvement and connection
- Team and project communication with the entire organization
- Internal team and project communication
- Administrative communication
- Dynamic team creation

PROJECT MANAGEMENT

Project management is all about ensuring that people stay informed and motivated while also staying on deadline. Project management tasks fail for lack of information and lack of communication. Project management blogs strive to achieve four goals:

- Keep everyone informed on the project's progress.
- Archive important documents.
- Raise discussion points.
- Involve all members of the project team.

Because project management is inherently decision-making based on information, project management blogs allow the project manager and the team to communicate back and forth. Some project management blogs are completely open, allowing anyone on the team to post and comment. These are often strong ways of ensuring that the project is pushing forward while encouraging contributions from anyone and everyone involved. Some companies who use blogs for project management simply don't *need* a project manager because the team completely owns the process and reaps the full reward for success.

In teams large or small, document management can be one of the most difficult aspects of project management. Finding out who has the most up-to-date copy of an important document, who is working on which document, and who each document has to go to can be difficult to track, even with advanced project management software. Project management blogs can be set up to allow people to contribute to documents in an organized manner.

An example of an externally based project management system that uses blogs is Basecamp (www.basecamphq.com), shown in Figure 6-1. For a low monthly fee (or even for *free*), team members can post messages, share documents, maintain to-do lists, and set project milestones. Most successful project management blogs, whether they're externally or internally run, will allow at least these basic project management features.

A strong feature of project management blogs is their ability to raise discussion points. This is accomplished by putting up a post that asks for feedback. These discussion points–based posts can

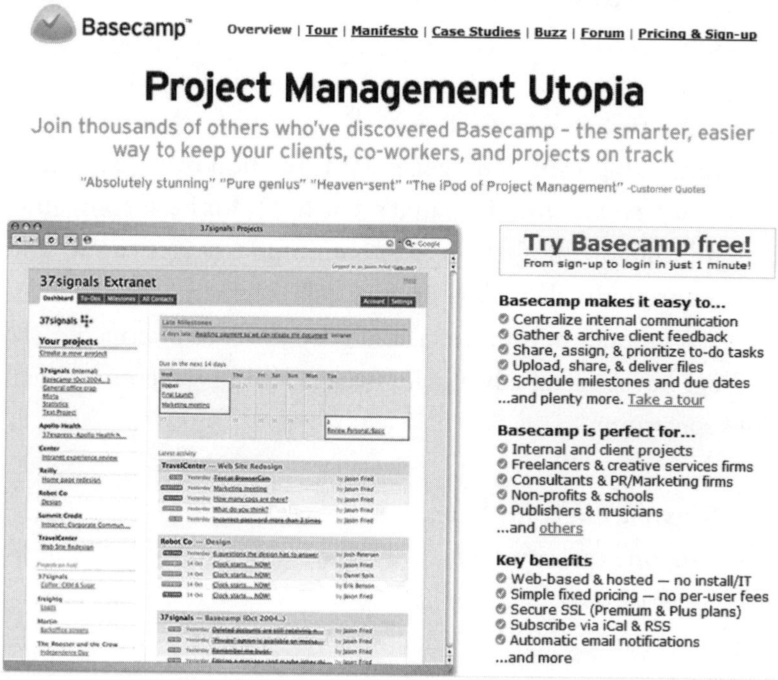

Figure 6-1   Basecamp, built by 37signals, is a fantastic project management system built around the concepts of blogging.

often alleviate the need for a meeting, a series of e-mail exchanges, or a conference call.

Finally, using a blog for project management is *participatory*. It ensures that everyone has ownership of the process and allows everyone to contribute. A well-oiled project management blog should be low maintenance and highly effective. A number of solutions are available for project management, but using even a simple solution such as Movable Type (www.sixapart.com) or WordPress (www.wordpress.org) can work well for motivated teams.

INTERNAL COMMUNICATION IS KEY

Internal communication at any sized company can be difficult. For most small companies, it may not be too difficult to do, but sometimes even small companies want something more permanent than e-mail.

E-mail is one of the greatest communication advances in recent memory, but it is also one of the most difficult to maintain. Between spam, scams, and general information overload, e-mail can often be more trouble than it's worth. Yet for most companies it is still one of the best ways to communicate, get input, and gather consensus. E-mail is used to call meetings, review documents, announce new projects, and post new jobs internally.

Blogs have several advantages over e-mail in the communications spectrum:

- Anyone can contribute.
- Anyone can comment and their comments can be seen by everyone.
- All posts are archived indefinitely.
- Blog posts are categorized for ease of viewing.
- Past posts can be searched quickly and easily.

Blogs are a powerful internal communications tool for a variety of purposes. While internal blogs may not supplant e-mail as the king of corporate communication, they are definitely finding their place in the royal family.

Some great uses for blogs internally are for project sites, new project announcements, recruiting, and as a way to filter down official company news and information from executives. One other great use for an internal blog is as an *industry aggregator blog*. (We talked about aggregation blogs in Chapter 5.) An internal aggregator blog is a fantastic way to keep your employees informed on what is happening in the industry.

In fact, each of these areas offers a great amount of freedom, and the software to power each of these can be as inexpensive as $500. Starting a new blog can actually be as simple as downloading and setting up WordPress (www.wordpress.org) or Community Server (www.communityserver.org) software, both of which are completely free to download.

The power of internal communications blogs comes from their archived nature and their searchability by keyword or date—along with a number of other benefits. It doesn't matter whether you're working at Microsoft or Aunt Minnie's Bakery, having a permanent blog location for official correspondence, industry news, company matters, new jobs, projects, and products can be an inexpensive and effective way to get news. In addition, because blogs are web-based, they ensure that even people who are away for a few days can quickly catch up on what happened while they were out.

IDEAS MATTER

One of the challenges facing today's companies is staying relevant and/or ahead of the curve and generating enough new ideas to keep the business profitable and on the forefront of the industry. Most companies realize that if they could get their employees' ideas out of their heads, the company would be able to accomplish much, much more. Some companies offer significant incentives for new ideas (such as profit sharing); others simply have a suggestions box and encourage employees to use it. No matter what your level of commitment to employee-generated ideas, it's hard to argue with the fact that 200 heads are better than 2.

It goes without saying that no ideas system will work unless you actually value the feedback employees provide. One of the best ways to do that is to acknowledge new ideas, and, if you decide not to go with them, to say honestly why you aren't using that feedback right now.

For most companies, the most difficult part isn't really what to do with great ideas after they're submitted, it's finding great ideas in the first place. And while a suggestion box can be helpful, and incentives are great ways to reward free-thinking employees, the real challenge is in taking an idea from its original state to something that can actually be created or accomplished.

This is one of the reasons that idea blogs are taking off internally at companies: they allow anyone to contribute to an idea and then allow anyone else to comment on the idea, refining it from its original proposal. Much like having employees submit new ideas can improve your business, so, too, can having employees refine other ideas.

Some companies even go so far as to air new ideas that are proposed at the executive level through idea blogs to see if anyone can spot holes in the plans. I know of a Canadian fabric company that ended up dismissing an entire product line because the factory manager was able to spot a production difficulty with a new idea. Thanks to his observations, the only cost to the company was the time lost in meetings.

Successful idea blogs share several common characteristics:

- Anyone can contribute (anonymously if they so desire).
- Anyone can comment (again, anonymously if they want).
- All ideas get reviewed and responded to at the senior level.
- Great ideas get picked, and employees get rewards for their ideas (profit sharing and cost savings bonuses being great rewards).
- Everyone is equal.

A great idea blog may not be enough to save your company, but then it doesn't exactly cost you much to start up such a simple blog. Plus, an idea blog can be a great way to communicate to employees that you value their ideas and, by extension, that you value them.

EMPLOYEES WHO BLOG

Internal employee blogs can be a fantastic catalyst within your company. Internal employee blogs help forge connections *inside* the company. External employee blogs are also great because they allow employees to connect with like-minded individuals *outside* the company.

> The best employee blogs keep people informed, allow for open brainstorming and problem-solving, and improve efficiency across the organization.

It doesn't matter whether you have a dozen employees or 2000, having your staff members connect creates fantastic new opportunities—especially if you're using idea blogs, as these pairings and groupings can often come up with great new ideas. One of the keys to successful employee blogs, beyond encouraging and getting employees to blog in the first place, is to provide them a way to connect to one another. I've said this time and time again, but blogs are equalizing forces. If a janitor has a blog, there is nothing to stop an executive from connecting with the janitor on a subject they're both passionate about—something that would be nearly impossible in the non-blogging world.

Getting successful employee blogs going requires that you provide a variety of ways for bloggers to find each other. At the least, a search engine for posts, subjects, categories, and blogger names is essential. But some companies go so far as to provide a single website that lists new posts, features individual bloggers, and links comments made by a blogger to that blogger's internal blog. The more ways you provide for your employees to connect, the more connections they will make.

The challenge is that implementing these features is more expensive than simply allowing employees to set up blogs. Although free products like Community Server (www.communityserver .org) shown in Figure 6-2, WordPress (www.wordpress.org), and Drupal (www.drupal.org), can help, it's likely they won't provide the whole solution to the puzzle. Starting employee blogs must be considered strategically: it isn't just about whether you value connections, but about *how much* you value those connections and what you're willing to do to facilitate them.

The best employee blogs keep people informed, allow for open brainstorming and problem-solving, and improve efficiency across the organization; for these reasons, IBM turned to blogs for its more than 150,000 employees in early 2005. IBM realized that if employees from around the world could connect on problems and subjects they were passionate about, they could begin leveraging those connections by creating *dynamic teams*, which we'll talk about more in a bit.

Whether you choose to leverage the connections that employee blogs allow, or you simply realize that having employees making more connections makes them smarter, more informed, and more

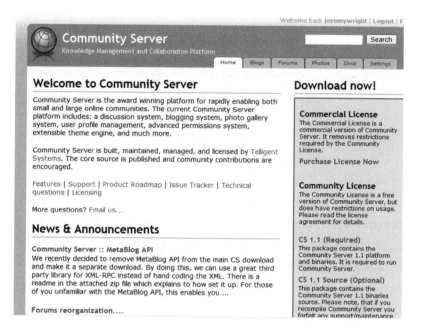

Figure 6-2   Community Server is one of a growing number of free tools that may help your business get started on the road to blogging.

productive, employee blogs are a great way to increase the value that your employees bring to the table.

BECAUSE THE TEAM SAYS

Official team blogs are a pretty new breed of blog. For companies with more than 20 employees, teams can basically run the company. Whether product teams or task teams such as IT and marketing, the teams in the majority of today's companies are self-sustaining, which is why it should come as no surprise that they are increasingly writing their own official blogs.

An official team blog is to teams what an official company blog is to the company: a clear and concise way to describe what is happening in the industry, to post new jobs, talk about team matters, post memos, and discuss other important work-related issues. Team window blogs (see Chapter 5) provide information to other teams, individual employees in the company, and corporate leaders. Several companies I know actually require that all teams publish official team blogs, because it enables executives to find out what is happening in all the teams simply by subscribing to various feeds.

Official team blogs also allow anyone to comment on news and to provide new ideas for the team, thus increasing the team members' ability to do their jobs and remain productive. Smart teams can also make use of other internal blogging tools available, such as administrative blogs, idea blogs, and project management blogs, within their team to make them more effective, whether or not the rest of the company is blogging. They also make use of exclusive internal team and project blogs.

INTERNAL TEAM COMMUNICATION

Sometimes teams want to toss around idea among themselves—perhaps for confidentiality reasons or because small groups can be more effective than large ones. As a result, internal blogs designed to be read only by team members are becoming increasingly popular. These blogs allow for document sharing, brainstorming, and archiving thoughts and discussions.

The goal is to reduce team-wide e-mail by putting most of the official correspondence on the blog so that it can be archived and searched, but the blog also allows responses to occur in a cohesive manner. One of the problems with e-mail is that as e-mail is sent to multiple people, it often results in multiple threads of conversation, with ideas crossing and confusion reigning. Blogs solve this dilemma, since all comments are chronological, so that people who respond to the original post are also responding to previous comments. This means that, generally speaking, internal communication is linear—from original thought to final thought—instead of jumbled among different conversational threads that then need to be recapped so that everyone is included in the loop.

Document sharing is important among teams. Blogs ensure that everyone has the same version of every document, that everyone can see when new documents are posted, and generally that it's impossible for someone to lose a document. E-mail can be deleted, but blog posts are much harder to lose. Blog posts can also be exported—in fact, creating regular backups of the posts and files on a blog is just as important as the blog itself.

In a blog-enabled team environment, every thought is a conversation waiting to happen and every idea has potential for expansion. Obviously, this requires a healthy team environment and, much as with e-mail, unhealthy teams simply won't be able to maximize the potential that blogs bring to the table. But even unhealthy teams can appreciate never losing a document, always being in the loop, and never having someone steal your idea (because your blogged ideas are credited to you).

An internal team blog, much like an internal company blog, is an archived record of a team's thoughts and actions. For smaller companies, one blog may fulfill this purpose for the whole company. Whether you're a small company or a large company using internal team blogs for individual teams, the strengths remain: less e-mail, clearer information that is archived and searchable, strong document sharing, and the ability to brainstorm openly. These are valuable assets to any team.

ADMINISTRIVIA DISTRIBUTION

Your company's ability to communicate clearly is inversely proportionate to how large it is. The larger your company, the more difficult it can be to get the message to people in an understandable way. Memos are a standard means of communication, but unless you plan to e-mail everyone in your company every memo, it's unlikely that the right people will always have the right information at the right time. This is where blogs come in.

Today's administrative world is littered with status reports, meeting notes, sales reports, and all kinds of trivial information that is completely essential to running the company. The challenge is that the people who need that information often don't have it when they need it.

One reason that blogs are so strong at document management is that information is never lost. Not only are blogs categorized, but they are also searchable. Having these documents available on an administrative blog (with permissions set so that the right people can see the right documents) is a great way not only to decrease e-mail and get the information out quickly, but also to ensure that documents are never lost *and* that people can comment on new documents as they are posted.

In addition, a successful company administrative blog can report on changes to HR (such as each employee getting an additional three weeks of vacation per year) and important company meetings (such as the one you're about to schedule about each employee getting an additional three weeks vacation per year). An administrative blog is, in many ways, the lifeblood of a company: without the mundane and the day-to-day, many companies would simply shrivel up. Thankfully, blogs make everything easy to post and easy to subscribe to.

While administrative information can be boring, having a blog on the subject means that when employees actually need to find certain information (such as vacation forms), they know exactly where to go. Blogs can be like a company intranet and document site all rolled up into one package. And you probably don't need any expensive software to accommodate this, as both WordPress and Movable Type are more than up to the task (though they may need minor customizations if you are going to try and lock out certain people from certain information, such as how much vacation senior executives get).

TEAM CREATION ON THE FLY

Dynamic team creation isn't technically a kind of blog that can be created, but it is one of the possible and amazing by-products of a healthy internal blogging culture. The most dynamic and valuable

Strange and wonderful things happen when you create a space for people to get together as equals.

team members are those who work well together to tackle problems creatively. I've been a member of such teams, and the single truth is that there is no way to plan them. A great team simply *happens.* Some teams are great, some teams are just good enough to get the job done, and some are a hassle even to be a part of.

Because blogs allow anyone to vent his passions and interests in a real way (instead of in an "interests" column in the employee database), people are able to connect more easily. The more easily people can connect, the more they get to work together. A healthy blog environment will naturally create teams, no matter how small the company. In fact, the greatest challenge to dynamic team creation is breaking down barriers of thought. For example, I worked with a company where the janitor was actually the perfect person to help with a team that was tasked with merging two companies. His perspective and passion for people, which is why he took the job in the first place, was put to great use in the meetings. Strange and wonderful things happen when you create a space for people to get together as equals.

As you begin creating a culture of internal blogging, realize that unexpected things are likely to occur. Don't judge your teams or assets by their covers, as even the rattiest-looking book could be a Pulitzer winner.

IT'S ALL ABOUT THE BENEFITS

Internal blogging empowers employees, increases communication, reduces e-mail, simplifies document management, and provides a solid framework for employees to stay informed, learn about new opportunities, and be involved in the company. But what does all this really mean for your business?

AVOID EVIL E-MAIL

Reducing e-mail is a huge job. On average, it takes someone 7 to 15 seconds to read, process, and do something about a single e-mail message (even if that something is to leave it there to deal with it later). If you can reduce the amount of e-mail your employees receive by even 100 messages per day, you will save them roughly half an hour of time per day.

Blogging doesn't simply eliminate e-mail, though, because the communication that is in the e-mail still needs to happen. What it does increase is the effectiveness of e-mail. E-mail becomes about "now" items: a meeting reminder, an urgent request, or a quick note. The blogs are the place where official, lasting communication happens and where feedback is made.

For many companies, this is a paradigm shift. And while it isn't necessary to enjoy the other benefits of blogs, the arguments for saving your employees' time, never losing a document, and getting employees involved in the company and empowered for change are difficult to dismiss.

Simply implementing blogs won't do all these things, though. You need to be prepared to raise up champions for the cause by training people to use the blogs, supporting new ideas, and responding to what is happening on the blogs. One of the challenges for companies that begin making their communication more blog-centric is that everything is out in the open: all initial posts and all follow-up comments can be read by anyone. For some companies, when discussions are then taken *off* of the blogs (as will happen), employees can feel left out of the loop.

This is how a blog communication loop works:

1. Initial idea is created.
2. Employees, managers, and executives post comments (anonymously or otherwise, depending on your company). Some companies let this process last for a set period of time.
3. The idea is reviewed. For some companies, this will mean an individual vetting each idea and then passing it up the chain. For others, executives will meet at the beginning of the week to go through new ideas. Some companies actually form a team of employees who are tasked with passing new ideas to executives, thus empowering employees not only to create ideas but also to review them.
4. For ideas that are rejected at this stage, whoever is reviewing them leaves a comment or sends an e-mail briefly explaining why an idea was not used. Sometimes an idea can be a catalyst for an even better idea, but if nothing else it lets everyone who submits ideas know that they were actually *heard*, which is incredibly important, especially at the early stages of building an ideas blog.
5. A decision is made. The ramifications of that decision may not be made public right away; however, posting to the blog or letting the originator know is common courtesy.

The goal of all of this is to provide a complete feedback loop so that nobody ever questions what happens to ideas. If an idea is turned down, the originator knows about it and knows why; similarly, if an idea is accepted, the originator is informed.

Smart companies will let the individual be involved, where appropriate, so that each person can see an idea come to life. Just as positive experiences with customers can create customer evangelists, so, too, can positive experiences for employees create employee evangelists. An excited employee is contagious.

LESS NOISE, MORE EARS

Internal communication can be a challenge. In some companies, too much noise exists—people send jokes and all kinds of other unproductive e-mail—and that can wear down a company's communication channels. The ratio of valuable communication to noise (or useless communication) is fairly high at most companies. For companies that don't take control of their e-mail culture, the culture is often driven more by quantity than quality.

Blogs provide a type of solution for e-mail noise and clutter in two areas. First, the culture around blogging is one where you decide whether what you're posting has value first, because anyone in the company can read it, and posting useless drivel doesn't go very far very fast (if nothing else, nobody will comment on the drivel, so people eventually stop posting it).

Second, the concept of the useless message is far more hidden in a blog post. In e-mail, the final "wow!" or "thanks!" message appears just as visible and important as the original thought, meaning that most of the time, the original thought is lost in a sea of extraneous e-mail. But on internal blogs, the original thought is *all* that is visible, unless someone *chooses* to take a look at the comments. And while there will likely be "thanks!" and "cool idea!" messages in the comments, they don't share the same level of intrusiveness that they do in e-mail, because you can skim past a dozen of them in just a few seconds; you don't have to click open each response.

POWER TO THE PEOPLE

Blogs empower people. In the public world, this is debatable, but in the world of internal blogging, it's an essential truth. The more blogs are properly used, the more valuable they are. I've talked about idea blogs a fair amount in this chapter, because they are all about empowerment—letting employees get involved in the health and future of the company. But every type of internal blog is about empowerment. If it reduces e-mail, it allows people to take control of their inbox. If it makes document management easier, it means your employees don't need to go looking around for the right file. If it helps everyone stay informed about mundane (yet important) administrative and company information, then nobody is left guessing.

DEVELOPING AN INTERNAL BLOGGING STRATEGY

Whether you are part of a small company or a multinational behemoth, getting the right information to the right people at the right time is important. And blogs, combined with feeds, provide that type of framework. Of course, a blog is only as good as the information being put into it and that information is only as good as how it's being put to use. So before you begin your blogging journey, ensure that you have an internal blogging strategy. With so much potential here, mismanaging it would tragic. Get excited. Encourage people. Find great new ways to use blogs. But make sure you do it because you want to improve your business, not just because blogs are new and exciting.

Developing a strategy is a three-part exercise: discovery, exploration, and excavation. The *discovery* phase of creating a successful blogging strategy is laying out your current challenges, your values, and your objectives as a company. Any blogging activity you take on needs to fit with these. Secondly, you need to *explore:* brainstorm new ideas, determine which of the ideas presented in this chapter work for you, and decide what types of activities you believe will make the best use of your resources. Finally, you need to *excavate*: do the work, get employees involved, get them motivated, help them save time and work, and generally make their lives easier, more fulfilling, and more exciting.

DISCOVERY

The discovery phase of any project is the most important part. What you create in this phase will determine not only the metrics for success, but also whether or not you'll succeed in the first place. Too many companies skip over this phase, which is kind of like an architect ignoring the plan of a house and looking at lighting fixtures first.

Planning never killed a project, but ignoring planning has laid waste to many great ideas. Your discovery phase should deal with several key points:

Challenges

Identifying the challenges facing your company is an important component of any new project. If something isn't solving one of your challenges or meeting one of your objectives, why are you doing it? Your challenge as a company could be that your employees are being flooded by e-mail, that you aren't generating enough new ideas, or that internal communication isn't as effective as it could be.

Values

While most people wouldn't add values as part of a project to-do list, I'm a big believer in everything that your company is doing emerging from your values, the dream you are proposing, or the promises you are making to yourself, your employees, and your customers. If your company doesn't have a set of overriding values, promises, or dreams (and, no, a typical vision statement probably doesn't cut it here), it's entirely possible that you are floating in the marketing wind. Values provide stability, and they're a great metric against which to test new projects and ideas. Your values, dreams, and promises might be that you love new ideas, that you will support employees' dreams, and that you will be a market leader in your industry no matter what.

Objectives

Setting objectives for a project allows you to determine metrics for success. Without objectives, you'll never know whether what you are doing is the best thing for the project. Your objectives must match to your values, and as such your objectives may be as simple as improving communication, giving employees the information they need when they need it, and helping to build healthy business relationships among employees and between employees and management.

Metrics for Success

Metrics typically map to your objectives. If your objective is to create new ideas, your metric for success might be that you've received at least 50 ideas during the year, that you've reviewed and provided feedback on all of them, and that you've acted on at least three of them.

EXPLORATION

The second phase in developing a successful blogging strategy is to . . . well, develop a blogging strategy. Discovery was all about setting the ground rules—most companies need to do this only once, and then those values and challenges can be applied to any project. Having done that, you can now enter the three phases of exploration: expanding, contracting, and deciding.

Expanding

This is your brainstorming phase. Take a look at this chapter's eight great ways to use blogs internally. Then look at Chapter 4's big list and brainstorm ways that your company can use blogs. For some companies, this might be a small list, for others it could be longer than the master list in Chapter 4.

Contracting

Having expanded the possibilities for blogging at your company as much as you can, now is the time to match the possibilities to your values, challenges, and objectives. This may mean your list goes from 20 possibilities to 3 possibilities. Find the areas that will provide value to your company where it's at right now. It's okay if blogging doesn't fit right now, because you can always redo this exercise every six months to see if things have changed.

Deciding

Having narrowed down the list, you need to decide which projects will be done and specifically what the metrics for success will be for each of those projects. At this point, you may want to look at proposing resources to be assigned to the project, and you may want to bring on a project manager and/or an employee champion.

EXCAVATION

Having decided *what* you're going to do, the final phase of developing your blogging strategy is deciding *how* you're going to do it. If you're setting up an idea blog, will you allow anonymous posting or commenting, who will review the ideas suggested, and will you give feedback? If you're doing official team blogs, how will you go about getting teams motivated to do this extra work? Will you create time in their schedules for this or is it just another task they need to take care of in their already busy schedules? No matter what you do, the excavation part of your project is a three-phase part: buy-in, execution, and follow-up.

Buy-in

Because blogs are generally employee-driven affairs, you should get buy-in early on, as well as feedback. Launching new projects is difficult in any company, but trying to implement internal blogs from the top down probably won't work. You can use a variety of tactics to get employees to embrace new blogs—simply opening the door to choice or getting employee champions involved will help. The success of the project depends on how much buy-in and participation you get, so don't discount this phase.

Execution

Launching the various blogs your company will be using can be a challenge. Will you start them all at once? Will teams be responsible for setting up and maintaining their own blogs, or will the IT department do it? Lots of questions must be answered, but thankfully actually installing blogs is largely an IT issue, and most blogging software packages are fairly simple to install and configure (for trained personnel). If you don't have the internal resources to handle this, you may need to hire a blog consulting company or bring in general technical consultants. In fact, bringing in consultants with blogging experience, specifically blog consultants, often isn't difficult, especially if they simply review and comment on your plans and do nothing else (many blog consulting companies have a set fee for this, which is fairly low).

Follow-up

For any good project, the worst thing you can do is never check to see how well it's going, whether it's matching up with your values, and whether the people who use the software are happy. Whether you conduct monthly reviews or weekly reviews, make sure you do a high-level evaluation of success on occasion, at least once a quarter. If you find that the venture is unsuccessful, you and your employees can determine how it needs to be fixed.

Because internal blogging has such a huge amount of potential for most companies, it's always sad when an internal blogging project fails because of lack of planning, poor execution, or a lack of follow-up. So do your homework, and treat your internal blogging project with the same respect with which you should treat your employees. After all, it's most likely they who will be using the blogs on a daily basis, and if it doesn't make their lives easier and better, it might not be worth doing.

WRAPPING IT UP

This chapter provides reasons to do internal blogging, offers some solid examples of ways that nearly any company could make use of internal blogging, and introduces some tools for you to use to set up and maintain a blog.

This chapter closes the "how to get started with blogging" portion of this book. At this point, you should have a solid understanding blogging's usefulness and how it can be applied internally and externally to grow your business, improve your relationships with customers, and increase your visibility—among other things.

In the next three chapters, we'll look at how to monitor what's being said about you and your products, how to participate in your blog, and (the all-important) how to deal with negativity.

7

LEARN WHAT'S BEING SAID ABOUT YOUR COMPANY AND PRODUCTS

Sometimes the problem with blogs is that they create a lot of noise, and as a result you can't tell what's relevant. It's a bit like trying to find someone you know at a major rock concert—everyone's yelling, and the fact that you are one of the few not yelling doesn't help you find what you're looking for; you still get lost in a cacophony of voices. As your company gets into blogging, instead of being lost in the crowd, you need to know not only what the blogging voices are saying, but what individuals within the crowd are saying.

In this chapter, we cover how to keep track of "the conversation" as well as how to track individual bloggers, how to monitor and establish metrics for your blog, and how to respond to events that happen in the world of blogs.

KNOW OR DIE

One of the challenges with blogging isn't finding blogs, finding posts, or even finding posts about your company. A massive amount of information is available around blogging, so the challenge isn't in finding that information. Instead, the challenge is to find the *right* information and apply it in a meaningful way.

Thankfully, bloggers have found a noble reason to start sifting through the information: *ego surfing*. Ego surfing is an incredibly precise art form that involves surfing the Web, specifically using Google or other search engines, to find out who is talking about *you* and what they are saying.

Early bloggers decided that searching Google on a nearly daily basis was not only inefficient, but slow. After all, it could take more than three days for new links to your site to show up in Google, and that was simply unacceptable. In fact, Dave Sifry, one of the earliest bloggers, got so fed up with using Google for ego surfing that he created his own website called Technorati (www.technorati .com) to begin tracking how blogs linked to each other.

In the summer of 2005, Technorati began tracking its ten-millionth blog, which caused Sifry to reflect by writing the following (at www.sifry.com/alerts/archives/000312.html):

> The reason why I created Technorati in the first place—I wanted to know who was talking about me and the things I cared about—hasn't changed.... It provides me with a drop of joy and a lot of wonder that we've been able to contribute our small part to the greater good, and to help people make sense out of all of this remarkable creativity in the blogosphere.

Technorati started out small, tracking only a few thousand blogs. As the blogosphere grew, so did Technorati's database. Over the years, other services have come online such as BlogPulse, IceRocket, and PubSub, each of which is discussed in detail later in this chapter. As this book and the blogging community matures, these sites will undoubtedly add new features and new sites will surely come online.

I believe that only two things will remain true in this life: People won't agree on God, politics, or sports; and bloggers will never stop perfecting the art of ego surfing! Thankfully, your company gets to benefit from at least one of these truisms.

FINDING VALUE IN A CACOPHONY OF DATA

As we'll see later in this chapter, services such as Technorati, coupled with smart web analytics, can provide you with a veritable treasure trove of data. But what do you do with all of that data?

We'll look at specific uses for data that each system generates; however, you'll see that you are usually looking for three main pieces of data as you begin to baseline and do trending:

- Where, why, and how you are growing
- Trends you are starting or of which you are a part
- What people are saying about you and how you should best respond

Most companies—even those using low-cost shared website environments—will have some kind of blogging and reporting package installed, commonly known as *web stats*. If you don't have such a package installed, you can use free or paid *stats trackers*, which are available at a variety of websites in a variety of configurations. None of these will be as accurate as the statistics provided by your server or hosting company, but they will provide you with the three main pieces of data.

The reality of web analytics, and with blogging in particular, is that the actual numbers matter very little. What *is* important is the *growth* of those numbers and what that growth means. Starting out with 10 readers and progressing to 100,000 is incredibly impressive and should be studied and acknowledged. Starting with 80,000 and growing to 100,000 is also important to note, but the growth isn't nearly as impressive. What matters is what the numbers represent: growth, links, trends of which you are a part, growing customer satisfaction or dissatisfaction, and other such important issues.

"Tripping over the Long Tail" looks a bit more at why numbers themselves matter—but in a different way than most people think.

TRIPPING OVER THE LONG TAIL

Chris Anderson, editor-in-chief of *Wired* magazine, first coined the term *Long Tail* in a now-famous article published in the fall of 2004 (www.wired.com/wired/archive/12.10/tail.html). Chris's basic premise, as it applies to blogs, is that while mega blogs are certainly out there with audiences rivaling major news organizations, the influence and size of those blogs is about the same as all of the small blogs.

Chris illustrated this with the following graph:

Practically speaking, this graph shows that a handful of super large blogs exist, but also a long tail of millions of other blogs are out there and just as, if not more, important than the largest blogs. In fact, much of the power of blogging is found in this long tail—conversation happens in the long tail, and your customers are in the long tail. And, most likely, *you* will be in the long tail.

While knowing your numbers is important—in that they allow you to graph your growth—they are also less important than you might think, because ultimately what matters is how the rest of the long tail responds. Don't look only at your stats—make sure you also look at how well you are speaking to, or pitching into, the long tail.

Check out Anderson's blog, which details how companies are interacting with the long tail: http://longtail.typepad.com/.

Your web stats will provide the first points of importance for you: if, where, why, and how your blog is growing (or shrinking). The answer to the *why* may be fairly vague, such as "Google is sending us more traffic." This is where trend analysis and link patterns start to come into play. Of the three main blog tracking engines (Technorati, BlogPulse, and PubSub), BlogPulse is the best at offering a historical analysis and is often able to spot the trends of which you may be a part. Finally, services such as Technorati and PubSub are great at finding out what people are saying about you (and who those people are).

Taken together, web stats, trend analyses, and link tracking provide not only a valuable amount of information, but also clues as to how to use that information. At the end of the day, though, your blog's success is rarely measured by these numbers. They are merely indicators of overall health, visibility, and the relative passion of your blogging and blog-reading audience. As such, while important, they should be measured against your overall strategic goals and specifically your blogging goals.

RESPOND TO FEEDBACK—GOOD AND BAD

Having tracked conversations, analyzed trends, poured over your web stats, and otherwise looked deep into how the blogging world feels about your company, brand, and products, you will undoubtedly come to realize that actual feedback is buried in there. Some of that feedback will be good, some will be bad, and some will simply be questions to which you should respond. But no matter what kind of feedback you get, all of it deserves an answer.

Dealing with good comments can often be the most difficult thing, because the temptation is simply to acknowledge the feedback and move on. However, a positive comment is an open door for you to move that customer one step closer to being an evangelist for you. It's an opportunity for you to create yet another positive experience with your company and begin building a relationship. Take that responsibility seriously.

The best way to make a great impression is to respond to a comment in as short a timeframe as possible so that the comment's importance has not diminished.

Likewise, a bad comment should not be ignored. I've said time and time again that an unhappy customer is a passionate customer waiting to happen. And, like the good comment, someone posting a bad comment is giving you the opportunity to interact with her. Not only is it welcome, but in many ways it's expected: because she has interacted with you, ignoring the poster would only drive her farther away. In this case, inaction is just about the worst thing you could do.

Questions, support issues, and other customer relations types of comments should be handled quickly. In an ideal world, all comments—even questions—should get a response in less than 24 hours. Even a response like this is better than nothing: "Thank you for your comment. I have routed this request to the appropriate team. If you don't hear back from them in a few days, let me know and I'll follow up." When someone uses your blog to comment on one of these topics, she isn't just stating that she has an issue—she expects to get help. She is asking for you to create a positive experience for her.

RULES FOR RESPONDING TO COMMENTS

Here are three cardinal rules for responding to comments:

- Respond quickly.
- Be human.
- Follow up to ensure resolution.

The best way to make a great impression is to respond to a comment in as short a timeframe as possible so that the comment's importance has not diminished. Twenty-four hours is a good amount of time, eight hours is better, and under an hour is best. For large companies, these comments can go into existing customer relations pools (assuming they work well enough to produce a response that is not only timely, but respectful). For smaller companies, treat a comment on your blog as you would treat a customer who came into your office with a question: you would probably drop everything to help, and someone commenting on your blog deserves no less because *she* is approaching *you*.

Responding with a human voice, and not with an automated reply, is important. It can also be the most difficult part of this process, because some comments on blogs can become repetitive. Several companies have started responding to repetitive comments within their own posts, and then (nicely) pointing future commenters back to that post, with a note to the effect of "Thanks for the comment! We recognize that this is an area we need to improve on, and we've jotted down some thoughts for how we plan to do that here: [include the link]."

Follow-up and effective customer relations go hand in hand. This is one of the reasons having individuals responsible for blog comments is more effective than having departments responsible for them. Allow the individuals to own a customer interaction, and allow them the freedom to ensure that customers are properly dealt with and that they go away with a smile. The people who respond to your blog comments are like frontline sales people in a retail store: they offer you the best chance at making a great impression.

LEAVE COMMENTS ON OTHER BLOGS

While responding to comments on your blog may seem fairly obvious, it isn't the end of the road for feedback. As you've no doubt seen if you've used Technorati and other tracking services, comments about your company probably appear on other blogs. Bloggers who post impressions of companies on their blogs are practically begging for you to provide feedback. These posts provide an opportunity for you fix any problems and entice bloggers to try you again.

A friend of mine experienced an incident with an airline and missed a flight due to delays; he ultimately ended up missing a job interview and therefore not getting the job. He contacted the airline's customer service, but there wasn't much they could do about a lost job opportunity. After writing about the experience on his blog, a senior airline executive contacted him and asked, "Is there anything we can do to make it up to you?"

This simple response changed my friend's outlook about the airline. He realized that there really wasn't much the company could do, but the fact that someone cared enough to reach out to him

TECHNORATI RESPONDS

In the spring of 2005, my friend Stowe Boyd from Corante (www .corante.com), posted on his blog that he was experiencing some problems with how Technorati was tracking his links (www .corante.com/getreal/archives/2005/05/16/whats_going_on_at_ technorati.php). He said he was being updated on new links, but his overall position among the top blogs wasn't changing.

Within a couple of hours, Adam Hertz of Technorati responded to Stowe's comments, as shown next, explaining that the numbers issue was due to some growing pains—something Technorati was working hard to fix. Hertz made no excuses, but he was honest about the issue and the solution.

Arieanna Foley is a Professional Blogger and marketing specialist. She is a blogging consultant, and is a member of the marketing team for Qumana. Arieanna is an avid proponent for online tools in business communication. She follows social technologies and their impact on the way people interact. Her personal blog is Blogaholics.ca.

GUEST AUTHOR

David Coleman is the principal consultant of Collaborative Strategies, and the author of *Groupware Technologies and Applications (Prentice Hall*

COMMENTS

Adam Hertz on May 18, 2005 11:36 AM writes...

Stowe,

Thanks for your thoughtful comments, and your support for Technorati. Please forgive the length of this comment; you raise some important issues, and I felt they deserve a substantial response.

Our mantra at Technorati is Be Of Service. We take this really seriously. We're very proud that we've created a valuable service that people depend on every day. We strive for perfection when it comes to accuracy, and we try to stay as close to real-time as we can get. It's not easy, and we don't always measure up to these lofty goals.

Another value of our company is transparency and honesty. That's why I wrote you back so quickly with an explanation of the behavior you were seeing. I've worked at companies where responses to criticisms are "spun". That's not our style.

Having said that, we don't always go into excruciating detail in our responses. Our users just want our service to work, they don't necessarily care about the details. In this case though, perhaps I could have been more explicit. The problem was not that we hadn't indexed your post with the Dodgeball tag. It was a transient failure in the application that produces the tag results page. So as such, it wasn't a symptom of not "keeping up".

There is no doubt that keeping up with the growth of the blogosphere is a major technical challenge. You probably noticed that we just passed 10

Corante sPACAmouth
› Blog Antihype
› CTC 2005
› Nerdvana
› Technorati Beta
› Unlinking From Social Networks
› Death To All Panel Sessions
› Remote Tags
› Continuous Partial Attention

RECENT ENTRIES
› Is Microsoft Buying the Market?
› Collaborative Consolidation Again?
› Mary Hodder on Social Architecture
› True Voice: A Conversation with Amy Gahran about Women in Podcasting
› NodeTime Project
› Too Much Collaboration
› Tom Coates on How Blogging Impacts Conference Going
› Plazes Integrates With Google Maps
› Google homepage turns into an RSS aggregator
› JD Lasica Jumps In On Open Tags
› BlogPulse Profiles Beta
› Derek Powazek on How Tags Happened at Technorati
› Communities Are About Trust
› Kevin Marks on Tag Decentralization
› Yahoo scoops up Konfabulator
› Seb Pacquet's Dreaming Of Something New
› More From Adam Hertz on Technorati Link Counts
› Mary Hodder Digs Into Various Link Counts
› AttentionTrust
› Open Tags: Made For A Distributed World
› Feedback from Adam Hertz

(continues)

> Not only did Hertz find Stowe's post, and not only did he respond to it, but he also responded to a comment left by another user later in the day and helped her through issues involving her blog and how Technorati was tracking it.
>
> Because Technorati execs are so responsive to bloggers and customers' needs, user support for Technorati's services continues to grow.

changed his entire perception of the event. Whereas it used to end on the sour note of "that company wouldn't even talk to me," the story now ends with "I can't believe a an exec read my blog!"

Any time any kind of comment about your company or products appears on a blog, it is an open invitation for you to comment or contact the blogger directly; in fact, the blogger *wants* to be contacted. Don't be afraid to leave comments on others blogs. Nothing makes a blogger happier than hearing from you.

HOW TO WATCH BLOGS

Some people equate *watching* as a passive thing—you watch TV, for example. Others equate it as an active thing, where you are nearly a participant—like watching sports. And others like to watch after the fact—for instance, by analyzing yesterday's stock performance.

Watching blogs can be a similar situation: you can watch actively or passively, and you can analyze past behavior to determine future outcomes. Active watching is done via free services such as Technorati (www.technorati.com) and BlogPulse (www.blogpulse .com), while passive searching is done via free services such as Pub-Sub (www.pubsub.com) and Feedster (www.feedster.com). If you are a "next-day trader" type, you can glean similar information by looking at your website statistics.

HOW BLOGS CAN DELIVER BUSINESS RESULTS

by John Nardini, executive vice president of Denali Flavors

Denali Flavors' Moose Tracks ice cream is a top seller and popular with those who have tried it. Still, many people have never heard of the product. As such, one of Denali's business objectives is to generate awareness of Moose Tracks, which would then lead to a trial of the product. Once a customer tries the ice cream, Denali's experience shows that the product's impressive taste drives the customer to buy more.

The company decided to accomplish its marketing objectives by creating a series of blogs aimed at different consumer groups (see the illustration). The blogs would link to the Moose Tracks website (www.moosetracks.com) and be designed to funnel visitors to the site. This way, awareness of the product would happen naturally. In addition, the advertising/promotion costs would be low compared to a traditional media effort.

(continues)

Denali developed the following four blogs to address various consumer interests:

- **Moosetopia (www.moosetopia.com)** A fun entertainment blog written by the Moose Tracks moose. The blog reinforces the fun nature of the product, and every post is an awareness-generating effort for the brand, even if the author doesn't talk directly about the product.
- **Free Money Finance (www.freemoneyfinance.com)** This blog deals with personal finance with a tagline of "free and simple advice on money and finance designed to maximize your net worth." As Denali's top-rated blog, because of the popularity of the subject matter, this site is sponsored by Moose Tracks ice cream (a fact that is positioned prominently in the top-right corner).
- **Team Moose Tracks (www.teammoosetracks.com)** This blog details the efforts of Denali's cycling team to raise money for an orphanage in Latvia. It contains biking tips as well as details on the fundraising. This blog serves several purposes: It gains brand exposure for Moose Tracks and links back to the main site; it reflects positively on the company's (and the brand's) efforts to help a charity; and it raises a significant sum of money to help the orphanage.
- **Denali Flavors (www.denaliflavors.com)** Denali's most recent blog gives an inside glimpse at what goes on in the company. This site will serve to attract comments and feedback directly from consumers on a wide range of topics.

As each site was developed, it was marketed using tactics such as posting comments on other blogs, trading links with other sites, asking other sites for referrals, and writing articles on sites that link back to the blog. All of these drove traffic to the blogs which, in turn, drove traffic to the Moose Tracks website.

Denali measures the impact of blogging by the effects on the main site. To date, the blogs have helped Denali achieve the following results:

- Site visits up 18 percent
- Hits up 11 percent
- Total time on site up 27 percent

There's still a lot of work to do (including potentially launching additional blogs), but the initial results are positive, while the costs are very low. In addition to the time spent by Denali's blogger, the company has spent less than $500.

USE TECHNORATI TO TRACK A LINK

Active blog tracking is done in *real time*—that is, the results of your searches are up-to-the-minute views of what is happening in blogging. The most popular active blog tracking service is Technorati. Developed as blog use was beginning to explode, Technorati's main purpose and main feature is tracking what blogs are saying about a specific subject and what blogs are linking to other blogs by listing the newest entries first.

Technorati ranks all blogs based on the number of links that point to that blog and calls this measurement *authority*. If your blog has 50 links, it has more authority than one with only 10. Many blogs have hundreds and thousands of links.

By going to Technorati's website and entering the address for your blog or your website, you can see how many blogs are linking to your site. While Technorati doesn't currently track all blogs, it does track more than 14 million sites. If, for example, you entered *CNN.com* as the searching entity, you'd find a large number of links to CNN—nearly 75,000 links from more than 40,000 sources, as shown in Figure 7-1. (Throughout this chapter, we will use CNN as an example for our searches.)

Technorati presents the following information to its users:

- Number and authority of links back to a website (known as *backlinks*)
- The rank of the blog being searched (if you own that blog)
- The number of links in the last week
- Watchlists that notify you via e-mail of new links to your blog

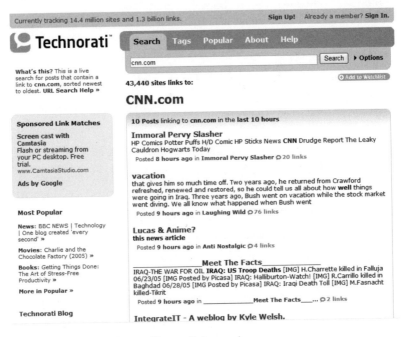

Figure 7-1   CNN shows off some link muscle.

You can use the information from Technorati in a number of ways. You could, for example, contact the most influential bloggers who have linked to your site and ask them for feedback on your products, service, or brand. Several companies have even given such bloggers free samples of new products to demo and review. (I also recommend that you thank bloggers now and again for their links. It's a small gesture and takes little time, but it's appreciated. It's the blogging equivalent to sending a note or a box of chocolates.)

Because Technorati sorts results based on time of creation as well as authority, you can also respond to new links in a timely way. You could respond to negative comments, thank the user for positive ones, and create positive new experiences largely thanks to the information that Technorati provides. As a result of being able to see who is linking to you, you can begin to see the community of people who link to you and link back to them to keep their interest. In the world of blogging, nothing says "thank you" like a backlink.

Sorting results based on authority lets you know who are the most "important" bloggers linking to your site. While linking isn't the only metric of a blogger's success or influence, it's always a good place to start. By being aware of the popularity of bloggers linking to you, you can also be aware of your authority in the blogosphere.

Finally, if you sign up as a member of Technorati, you can see your link rank relative to other links. Once again, if your rank goes up, that means you are growing in popularity faster than the blogs next to you in terms of links—so, for example, moving from a rank of 2000 to 1000 means that not only have you grown in popularity, but you have grown in popularity much faster than the other blogs who were in the 2000 range when you were.

Overall, Technorati provides a helpful snapshot view of your blog's visibility and is very good at allowing you to stay up to date on new links so that you can track issues quickly and easily. Using this service wisely will not only enable you to stay on top of what is being said about you, but it will also allow you to see the growth of your visibility to bloggers.

ICEROCKET DOES BLOG SEARCH

IceRocket emerged in 2005 as a major contender for Technorati. It boasts many of the same core blog search features but distinguishes itself largely on *speed.* To put it simply, IceRocket finds posts faster, makes them searchable more quickly, and returns results much faster than Technorati.

IceRocket also includes a handful of features that Technorati doesn't offer, including the ability to "trend" your search over time (to see how many results there were, for example) as well as the ability to subscribe to a search quickly and have those results returned as a feed. This allows you to find out about new information quickly and easily in areas of interest to you or your company. Much like PubSub, which we'll talk about a bit later in this chapter, IceRocket's feeds can be used to keep you up to date about who is saying what about your company, thus allowing you to respond quickly to customer concerns, customer questions, media coverage, or even competitor news.

Smart companies make use of searching via feeds to keep track of the things that matter to their business: product names, competitors products, people who are happy or unhappy about the company, and even media attention.

MONITOR BLOGS WITH BLOGPULSE

Like Technorati, BlogPulse is an active tool for monitoring blogs and, also like Technorati, it is free. Among the newest entries to the blog monitoring field, BlogPulse is run by Intelliseek, one of the world's foremost business and consumer intelligence companies.

BlogPulse's main feature set centers around trend analysis. Blog-Pulse is adding new features at an exciting rate, and you could definitely do worse than subscribing to the Intelliseek blog (www .intelliseek.com/blog) or the BlogPulse blog (shown in Figure 7-2).

BlogPulse's trend analysis is incredibly useful because it goes beyond the "point in time" figures provided by Technorati. Technorati's greatest weakness is that while you can tell from memory if your stats are growing, you don't have historical context for how quickly your links are growing as a trend. BlogPulse provides this information, as well as a large variety of other trend-based figures.

Figure 7-2   Intelliseek's BlogPulse service is strong and diverse in its trend searching capabilities.

As an added bonus, the graphs are pretty enough to include in any presentation, as shown in the visibility chart provided for CNN .com in Figure 7-3.

We'll examine several of BlogPulse's tools and discuss how to take advantage of the information they provide, including the following:

- Link Search
- Comparative Search
- Variable Timeframe Search
- Conversation Tracker
- Industry Trends

Link searching (Figure 7-4) returns a list of recent links back to the specified blog or website. Because BlogPulse tracks roughly 10 percent more blogs than Technorati, this figure will often be higher than Technorati's estimates.

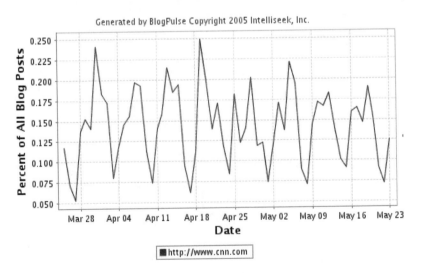

Figure 7-3   CNN.com's visibility according to BlogPulse.

Search for **http://www.cnn.com**

① **Trend Term(s):**   **Display Label(s):**

Ex= "digital camera" OR digicam   Ex= Digital Cameras

http://www.cnn.com	→	CNN
http://news.bbc.co.uk	→	BBC News
http://www.foxnews.com	→	Fox News

② **Date Range:** last 6 months ▾

Get Trend

Figure 7-4   BlogPulse link searches provide a variety of options.

When performing link searches, a variety of options is at your disposal. You can search competitors, assign labels (for clearer searching), and even modify the date range if you are hoping to compare who is talking about what in a given time period—for example, you could determine which news service had the most popular coverage of a particular event (Figure 7-5).

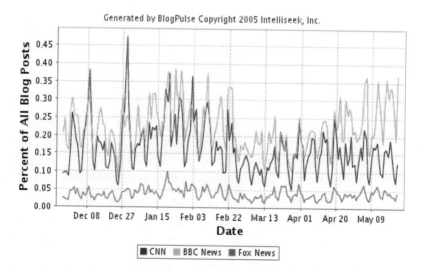

Figure 7-5   Links for top news services according to BlogPulse.

The graph information provided by BlogPulse is generally noted as a percentage of overall blog posts for that period, as opposed to a specific number of links. Here are a few examples of uses for this type of information:

- Comparing your historic visibility to a competitor's
- Tracking conversation about your company
- Tracking mentions of your company after a crisis
- Comparing responses to your press releases to responses on your blog

BlogPulse Profiles

BlogPulse recently extended its offerings to include BlogPulse Profiles (www.blogpulse.com/profile). A profile of your blog provides an overall rundown of important things to know: how popular it is, how many links it contains, what other blogs talk about similar things (great for reaching out into the blogging community), and a wealth of other information. This isn't the kind of thing you'd need to view daily—monthly is more appropriate—but it proves that lots of information is contained within each BlogPulse profile. Not only is it a great tool for tracking your blog, but because profiles are public, you can also track competitors' blogs or websites.

Track the Conversation

Another major feature of BlogPulse is the Conversation Tracker, shown in Figure 7-6. This tool allows you to see how the blogosphere is responding to a specific event or a specific post.

Remember the Kryptonite lock scandal discussed back in Chapter 3? BlogPulse's Conversation Tracker shows the results of a search on this particular issue in Figure 7-7 (http://showcase .blogpulse.com/kryptoniteconversation.html):

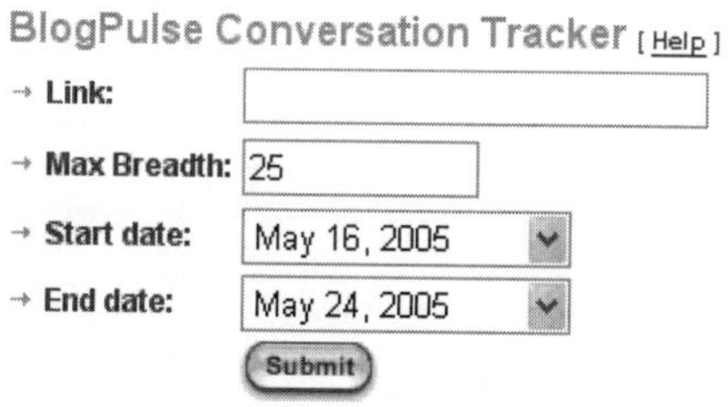

BlogPulse Conversation Tracker [Help]

→ **Link:**

→ **Max Breadth:** 25

→ **Start date:** May 16, 2005

→ **End date:** May 24, 2005

Submit

Figure 7-6 BlogPulse's Conversation Tracker.

Technorati's semiregular "state of the blogosphere" report shows the scandal in context, as shown in Figure 7-8.

Overall, BlogPulse's service is ideal at measuring reaction to an event, visualizing linking trends, and comparing individual blogs, websites, or pages for popularity and visibility. BlogPulse provides a level of context that the other search and trend services don't allow—one that your company should take distinct advantage of.

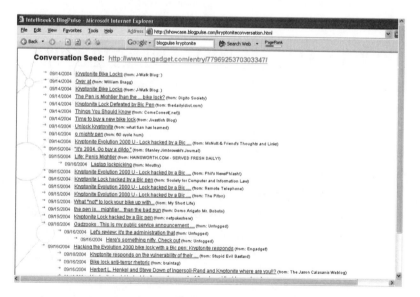

Figure 7-7 A small portion of the Conversation Tracker results for the Kryptonite lock scandal.

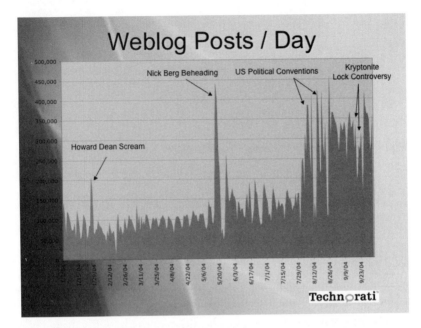

Figure 7-8   The Kryptonite lock scandal report.

PUBSUB: TELL ME WHAT I WANT TO KNOW

While active searching is helpful, the problem with active searching is that it requires that you go out and get the information. You might find it more helpful if the information simply came to you instead of you having to go find it. This is where passive searching comes into play.

Passive searching provides much the same results provided by Technorati, but it provides them as a feed to which you can subscribe. Every time a new link (or whatever you're looking for) is found, the feed is updated so that you get up-to-the minute results for the particular issues that interest you.

The fastest, most popular, and most versatile passive search engine in the world is PubSub, shown in Figure 7-9.

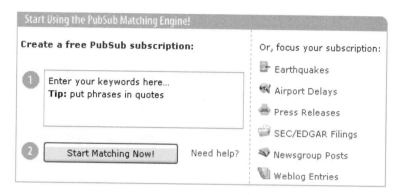

Figure 7-9   PubSub's interface provides a variety of features right up front.

PubSub allows you to focus on one or more areas of interest, including press releases and newsgroup posts, as well as the all important weblog entries. If we do a search for *CNN*, we get a very different type of response from PubSub, as shown in Figure 7-10.

Unlike other search services, PubSub doesn't actually display search results. This is because PubSub isn't designed to search the past—it's designed to search the future. PubSub's database grows by thousands of entries every minute and, as it does, PubSub notifies you by updating your personal feed.

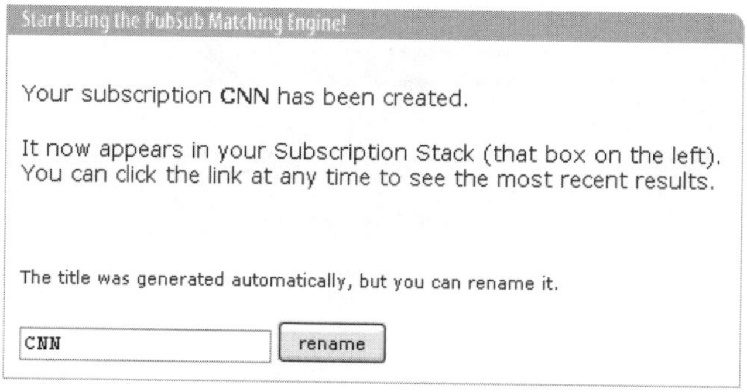

Figure 7-10   PubSub doesn't display your results; it simply produces a feed to which you can subscribe.

Your Subscription Stack, shown in Figure 7-11, is a list of the items for which you are searching, the results of which will be displayed in your feed reader, thanks to your own personal feed. You could add other terms here, such as BBC News, Fox News, ABC News, and so on. You could also search for specific products, phrases, or other specific information. There is no search too small for PubSub to track for you.

After you have created your Subscription Stack, simply subscribe to the feed and wait. As PubSub finds new items related to your queries, it will notify you by updating the feed.

You can use this information in a variety of ways. Most important, though, is that this information allows you to be able to respond to issues in a timely manner. If you find out within 20 minutes that a customer is having issues getting your product to work, it prepares you to respond to that issue more effectively than if the first time you hear about it is in *The New York Times.*

By the time an issue hits the wider blogosphere, you are already in crisis prevention mode. Subscribing to PubSub feeds means you can find out about issues faster than most bloggers, and it means you can take care of issues before they become crises.

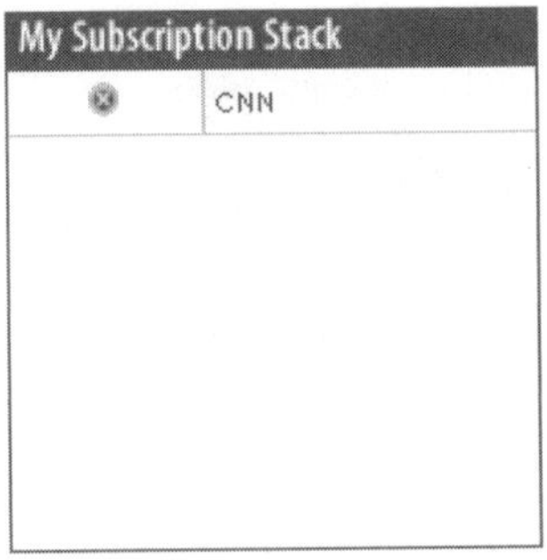

Figure 7-11   PubSub's Subscription Stack lets you combine searches into one feed.

SUGGESTED PUBSUB SEARCHES

You can use PubSub in a variety of ways. Here is a list of some valuable search ideas:

- Your company name
- Your main products
- Your competitor's names
- *I love* followed by your company name
- *I hate* followed by your company name
- Similar *I love* and *I hate* searches for your main products, your competitors, and your competitor's products

CHOOSING HOW TO SEARCH

As you can see, a vast array of blog search engines are out there, and the information I've presented so far doesn't cover all of them. You'll find blog search offerings from Feedster (www.feedster.com), Bloglines (www.bloglines.com), and even Google (http://blogsearch.google.com). This space will continue to grow over the coming months, fueling new innovations, better tools, and better tracking and ultimately providing the information you need when you need it.

Most companies use a balance between active searching via services like BlogPulse, Technorati, and IceRocket and more passive searching via services like PubSub, Feedster, and Google's Blog Search. Using each tool to its fullest potential, and being aware of new tools as they emerge, will help you not only stay on top of who is talking about you, but will ultimately enable you to participate more effectively in the conversation.

WEB STATS, YOUR WAY

The best way to view what's happening on your website or blog is to view the statistics related to your site. Looking into the past for trends, inflection points, and depressions can be incredibly valuable both in the predictive sense as well as by providing a framework for making decisions. Depending on how your website is configured, you can check the stats for your blog and your overall site in a variety of ways.

Three key types of past activity statistics can provide important information:

- **Web stats**   Such as those about who is accessing your site and what they're doing
- **Position stats**   Such as where you fit into the rest of the web based on visibility
- **Google stats**   Such as how many people are linking to you

Web stats are generally used with some kind of tool that aggregates what visitors to your site have done, where they came from, and various kinds of information about your computer. Like reading the *Wall Street Journal* or *The New York Times* to see how your stock is doing, you aren't really seeing individual trades, or visits—you are seeing the overall result of a day's worth of trading, or visiting. Web stats programs are similar in nature: they display a variety of information, a summary of what has happened that day or month.

If your website is not configured to disclose web stats, you can use external statistics tools such as StatCounter (www.statcounter .com) or 3DStats (www.3dstats.com). Both of these require that you modify your site to contain a snippet of code that tracks visitors the same way a regular web stats package would. The only downside is that because of the way the code snippets work, many of these are not as accurate as more traditional web stats programs. Either way, as long as you have the stats, you can begin to analyze them. The important thing with web stats isn't the numbers themselves—as with stocks, the upward or downward trends matter.

In addition to general web stats, you can track the value your blog is bringing to your company by using *Google stats* to track how many people are linking to your site (use the search term *link:mysite.com*), how many pages Google is of aware of on your site (use the search term *site:mysite.com*), or even how many other pages are aware that your site exists (use the search term *allinurl: mysite.com*).

You can also use other services that provide *position stats*, such as Alexa and MarketLeap, to gauge your visibility in your industry relative to that of your competitors.

ALEXA, MY DARLING

Alexa (www.alexa.com) provides a set of tools designed to help you ascertain the popularity and visibility of your site. On the downside, Alexa stats are based on the traffic behavior of it 50 million users, which, while good, isn't necessarily accurate. The goal with Alexa stats is to look at upward and downward trends more than specific figures.

One of the key pieces of information Alexa provides is *overall rank*. Generally speaking, it is more important to know what *class* of rank your site belongs to than actually monitoring the rank specifically. A site outside the Top 150,000 is considered irrelevant to the Internet at large. A Top 100,000 site is visible and likely popular within a niche. A Top 50,000 site is visible to the wider Internet, and so on and so forth. The rank isn't the most important piece of data, though in CNN's case, as shown in Figure 7-12, a rank of 24 means it is a very, very popular site.

Figure 7-12   Alexa presents basic information about CNN.com.

On the main Alexa results page, you can also see what similar sites users are visiting, some general stats, and user reviews. The meat of what Alexa provides is located under the See Traffic Details link.

While experts debate the actual usefulness of Alexa's stats overall, the stats do have a unique way of capturing exactly the type of data you may be looking for. Not only does Alexa plot and graph (up to two years in the past) page views and Alexa rank, it also establishes a "Reach" rank, which represents how many users out of an average million are not only aware of your site, but visiting it.

Alexa also provides information about similar sites, which can be useful for finding sites like yours, as well as information about sites linking in, which provides a list of sites that link to yours. While this information is useful, more effective ways of finding this information, such as IceRocket and BlogPulse, are available.

TAKING THE LEAP

While Alexa is largely a measurement of visibility, it is not the only measure of visibility. Marketleap (www.marketleap.com) provides a series of tools designed to verify your search engine visibility. Because most people arrive at new sites via search engines, most industry experts consider search engine visibility at least as important as overall visibility.

Unless you are a search engine expert, the only tool you will likely want to use will be the Link Popularity Check. This tool will rate your site based on the number of links through all search engines to your site.

In addition, you can select an industry so that you can see where your site is positioned within your industry, and you can even compare your site's results to other specific sites. You enter other sites' URLs, as shown in Figure 7-13, and Marketleap will provide information about your site's visibility relative to these sites.

Marketleap counts each of the links in a selection of top search engines and then adds those figures together to determine the overall score, as shown in Figure 7-14. This allows you to determine your overall Internet visibility, as determined by search engines. While this figure isn't as pretty as Alexa's, it is more accurate in terms of how easily users can and will find you.

These figures are interesting to watch as you begin blogging, as blogging makes you several times more visible to search engines than just having a regular website.

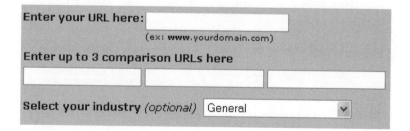

Figure 7-13 Marketleap allows you to see your site's visibility relative to competing sites.

abcnews.com ★	367,848	30,000	30,000	90,440	215,000
foxnews.com ★	463,544	47,000	47,000	295,144	74,400
www.abcnews.com	500,635	28,700	28,700	90,235	353,000
news.bbc.co.uk ★	6,416,380	93,900	93,900	638,580	5,590,000
www.cnn.com ★	8,125,256	158,000	158,000	1,109,256	6,700,000

Figure 7-14   Marketleap shows CNN.com relative to other major news sites.

GOOGLE IS KING

Google (www.google.com) is the Internet's most popular search engine, by several orders of magnitude. You can use Google in a variety of ways to determine your overall visibility as well as your importance to Google. Generally speaking, you can look for three key measurements from Google:

- Number of backlinks
- Number of pages indexed
- Your Google PageRank

More backlinks are better than less, because Google counts backlinks to determine how important your site is overall. This "how important" measurement is then reflected in a subjective figure called your Google PageRank. You can see your Google backlinks by entering **link:*mydomain*.com**, as shown next—which shows that CNN.com is linked to more than 150,000 times.

Obviously it's important for this figure to grow. The more people link to you, the more people find you, and the more Google sends people to you. It's a glorious circle of visitors and visibility that, ideally, grows over time. This number of links is then reflected in the subjective Google PageRank. PageRanks are numbered 1 through 10, with each one being an order of magnitude more important than the last, much like the Richter scale. If it takes 100 links to get a PageRank of 3, then it takes 1000 links to get a PageRank of 4, and 10,000 links to get a PageRank of 5—you get the idea.

To check your PageRank, download the Google Toolbar (http://toolbar.google.com). Then go to your website, and the PageRank will be displayed as a green bar, as shown here (you hold your mouse over the bar for a second to see the numerical rank).

You don't need to check PageRank very often, as it isn't updated by Google very often. By checking it once a quarter, or once every six months, you will see if your site is rising from obscurity to mega-importance in Google's eyes. A PageRank of 5 to 6 is healthy, a PageRank of 7 to 8 is amazing, a PageRank of 9 to 10 puts you among a handful of top sites on the Internet.

WRAPPING IT UP

In this chapter we looked at how and why you should monitor your overall and blog presence and how to respond to comments effectively. We also looked in depth at a variety of tools and how they can be used. Each of the tools outlined in this chapter allows you to respond to different issues in different ways, as well as providing context for the success of your blogging endeavors.

Knowledge is power, and the information gleaned from these search methods will give you a major advantage over your competition, because you will *instantly know* what your customers, partners, and the media are saying.

In Chapter 8, we'll look at how to participate in your blog, including how to start your own. Then, in Chapter 9, we will look at one of the most important tools in your toolbox: negative comments. Most companies are afraid of negative comments, but the reality is that a negative comment might just save your company, if you respond to it in the right way.

8

PARTICIPATING
IN YOUR BLOG

The blog had been up for a month before the trouble began. Every day, Arnold had posted a different idea about how companies could use effective signage to improve business. Writing the blog had been surprisingly easy—he just followed the conversational format that June had recommended. He usually blogged about whatever came up during the day.

Late in the week he had blogged about a sign he had made for Zylon Industries. It was a beautiful piece of work, an enormous banner that stretched across the front of the Zylon building downtown. The sign had been printed in pieces and then assembled on the site. It featured a multicultural assemblage of people and the tag line, "Employees—Our Greatest Asset."

On Monday morning, he saw a very nasty response to his post:

> *u suck! zylon crooks defraud investors and laid off lots of their "assets" last yr! i hope they don't pay u like they don't pay us. signs stupid. u stupid.*
> *Friday 11:12 PM by anonymous*

*The comment had been up all weekend! And several more
comments of the same vein were all undoubtedly from past Zylon
employees and all displayed some rather colorful profanity. Any
of his customers who had visited his blog would've seen this—not
to mention Zylon bigwigs, who were probably wondering why he
would allow such defamation on his blog. And they were
a $100,000-plus account.*
"June!" he yelled. "We have to delete this immediately."
*June read the post over his shoulder. Her hair was now fluorescent
green. "Not so fast, boss."*

—Part 3 of "Blog," a short story by Joe Flood

The key to succeeding in this new blog-enabled world is to go
beyond simple awareness into monitoring what's going on,
respecting the people involved, and participating in the conversation. It simply isn't good enough to know that a massive community of people who are important to your business are all blogging,
reading blogs, and being influenced by bloggers. You need to begin
creating meaningful and memorable experiences and conversations with your customers.

DON'T TREAT PEOPLE AS CONSUMERS

Your customers are not just consumers. They are your marketing department, your product development specialists, and the
secret to your success—an untapped resource waiting
to be invited to the table.

**Successful blogging means that you treat
people as people and not just customers.**

The concept of involving your customers in your business isn't
a new one; blogging just takes it to a new level, largely because you
often aren't inviting just one or two people to become involved,

you're inviting the whole world. By inviting the whole world, you open yourself and you business to a great opportunity to create positive and memorable experiences with your customers and to establish long-term relationships, thanks to those experiences.

As long as you can remember that people are people, and not just customers or consumers, you will be able to meet them where they're at—whether they are having a bad day and just need a little help and understanding or they are so happy they're floating on air. Successful blogging means that you treat people as people and not just customers.

MEETING CUSTOMERS WHERE THEY'RE AT

My friend Paul loves to bike. He claims that he spends roughly $2000 a year on his mountain bikes, adjustments, parts, and gear—and based on the looks he gets when he's riding in the street I believe him. Until recently, Paul was a typical consumer: he shopped all over town looking for minor savings here and there, grilled salespeople on the minutiae of mountain biking, and generally was a pain in everyone's behind. That is, until a fateful day in late 2004 when his front tire blew out on a country road in the middle of nowhere.

Paul stood around for nearly an hour debating whether he should hide the bike, walk home, and pick it up later, or stick around a wait for someone to help, but he felt paralyzed by the fear his bike would be stolen. While he was agonizing over the decision, a friendly samaritan came along. He offered to put the bike in the back of his truck and take it to the nearest bike shop; Paul gratefully accepted.

It wasn't until they arrived at the bike shop and the kind citizen went to the back of the shop to find Paul the right tire and tube that Paul realized the samaritan was actually the shop's owner. This small businessman not only went out of his way to help Paul, but he serviced Paul's bike free of charge. Since that time, Paul shops at *only* one store with no grilling, no bartering, and no hassling. He trusts that the business owner won't rip him off, will keep him informed, and will be a partner in his passion.

This business owner is an example of some of the best relationship-based, customer-centric marketing possible—the quintessential example of a business owner who respects his customer. First and foremost, he respected Paul, his situation, and his passion. He also went above and beyond the call of duty to meet Paul where he was at. If he hadn't seen Paul standing on the side of the road stranded, he would never have earned Paul's trust and, ultimately, would have lost a lifelong ally.

When approaching blogging, bloggers, and your customers who are participating in or reading the conversation, respect is the most important component. Once you've learned to respect your customers, their experiences, and their input, you will be able to contribute effectively to the conversation in a real and meaningful way. Thanks to blogs, you can find customers who are stranded on the side of the road, and you can offer them a lifelong relationship. The challenge for you is in realizing that customers are people, too, and they deserve respect.

DIRECT FEEDBACK

When you blog, you'll receive customer feedback in three ways:

- E-mail or comments posted on your blogs
- Comments posted on other blogs
- Posts on their own blogs

You succeed in respecting these people in the same three ways. Each of these presents unique challenges but also unique opportunities for success and for creating positive experiences.

Generally, comments on a blog are short and succinct. Some comments may be long, but the vast majority will be simple feedback that comes in at under 100 words. Some people simply aren't comfortable leaving comments or aren't aware that comments are even possible, which is one of the reasons having a clear way to e-mail your company from *every* page is essential. These e-mails will often be longer than a blog comment would have been, purely because e-mail is the type of medium for which a 100-word response isn't enough; that's because in e-mail, people provide *context*, while in blog comments they mainly provide *reaction*.

In a blog comment, someone is reacting directly to your post, sometimes viscerally, often without providing context. This is one of the reasons it's important for you to respond to the comments you receive regarding your blog.

Ten Tips for Comment Response

Here are 10 tips for responding to e-mail or comments successfully:

- *Thank them for their feedback.* Realize that it took effort both to find you and write a comment or e-mail. It's important that you respond with thanks instead of anger, annoyance, boredom, or any of the other emotions that are so easy to slip into when dealing directly with people—especially angry people.
- *Acknowledge the issues.* This doesn't mean you have to say you were wrong when you weren't; it means you acknowledge that the person *has had an issue*, and that you will do your best to resolve it.
- *Admit where you've failed.* Admitting failure can be difficult for companies, especially in these days of massive lawsuits and the like. However, being real will not only calm people down, it will likely dissuade further anger.

- *Solve any problems.* Having admitted that someone is upset and admitted any failures on your company's behalf, *solve the problem.* People are accustomed to responses such as "That's our policy" or "We regret any inconvenience this may have caused." You can do better than this.

- *Take ownership.* Treat the problem as if it were your own. Call in resources as necessary. Note how processes aren't working and get your company in gear to fix them.

- *Respond quickly.* Responses in under 24 hours are the most effective. If it's taking you more than 24 hours to respond to a query, you're having problems. Responses in under an hour are a *conversation,* and conversations are powerful vehicles for positive experiences.

- *Answer questions.* Sometimes, people just want to know a simple answer. Instead of dismissing a question as unimportant (after all, the customer isn't upset), look at it as an opportunity not only to create a positive experience, but to begin a dialogue with the questioner and start a relationship between that person and your company.

- *Be friendly and courteous.* Treating customers with the respect they deserve, and treating them with the respect you'd appreciate from others, is central to any customer responses.

- *Don't use form letters.* As a rule, people do not like to be told that your time is more precious than theirs. A form letter does exactly that: it says that you didn't have the time to craft a personal response, so you've sent them a canned one. People not only feel disrespected when they receive form letters, it's almost a betrayal of trust when they come directly to you with an issue in a comment or an e-mail and you dismiss it with a form letter. Be personal. Be real. Be human.

- *Follow-up on any issues or questions.* It may be that someone isn't actually having an issue at all. Maybe he or she just has a suggestion or wants to thank you for being so great. Either way, check back with people after a few days or a week to make sure that issues are resolved to their satisfaction, that someone has responded to their suggestion, and that there's nothing more that needs to be done to create *even more* positive experiences for them.

Most of these principles are simply common sense—good business and customer service practices. Some might be antithetical to your company's policies, but most likely they are already part of your customer service mentality—or they should be. Problem is, sometimes these things don't transfer onto blog comments or into e-mails related to blog posts, often because customers can be very *raw* in their responses, something that is difficult to respond to in the best of times. Treat all your customers as people, and they will treat you and your company as a valued part of their life.

RESPONDING ON OTHER BLOGS

Responding to comments on your blog is fairly easy, largely because if you decide to take the conversation into e-mail, you can easily do so. Responding to comments on other blogs is much more difficult, because the only place to respond is *in the actual comment postings*. As a result, you get only one chance to make an impression that conveys respect and deals with the issues.

To set the stage, here are some examples of *great* responses from companies in blog comments. Here's a comment made on a blog after a user explained that he couldn't install QuickBooks (from http://jkontherun.blogs.com/jkontherun/2005/05/intuit_responds.html):

> I'm the QuickBooks Online Edition General Manager as well as the Acting Leader for our Community efforts (another fancy title :-) for QuickBooks

customers like yourself. Speaking on behalf of our new team of Community employees, as well as for the good intent within all Intuit employees, your pain and vocal advocacy did not go unnoticed. While I'm not yet involved in fixing this specific problem, I will share that this pain of yours is making the rounds of executives and will be used with many Intuit employees as a powerful example of how Intuit employees can do more right by more of our customers.

Again, thank you very much for taking the time to write it down. I believe the power of blogs like yours isn't so much that it enables people to have a voice that compels companies respond, but that it's so easily visible to find out the pain in the first place that solving the problem becomes an easier process. While unfortunate that the world works this way today, blogs and people like you move us forward towards a better place.

And here's a comment in response to a user having issues with her site (from www.corante.com/getreal/archives/2005/05/16/whats_going_on_at_technorati.php#23458):

Kim, please see my comments on your blog. For some reason, we classified your blog as spam and stopped updating it. I reclassified it just now, so you should be seeing your recent posts in our index in a little while. Sorry.

Here are some tips for responding to a comment on someone else's blog:

- *Apologize.* You don't necessarily need to say you were wrong, but saying "I apologize that you had to go through this experience" can be enough.
- *Ask the commenter to e-mail or phone you.* Leaving your contact information means you've provided an opportunity for that person to contact you directly. It's their choice to pursue the matter, and the ball's in their court.
- *If appropriate, leave an explanation as to what happened and what is being done to fix it.* This works only if there was a failure on your part that is already being addressed or soon

will be addressed. Use this response sparingly. It's good to get that message out in public, but it's bad if the situation doesn't get better eventually (that is, you say something will be fixed and then it isn't).

HOW NOT TO RESPOND

The story of Joi Ito, a prominent blogger, and SMS.ac, an SMS communications company, is a great example of responding badly to a blogger. Joi, though, is one of the top 10 most popular bloggers on the planet, which makes this an even bigger misstep. Joi had complained about the service SMS.ac was offering. The company's response? A *cease and desist letter!*

Joi chronicles the story on his blog (http://joi.ito.com/archives/2005/02/22/letter_from_kevin_b_jones_of_smsac.html) in an open and engaging way. He received more than 70 comments and more than 20 trackbacks (links on other blogs pointing out this story). All considered, more than 200 comments about this issue are spread across various blogs. And what did the letter from the SMS.ac attorneys say?

UNLESS YOU IMMEDIATELY CEASE AND DESIST YOUR ILLEGAL ACTIVITY, YOU WILL BE PROSECUTED

While responding effectively to negative comments can be challenging, as we'll see in Chapter 9, a unilateral cease and desist (without any details of the "illegal activity") probably isn't the best way to deal with the situation. The key to responding to comments on other blogs is to keep the response short and sweet. Don't indulge your desire to write a long letter (remember that the typical blog comment is less than 100 words).

RESPONDING DIRECTLY

Since we have already examined how to find other bloggers who are linking to you, you may now be aware of some cases in which a blogger perhaps wasn't entirely happy with your company, service, or products. These things happen; it's impossible to be perfect even on the best of days.

You can easily find posts about your company; the challenge is to respond to them appropriately and effectively. A blogger's post is an invitation to dialogue, because bloggers are accustomed to (and value) conversation and relationships. As a result, the single best way to deal with a blogger's comments is to respond directly to them.

Here is how to respond to a blogger who has written something about your company to which you need to respond:

- Send the blogger an e-mail using the tools outlined in responding to comments and e-mails earlier in the chapter.
- Offer something that is appropriate, given the blogger's state of mind. (Later in this chapter we'll look at how Intuit offered James Kendrick a free upgrade of its software package.)
- Leave a comment on the post noting that you've e-mailed the blogger. This will let others know that you care and are dealing with the issue.

All of the rules of courtesy and respect hold true during this exchange. Some bloggers like to publish the e-mails and letters of companies who contact them, so be aware that this may happen, and be sure to word your letter with that in mind. Don't see this as a threat—bloggers are typically honored when a company responds directly to them (unless the response is a cease and desist letter, of course).

At the end of the day, each of these interactions offers you an opportunity to create a positive experience and to lead a blogger to become a passionate evangelist for your company.

CREATE PASSION

All of this talk about creating positive experiences is really all about one thing: turning people from consumers of your product (and therefore takers) into passionate evangelists and customers evangelists (and therefore givers).

> **The key to creating passionate customers is to evoke an emotional response in them and to give them a healthy outlet for that emotion.**

The process that defines the creation of passionate customer evangelists is an interesting one, as it involves *contact* with customers as people, *positive experiences* that reinforce their desire to have a relationship, a *reason* to be passionate, and a *space* in which to express that passion.

Creating true passion in your customers requires more than them being aware of you and having a positive experience. It even goes beyond a fantastic experience that exceeds their expectations. The key to creating passionate customers is to evoke an emotional response in them and to give them a healthy outlet for that emotion. A public blog should, at a minimum, hit these two points. It must evoke an emotional response and it absolutely has to be a safe location for your customers to convey that emotion.

VALUE YOUR CUSTOMERS

To get to this place, you need to go beyond the typical "customer" mindset. You need to make your customers mean more to you than your business does.

As you can see in the following consumer evolution chart, you need to go through a distinct process for your customers to want to participate in your company. Moving from a consumer to customer mentality is important, because consumers are a faceless group whose sole purpose is to spend money. Customers aren't faceless, but they are still a large *nameless* group that is hard to pin down.

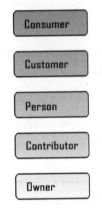

The challenge with consumer evolution is that the changes that are required don't happen in customers—*they happen in you.* And not only that, but the changes become exponentially more difficult the closer you are to valuing your customers as owners. Moving from a consumer to a customer isn't too hard, as it's just a simple change in perspective. But going from a customer to a person requires that you not only treat each customer as an individual with unique needs, moods, and passions, but that you be prepared to anticipate those needs and respond to them. Valuing your "persons" as contributors takes an even larger step, as it means valuing the input they provide for your company, even (and especially) *in ways you don't like* and in places *you don't want them to see.*

Truly valuing your customers as owners takes even more effort, as it means realizing that they are actually more important than anything else. For you to transform your customers into owners, you need to expend at least 10 times the energy keeping current customers happy that you spend acquiring new customers.

Thinking of your customers as owners is very much like how you treat your partner or spouse. If the only way you communicated was via newsletters you left on the fridge or neon signs on the front lawn, how valuable, important, and intimate would your relationship be perceived? Imagine talking to your customers as individuals every day and running important decisions by them. How healthy, valuable, and even (gasp!) profitable would your company become? Every customer would be just as responsible for your success as you are and would be just as prepared to promote your business, passionately advertise what is going on, and think creatively about ways for you to succeed.

DEVELOP A BLOGGING STRATEGY

Part of respecting the conversation you're about to begin having with your customers (or contributors or owners) is to participate with a purpose. The number of companies who simply hop into blogging and post whatever they want scares me.

One particular client of mine seemed like a dream opportunity. The company was willing to try new things, totally into the possibilities of blogging, and seemed to have that most elusive of traits—they really "got" blogging. However, after several months of working closely with the team, the company ended up doing its own thing—and doing it very badly indeed.

Originally, they launched their blog with the advice my associates and I had given them: they provided a "weird and wacky news from around the Web" kind of blog, largely because that's how they marketed themselves—"virally," via word of mouth. A week later, they changed the blog to a pornographic blog, arguing that the traffic would be higher. The final week, it degraded even further into a tangled mess.

Obviously, I don't feel comfortable naming this client, both for their sake and because it won't benefit the point of this story. The point is, if you don't know what you're doing, don't know where you're going, and don't have a real *strategy* in place for getting there, you're more likely to flounder around making a fool of yourself than actually getting any real returns from blogging.

As you begin looking at blogging, you need to start thinking of your blog in a strategic way. Do you have a public relations goal? If so, you need blog relationships. Do you have media tracking? If so, you need blog tracking. Do you have a business plan? If so you need a blog plan. Everything you do on your blog needs to have a reason, and you need to use metrics and measures for success. If you have no goals, then you can't determine whether you are succeeding in your blog or not.

CRAFTING A STRATEGY

Any successful blogging strategy includes a number of important considerations, and yours may have more or less of the following:

- **Reasons for starting** This includes your values, vision, objectives, goals, and motivating factors (such as competitors, market pressures, or parent company directives). Knowing how the blogging idea came up in the first place is important, because while it may have been the original motivating factor, that doesn't mean it's the best one you need to have in going forward.

- **Ways to determine success** What ideas are being proposed? What drivers can be evaluated and turned into metrics? Who do you need to relate to (the media, your partners, your contractors, your suppliers, or your customers)? How often will your success be measured? Ultimately, you need to know what blogs are being written, for what reason, and how you can ascertain their individual and collective levels of success.

- **Ownership and accountability**   Who is in charge of your various blogs, and to whom do they report? Do the blogs serve purely a marketing function, will they fall under IT (as many website activities do), or will they be addressed at the senior management level? Accountability is even more important than who will run your blogs, as accountability determines the long-term success of your blogs. Even if you have the right team running your blogs, if the wrong person is dealing with issues that come up, the blogs may be unsuccessful.

Many other considerations lead to a successful blogging strategy, but once you identify what you're trying to accomplish, how you'll get there, and how you'll know when you get there—as well as figuring out who will write which blogs—you're off to a good start.

Beyond creating your initial strategy, you also need to create a strategy for each blog. I've talked about GM's blogging several times in this book. GM has allowed each blog to take on an identity, and individuals and teams grow that identity through means other than blogs, such as via podcasts, video, and other consumer-driven media. Perhaps the goals for one of your blogs would be best served by adding a message board system, or maybe you want to invite some of your readers to contribute from time to time. Maybe you annually fly out a dozen of your most active commenters for a day of brainstorming. Whatever you decide to do, make sure you let each blog stand on its own and grow on its own. You will generate good ideas for not only one of your blogs, but for all of them.

THE ELEVATOR PITCH FOR BLOGGING

In April 2004, the Social Software Weblog (http://socialsoftware
.weblogsinc.com) hosted a contest to see who could write the
"perfect corporate weblog elevator pitch," as judged by a panel
of experts. The pitch would convince the executive "to sponsor
and resource a critical mass of weblogs in his/her organization
so that their benefits can be demonstrated in a meaningful
way." Following the illustration is the winning pitch, written by
Lee LeFever of Common Craft (www.commoncraft.com).

First, think about the value of the *Wall Street Journal* to
business leaders. The value it provides is context—the *Journal*

allows readers to see themselves in the context of the financial world each day, which enables more informed decision making.

With this in mind, think about your company as a microcosm of the financial world. Can your employees see themselves in the context of the whole company? Would more informed decisions be made if employees and leaders had access to internal news sources?

Weblogs serve this need. By making internal websites simple to update, weblogs allow individuals and teams to maintain on-line journals that chronicle projects inside the company. These professional journals make it easy to produce and access internal news, providing context to the company—context that can profoundly affect decision making. In this way, weblogs allow employees and leaders to make more informed decisions through increasing their awareness of internal news and events.

Beyond the Blog

Don't stop at blogging. Once you've begun a conversation with your customers, you can't stop doing it. Look for other ways within your company to involve customers as evangelists, product developers, marketers, spokespeople, and other roles. If there's one thing blogging will teach you, it's that people not only want to tell you how to run your company, they also want to tell you how to grow it.

Part of learning to listen, then, is learning whom to listen to. We covered the technicalities of searching earlier in this book; having a strategy for searching, and a process for dealing with what you find, are important components of an overall successful blogging strategy.

DEVELOPING COMMENT GUIDELINES

As you begin to blog, you will receive comments to your posts. It's great to know how to respond to those comments, but at some point you need to lay out the commenting ground rules—after all, you don't want to see comment spam, nor do you want to see distasteful comments on your blog.

Aspects of successful comment policies include the following:

- *Identify who owns the content.* As a foundational legal matter, it is important that you spell out whether the commenter or your company owns his or her content. If the commenter owns it, he or she can ask for comments to be removed at any time, while if the company owns it, your company will likely have to review each individual comment to ensure you aren't engaging in libel against other companies, for example.

- *Establish what types of comments aren't allowed.* Most blogs don't allow spam (comments that promote a product or service, unless of course it's related to the discussion at hand). Some blogs don't allow any comments whatsoever. Others don't allow links. Figure out what types of comments are or aren't allowed, keeping your blogging strategy in mind.

- *Determine whether or not comments are moderated.* Many companies, and an increasing number of bloggers, have begun moderating comments. This means that a comment won't show up on a blog until a human being at your company reviews it to make sure that it isn't spam, isn't vile, or isn't illegal. A moderator can protect your blog from all of these things. However, using a moderator may slow down the conversation. While this is a choice your company needs to make, it's also something you can revisit at a later date (for example, you may choose not to moderate comments until you begin to experience issues with spam or inappropriate comments).

- *Decide whether or not you will allow anonymous comments.* Anonymous comments are an interesting issue in the blogosphere. Until recently, most blogs allowed anyone to post as anyone, even anonymously. Increasingly, though, as people have begun posting either anonymously or as someone they clearly aren't (for example, Bill Gates, Bill Clinton, George W. Bush, or Michael Jackson), some blogs are beginning to remove comments that are obviously not from the actual person who left them, along with those that are anonymous.

- *Decide how you will deal with questionable situations.* If someone posts hateful comments, spam, irrelevant notes, or racist or other inappropriate information, how will your company deal with it? Will you remove these posts? Will you leave them on the blog? Will you edit the comments?

A proper set of comment guidelines is important to your blogging strategy, so ensure that as you begin to look at how you'll accept comments, how you'll respond to them, and how or if you'll remove them, you keep your blogging strategy close by to make sure that the comment guidelines match the tone, guidelines, and objectives of your strategy.

SEARCH FOR INFORMATION

When you are conducting searches, whether it's via Technorati, Pub-Sub, BlogPulse, your web stats, or even new methods that have yet to be invented, it's important that you search for the right things. Generally speaking, you want to search for four things:

- Positive posts from people who love your company and/or products
- Comments about your competitors

- Overall comments about the state of your industry
- Negative comments about your company and/or your products

Each of these searching goals is a distinct challenge and presents a unique set of opportunities for interacting with your customers and creating positive experiences.

THEY LOVE ME! THEY REALLY LOVE ME!

Searching for people who love you and your company is one of the easiest things to do—not because the technology for these searches is unusual, but because all of us *love* to hear good things said about us and the work we're doing. It can be exciting, uplifting, and a true joy to hear about how much people admire you and your company. It can be a vindication to hear people say you're on the right track, and it can make your day when you or your products improve someone's life.

But don't let this be the only searching you do. If you hear only the positive comments, nothing about your business will change for the better. Because the blogosphere is enormous, you can easily construct your own little echo chamber by seeking out blogs and running searches based solely on concepts that reflect well on you and your company, on your frame of mind, and on how you see the world. Although it's important to stay in touch with the people who love your company, you need to get the full spectrum of input to make intelligent business decisions.

When you're searching for information about your company, you need to do three distinct things:

- **Read blogs**   Whether you're looking for new blogs written by passionate advocates for your company or blogs written by people who hate everything you stand for, subscribing to the feeds of people who are in the trenches is absolutely essential to getting real day-to-day feedback.

- **Run searches**   Using PubSub, Feedster, or other tools discussed in this book, you can search for specific terms, depending on your goals.
- **Invite feedback**   Ask for feedback on your own blogs. Or e-mail bloggers that you know and respect and ask them for feedback. The world of blogging isn't passive, so get involved in figuring out where your company is at.

Searching Success

Let's consider two popular consumer companies: General Motors and Starbucks. Each company makes unique products for unique consumers, and the Internet blog search results for either company would therefore be very different.

In terms of blogs, try running searches on *Starbucks blog* and *GM blog*. Starbucks has a quite popular fan blog called "Starbucks Gossip" (http://starbucksgossip.typepad.com/), shown in Figure 8-1, while GM has no single particular fan blog—rather, because the company makes a variety of products, its fan blogs tend to be based on specific products, product lines, or types of products.

Starbucks has company fans, while GM has fans of specific products, product lines, or types of products. To find GM's particular fan blogs, you need to search at the individual product, product line, or type of product level. Search for *Corvette Blogs* and *Chevy Blogs*, and you'll find that each returns a number of results.

Next, you can search for particular words with regard to GM and Starbucks. This search is pretty easy; it involves adding the company name, product, or product line name with descriptive

Figure 8-1   Starbucks Gossip is *the* blog to read if you're Starbucks (or into Starbucks).

words, such as *love* or *great,* as well as actions that people do with your product, such as *drink* and *drive* (not together, obviously!).

Here are some suggested word searches that you could use for GM and Starbucks:

- **GM**   Search for *love corvette, corvette rocks, love chevy, drive chevy, car ride, road trip,* and *test drive.* Each of these searches will result in responses that include positive comments about areas in which GM is interested—specific products, product lines, and activities people engage in with their vehicles.
- **Starbucks**   Search for *love starbucks, venti, morning coffee, drink coffee,* and *star bucks.* Each of these searches tries to find information about the company, products, and activities in which the company is involved.

The challenge with running such searches is that many results appear to have nothing to do with what you're looking for, which is why you need to continue refining the searches so that you get both a wide range of results as well as useful ones. You don't want to narrow your searches so much that you don't find *all* the comments, but you also don't want to have to sift through hundreds of useless results with every search.

Finally, inviting feedback and creating dialogue is an important consideration. GM does this pretty successfully with its existing blogs, though the company could begin branching out to other products and product lines to expand this discussion. Starbucks, however, often relies on other means of direct customer feedback. One of the challenges for a company like Starbucks can be that the actual quality of products and service customers receive is largely dependent on individual stores and store managers. Starbucks needs to reach beyond the individual consumer level to the "passionate coffee drinker" level. Perhaps including searches for *addicted to coffee* or *coffee addict*, and regularly talking with people who write reviews at blogs like CaféGeek (www.cafegeek.com) about how the company is doing, what they think of the products, and so forth, would be a good idea.

SPYING ON THE COMPETITION

Knowing what your competition is doing, knowing what people are saying about your competition, and knowing how people *feel* about your competition are at least as important as knowing those things about your own company. Your company will live or die on its ability to outmaneuver, outthink, and outposition the competition, and blogs will help you do that like no other tool (except perhaps bribing competing officials, which I don't advocate).

The first rule of thumb is that for every search you run on yourself and your business, you should run a mirror search on your competition. If you want to know how much people love the Corvette, you'd better know how much people love the Mustang as well. If you want to know how much people love having WiFi in your coffee shop, you'd better know what the trendsetters think of WiFi in all coffee shops.

Consider the following when spying on your competition:

- *Watch them like a hawk.* This means knowing as much about what the blogging world is saying about them as you can. Search for every mention of their company names, for example, and have those results returned to you daily as a PubSub feed.
- *Know how they compare to you.* The statistical analysis you do weekly or monthly as part of knowing what people think about you is important, but knowing those same things about your competitors is an important leading indicator.
- *Know what customers expect out of your competition.* Often times, customers will be begging for new features, innovations, and so forth. Apple Computer users have, for example, begged for a G5 (Apple's most powerful processor) laptop for years. Knowing this allows Apple's competitors to position their laptops as being "powerful enough for those who want a G5."

Watching your competition like a hawk can be a challenge, but it can also be uniquely rewarding. One company with which I consult actually ended up starting a blog that cataloged all the information they were gleaning. As a result, many of their competitors' fans and passionate advocates began coming to this new blog to talk about why they loved the company. The net result was that they had more information on their competitors' most valuable customers than their competitors did.

Having the information on your competitors and their customers, and knowing what to do with that information, are two very different things. First, of course, you can make comparisons: how many people talk about your competitor on a given day versus how many talk about you, and how does that trend map on a day-to-day and week-to-week graph? Are they getting more popular than you? Did they get a larger response after the last tradeshow? Do people more readily compare them to another valuable brand? Do they compare your two companies side-by-side? All of these types of questions are important, and properly researching your competitors will prepare you to answer them.

Running searches on your company name *and* their company name will show you all blog posts containing both names, which is an important thing to see; it will tell you, for example, which products or company customers believe is of greater value, is more desirable, and is more "buzzworthy."

Overall, the tools you use to watch your competitors are feed-based systems such as PubSub and Feedster, active search systems such as Technorati and BlogPulse, and any other "creative" means (such as setting up a fan site for your competition) that you may start. Each of these will yield different types of results and should, therefore, be responded to appropriately.

THE STATE OF THE INDUSTRY

Knowing what people think about you, your company, and your products is important, and knowing what they think about your competitors and their products is crucial, but just as important as either of these is knowing what people think about your industry.

People, in this case, can be analysts, industry experts, prominent figures, and leaders in the industry, all the way down to the regular folk who actually keep you employed by buying your products and services. Determining where the whole industry is going requires that you listen to all of these levels of voices. You can subscribe to industry leaders' blogs (industry analysts, for example, *love* starting blogs, probably because they love seeing their words in print); for others, you may need to do searches.

Look in the following five places for industry information to get you a good idea where your industry is going:

- **Analyst blogs**   These are a gold mine. Successful analysts are actually quite smart. The folks at Jupiter Research, for example, host a number of successful blogs, including analyst blogs like David Card (http://weblogs.jupiterresearch.com/analysts/card/) and Joe Wilcox (http://weblogs.jupiterresearch.com/analysts/wilcox/); industry blogs such as Media (http://weblogs.jupiterresearch.com/toplevel/archives/cat_media.html), Marketing (http://weblogs.jupiterresearch.com/toplevel/archives/cat_marketing.html), and Commerce (http://weblogs.jupiterresearch.com/toplevel/archives/cat_commerce.html); as well as a blog by Jupiter Media CEO Alan Meckler (http://weblogs.jupitermedia.com/meckler/).

- **Press release wire services**   All of the major press release wire services supply feeds these days. As a result, you can either subscribe to all press releases for an industry or you can search on the feeds. Because press releases are so popular, PubSub allows you to search specifically on press releases, and it automatically filters out all other content (www.pubsub.com/pressreleases.php). You can also do this with blogs (www.pubsub.com/weblogs.php) or even newsgroups (www.pubsub.com/newsgroups.php). Heck, you can even search based on U.S. Securities and Exchange Commission (SEC) filings to stay truly on top of your industry (www.pubsub.com/edgar.php).

- **Industry blogs**   While finding industry-defining blogs can be a bit of a challenge (you'll likely need to poke around a little bit in blogrolls of bloggers who write on your industry), subscribing to overall industry news, information, and insider details saves you a lot of time and effort. In reality, a successful feed, search, and blog system means you likely won't have to read the newspaper to get this information—unless of course you want to.

- **Feed searches**   Try to do smart searches on PubSub or Feedster for terms that define your industry. You want to get an overall, high-level view of where your industry is at on a day-to-day as well as big-picture level.

- **Yahoo! News feeds**   Finding out specifically what's new day-to-day can be a challenge. Most people rely heavily on the newspaper, TV, or radio for this. Thankfully, you can also get your news delivered via a feed. Efforts are underway to let you download news to your MP3 player and then have it read back to you (like a radio show). Yahoo! News provides all of its news as feeds, including specific industries and categories, and it offers the capacity to search the news for specific keywords and have those articles returned to you as a feed (just as Feedster does). You can access Yahoo! News feeds at http://news.yahoo .com/rss.

Searching your industry, like searching for your company name, can provide a wealth as well as an overabundance of information, which is why you need to start small, limiting your individual searches until they are relevant and useful, and then build on that. Otherwise, you'll find yourself having to sift through quite literally thousands of results every day, which doesn't help you or your company make smart decisions.

You may choose to work with a blog consulting company or a media clipping company that specializes in blogs to create summaries of these for you on a daily, weekly, or monthly basis. If you are able to do this yourself, having a hands-on view of your industry, competitors, and your company is invaluable; however, make sure

THE WEB VS. BLOGGING

Andy Lark, a prominent marketing consultant and speaker, is often contrasting the world of blogs with the traditional corporate and marketing worlds. He compiled the following comparison list to show some of the main differences between traditional websites and blogs.

Web = Organized	Blogosphere = Chaotic
Web = Predictable	Blogosphere = Unpredictable
Web = Find	Blogosphere = Browse
Web = Comprehensively shallow	Blogosphere = Incompletely deep
Web = Broad	Blogosphere = Niche
Web = Slow/Web-time	Blogosphere = Instant/Blog-time
Web = Cold	Blogosphere = Warm
Web = Transmission	Blogosphere = Conversation
Web = Place	Blogosphere = Community
Web = Anonymous	Blogosphere = Personal
Web = Company	Blogosphere = People
Web = Content	Blogosphere = Expression
Web = Cookie Cutter	Blogosphere = Individual
Web = Closed	Blogosphere = Participatory
Web = Unresponsive	Blogosphere = Gives thanks

it doesn't bury you in information. Being aware and being productive can sometimes be two very different things.

NEGATIVE SEARCHING

The goal of searching isn't necessarily to feed your ego. The goal of searching for what your customers and potential customers are saying is to create more positive experiences, improve your products, and become able to relate to your customers more effectively.

In Chapter 7, I discussed how you can use a variety of tools to find information. More than any other search, the negative search will bring direct value to your company and blog because it presents situations you can tackle head on, in an honest and authoritative way.

A negative comment found in a search is like suddenly realizing your roof is leaking. It demands immediate attention. Thankfully, most of the people who send negative comments are in fact asking for you to make the situation better. They are commenting or posting about the experience because they believe they've run out of options.

Intuit, makers of QuickBooks and other financial software, is a shining example of the power not only of blog searching, but also negative searching. Earlier this year, James Kendrick blogged that he was having trouble activating his copy of QuickBooks. He had recently upgraded his computer and had to reactivate the software. But the QuickBooks website wasn't working for him, and when he called Intuit, he was told to update his information on the website. In utter frustration, he wrote about what was going on in his blog (http://jkontherun.blogs.com/jkontherun/2005/05/when_activation.html):

> At this point I cannot use my accounting software and am really stuck. This is a travesty considering the fact that QB is business accounting software

and moving/installing it on new computers is something that happens all the time in office settings. There is no one I can talk to, nowhere I can go for manual activation, nothing that I can see I can do at this point. Well, except switch to another product.

Within hours, Intuit's on-the-ball team found his post, sent him an e-mail, and resolved the situation. Less than 24 hours after the original event, James posted the conclusion (http://jkontherun .blogs.com/jkontherun/2005/05/intuit_responds.html):

> After ranting about my difficulties activating my copy of Intuit QuickBooks 2003 I was contacted by an Intuit customer advocate (nice title) who not only personally made sure my program was properly activated and registered but also informed me they were sending me the latest version of the program. This was all unexpected and a very fast response to my original blog post. I must commend Intuit for looking for customers who are having problems with their programs and then taking the steps necessary to make sure they are happy with the results. Maybe they should take a hard look at the current activation scheme and do what they can to improve the system to minimize potential problems such as the one I experienced.

Not only that, but Intuit's online general manager, Paul Rosenfeld, dropped by to apologize for the issue and to point to the official QuickBooks blog (http://quickbooks_online_blog.typepad.com/ blogmain/).

Overall, Intuit is a fantastic example of a company that not only listened, and not only resolved the situation, but also went above and beyond by creating a positive experience for Kendrick by offering him a free upgrade. Obviously, it would have been best if the situation had never occurred in the first place. But the next time Kendrick talks about Intuit and QuickBooks, which do you think is he more likely to mention: the fact that he had a hard time activating his product, or the fact that two separate Intuit reps helped him with his problem *and* they upgraded his software free of charge?

Rules for Negative Searching

A number of lessons can be learned by Intuit's example. The process for dealing with a negative comment can be best summarized by using the *FIND concept* that I learned early in my customer service career. FIND stands for Find, Investigate, Neutralize, and Deliver.

The idea behind FIND is that you'll never be able to create positive customer experiences out of negative events if you first don't look for and *find* the negative events. Second, you need to *investigate* the event to see what the customer's issue was, where the failure was, and what you can do to alleviate the customer's concerns. Next, you need to solve, or *neutralize*, the customer's problem. Finally, you need to *deliver* a positive experience. When I taught this in university, I'd argue that we should actually strive to over-deliver, as that creates not only a positive experience for the customer, but a memorable one. Under-promise, over-deliver, and thereby create fantastic experiences and memorable relationships in the process.

Dealing with negative comments using the FIND methodology allows you to ensure that not only is the customer properly treated for their distress, but that he or she is rewarded for helping your company become better at what you should already be best at: treating people like people.

But, if you aren't looking, you can't FIND it.

WRAPPING IT UP

Participating in your blog can be an exciting and scary business. How do you find and respond to comments, how do you treat your users with respect, and how do you ultimately create passionate and engaging customers are all questions that businesses struggle with in or out of the world of blogging. In the next chapter, we'll deal with the biggest challenge, and opportunity, of all: negative feedback. It can make or break any business. We'll look at examples, tips, and solid ways to turn negative feedback into a positive experience not just for your customers, but for your business as well. After the next chapter, you won't fear a negative comment or a frustrated customer again—you'll revel in them!

9

DEALING WITH NEGATIVITY

hroughout this book, I have discussed reasons for dealing with the negativity that may or may not come with your business blog. Dealing with negativity requires that you make a change, often at the deepest levels of your company. Ask yourself what promises your company makes and how any negative issues that crop up reflect on those promises.

Having a promise and standing by it can be the most difficult challenge in any business. Microsoft came to realize this early in the growth of the company. The company promise was, and always has been, to create great software that makes people's lives easier. At the beginning, all it took to realize this dream was to present an easy-to-use graphical system with which users could interact. These days, making great software has become synonymous with making *perfect software*, a shift for which the company simply wasn't prepared.

Measuring Microsoft's fall into popular culture derision is a difficult task, but the results are unmistakable. For example, the open-source software movement had, for many years, a primary goal of destroying what they called "Micro$oft," "Microshaft," or

"The Evil Empire." Even now, searching on the term *Micro$oft* returns *millions* of results in Google. (Open source software is free software that isn't created by companies but instead by thousands of volunteers. The Open Source movement is infamous for its zeal in mocking and deriding companies such as Microsoft.)

As with all truly great changes, Microsoft's response to the criticism started out small. At first, Microsoft employees began participating in newsgroups, which scared many developers, because they'd have to deal with real people. Then Microsoft began creating communities in which developers could interact with larger groups of users. Finally, Microsoft found blogs, which allowed company bloggers to ask the entire community directly what they were looking for, instead of asking a small subset of people to define the worlds' desires.

Trying to understand why people can be so negative toward your company, specifically on blogs, is a difficult thing. Jeremy Pepper, a leader in the world of public relations, chimes in with his piece "Why Negativity Happens." Over the course of this chapter, we'll examine the whys of negativity, as well as how to respond to negativity and how to ensure you've properly dealt with potentially damaging issues.

WHY NEGATIVITY HAPPENS

by Jeremy Pepper, blogger and president of POP! Public Relations

With the ability to post anonymous comments on blogs, to set up blogs with a *nom de guerre*, or to pretend to be someone you are not, the inherent nature of anonymity in the blogosphere lends itself to bravado. It is human nature that when one is hiding behind the pen—either via e-mail or on a blog—that the truer sense of one's self will emerge, and with the ease of posting to a blog, the chance to tear down and be negative is brought to the forefront.

How does a company deal with such negative attacks, whether legitimate or not? For the legitimate attack, likely worded in a less than sincere or kind way, the company should respond. That's just part of basic crisis communications. But what of the unwarranted attack and negativity on a blog that potentially can spread throughout the blogosphere? Should a company respond to false allegations, or is a response just going to fan the flames? In the new nature of blogs, the lack of a response unfortunately can appear to be acquiescing and confirming the complaint. And then the false allegation will spread like wildfire. Containment at the beginning is the best route to take, to quash and respond to the false rumors and negative attacks.

Attacking someone or something via a blog is easy. Being that forceful in a face-to-face situation is a different thing altogether, and since it is easier to stand on a soapbox on the Internet—where no one knows who you really are—we will begin to see more negativity and attacks on blogs.

THE VALUE OF NEGATIVITY

As Pepper mentions, and as I'm sure you've realized by now, being in business sometimes means customers will be unhappy. In Canada, where I live, one of the national landmarks is Tim Horton's, a coffee and donut store. Tim Horton's makes coffee that regular Canadians love. To a coffee aficionado, it probably isn't the best coffee in the world, but to most Canadians it's soothing and reminds us of home, whatever that may be for each of us. However, even a place known for great coffee sometimes makes a bad pot, just as even the best software companies have bad releases, etc.

So it should come as no surprise that sometimes customers aren't impressed by these lapses in quality. The traditional response is something along the lines of "fix it, and make the customer happy." Sometimes that will mean giving a poor, cold Canadian a better cup of coffee. Other times it might mean a refund.

Once, at one of Toronto's better restaurants, I reached the bottom of my bowl and found a ladybug and an ant, both dead. I was so disgusted that the manager gave our entire party their meals free of charge, and then he gave us a $50 gift certificate. Sometimes, fixing the situation *and* making the customer happy can cost you. But letting an unhappy customer leave unhappy will cost you even more, as they'll tell their friends of their bad experiences, which will undoubtedly hurt your business more than a simple refund.

The restaurant in question managed to turn an extremely negative experience into a generally positive one. Each negative experience your customers have is ultimately an opportunity for you to turn it into a positive one, and therefore get your customers one step closer to becoming evangelists for your company.

OTHER TYPES OF NEGATIVITY

It would be nice to think that every type of negative experiences is due to minor lapses in quality. However, that simply isn't the case. Generally speaking, negative experiences can be grouped into four different types.

Lapse in Product Quality

Whether it's bad coffee or a fresh, new shirt with a loose hem, sometimes products aren't what they are supposed to be. Either way, most customers understand these lapses, unless, of course, they get poor service or get lost in a inefficient process when they're looking for things to be made right.

Poor Service or Support

Most customers have experienced bad phone service, such as interminable wait times or confusing phone systems. These are the baby steps that lead to poor service. Worse is having customer service reps yell at customers, tell them they're lying, or simply refuse to help. It happens, and these negative experiences are often enough to cancel any positive ones built up with a customer. It's been said that it takes four positive experiences to cancel out a negative one, so ensuring that customers get the best possible support (especially when they've experienced a minor inconvenience, such as a lapse in product quality) is essential to your business. It's also well-known that customers are more likely to report an unhappy experience than a happy one, and they'll report those experiences to more people.

Lapse in Process

Lapses in process are the worst possible negative experiences a customer can have. If a customer is having her cable installed at home and needs to take half the day off to do it, and then the technician doesn't show up, doesn't have the right tools, or simply can't make it happen, the customer is unlikely to be impressed. Similarly, if a customer is required to register for a new software product online, can't do it over the phone, and the website is broken, a major lapse in process has occurred. Some lapses are minor. But some are so major that customers leave unhappy and establish a mental boycott against your company. Sadly, such lapses in process often happen to customers who have had a bad service experience or who have encountered a lapse in product quality.

Abusive or Criminal Activity

These types of negative experiences are rare even in the worst of businesses; however, they do happen. Mechanics overcharge for work that was never needed in the first place, a real estate agent doesn't disclose issues with a home buyer, or a retail store sells a damaged item at full price. No matter when abuses or criminal activities happen, they are the worst type of negative experience a customer can have.

BLOGS CHANGE THE EQUATION

Whether the negative experience is a major one or a minor one, *it has still happened.* In the world before blogs, those negative experiences would be told to a few friends and, if it was bad enough, those friends would tell other friends. Experiences such as customers finding a dead rat in a new couch, having to wait three weeks for a new phone hookup, or finding out about corruption in your company may go even further: to the press. Generally speaking, though, most bad experiences before blogs were confined to groups of roughly a dozen people. They would affect your bottom line, but not to a degree that would actually hurt your business.

With the advent of the Internet, and blogs in particular, customers now have a completely different kind of influence. Thanks to the visibility of blogs, the audience that bloggers naturally gain, and the ease of publishing new posts, customers who have negative experiences can now broadcast that to hundreds or even thousands of their readers instead of just 10 or 12 of their friends.

Add to that the bloggers' propensity to link to other sites, and even minor customer service issues may be seen by thousands of people, while major lapses in service that would never have been picked up by the mainstream media are suddenly viewable to millions, simply because so many people are now reading blogs.

RESPONDING TO NEGATIVITY: YOUR CHOICE

When you are responding to negativity, you have a choice: you can ether create another negative experience for your customer and likely lose him or her forever, or you can create a positive experience that could, if nothing else, negate the negative experience.

If the positive experience is strong enough, you may gain a happy customer or even a customer evangelist.

Even better, by creating a strong positive experience in blogs, you allow other customers to experience it and be influenced by it as well. As negative experiences spread through the blogosphere, so do positive ones. Bloggers love to point out companies who "get blogs," and examples of companies who not only read blogs, but also respond on them, are few and far enough between that you'll benefit from a lot of linking and perhaps even more eyeballs than had read the original story of the negative experience.

Blogs make negative experiences exponentially more visible, which means that your company needs to be aware of the issues being raised in blogs, needs to be able to respond to them quickly, and needs to make sure the issue is fixed and that the original unhappy customer is made happy. Doing this in the public space can be both scary and dangerous, but there is a power to it that cannot be ignored.

HOW NEGATIVITY LOOKS

To understand how to deal with negativity that arises in blogs, you must first understand what that negativity looks like, where it can be found, and what type of negativity you are likely to encounter.

CUSTOMER TYPE AND RESPONSE

Back in Chapter 2, you were introduced to the five types of customers: saboteurs, occasional sufferers, reluctant customers, regular customers, and evangelists.

Respond to all of your customers on blogs like they're evangelists, or potential evangelists.

Each of these customers is created based on his or her negative or positive experiences and, as such, will respond in completely different ways.

Each of these types of customers *will* express their displeasure at negative experiences, but they'll do it in unique and varyingly passionate ways. More passionately negative customers will generally see any negative experience as reinforcing their perceptions of your company, while generally positive ones will see it as a one-off mistake. Either way, you need to treat these customers with respect, fix the problem, *and* make them happy.

Saboteur

A saboteur will treat any negative experience in a "last straw" type of manner and will broadcast the experience as loudly as he or she can. Most saboteurs are simply regular customers who have had either a few too many negative experiences or an overwhelmingly negative one, such as an abusive or criminal experience. These individuals can be expected to post comments whenever they encounter the name of your company, to blog about their experience, and to, at best, be sarcastic whenever they blog about your company in the future. While dealing with saboteur-type customers in blogs can be a challenge, you can realize a huge benefit not only by fixing the problem and making the customer happy, but also by turning him or her into a customer evangelist.

Occasional Sufferers

These types of individuals have had negative experiences with your company. They may or may not blog about their experiences, but they will definitely tell their story whenever someone else has a negative experience with your company, thus amplifying the effect. If they have a blog, they may have blogged about their experience when it happened but are unlikely to bring it up over time. These types of customers are often the types who have run into lapses in process or several lapses in product quality. They are important to the sustainability of your business, because they would normally be regular customers and regular purchasers of your products.

Reluctant Customers

Reluctant customers typically haven't had any truly negative experiences with your business, but they haven't had any truly positive ones, either. They shop at your business when they have to or when you offer the lowest price, but they feel no sense of commitment to your business. As such, these are the types of people who will be influenced watching you interact with other customers and will easily interpret those positive experiences as reflective of your company. These customers won't really post negatively or positively about your company in comments or their own blogs, largely because they have nothing overwhelming to say. As a result, it's difficult to reach out to these customers and push them along the path to becoming evangelists directly, but indirect positive experiences they see will, if nothing else, make them more aware of your business.

Regular Customers

Your regular customers keep your business going. Whether you're a small-town bakery or a huge box store, your regular customers are likely a significant percentage of your revenue and, as a result, keeping them happy and dealing positively with their negative experiences is key. Regular customers will blog about their negative experiences with businesses at which they enjoy shopping, largely because they *don't expect* to have those negative experiences.

They expect generally positive ones and, as such, are prime targets for you to make happy. These types of people blog about the positive experience you created and spread the news around in future posts about your company—but they wouldn't necessarily do that with negative experiences.

Evangelists

Your customer evangelists can, and will, change the face of your business. These people may eat at a certain restaurant three times a week, constantly trumpet the works of their favorite authors, and are the kinds of folk who buy only one kind of car because that manufacturer has always exceeded their expectations. Your evangelists will be downright shocked by any negative experiences—some will even try and contact you directly about them. It's important to remember that *any* negative comment you come across in your searches and travels could be from an evangelist. The worst part of an evangelist's negative experiences means that those people will quickly progress down to reluctant customers and, if the experience is bad enough, all the way to saboteurs. An unhappy customer is a happy one waiting to happen, a saboteur is an evangelist waiting to happen, and a negative experience with an evangelist is a saboteur waiting to happen. Respond to all of your customers on blogs like they're evangelists, or potential evangelists.

FORMS OF NEGATIVITY

Beyond the individual profiles of your customers, negative feedback can come in any number of forms, including e-mail, blog posts, and comments on blogs. Each of these shows a varying degree of commitment to expressing a given customer's concern over his or her experience.

- **E-mail** For non-bloggers who haven't read a blog post that set them off, e-mail is the method of choice for communication, specifically if a phone call hasn't worked in the past. E-mail is fantastic at one thing in particular: it allows you to respond directly to customer inquiries.
- **Blog comment** A blog comment typically means that someone has read a post and been reminded of his or her own negative experience. If it's recent, it may be passionate, or it may simply be a "oh, yeah, something like this happened to me, too!"
- **Blog post** A post on a blog shows that, as with e-mail, the customer was upset enough to set aside time to write down the experience, and this person does, in fact, want to hear from you. A blog post is an open invitation for response from anyone, including the business that created or allowed the negative experience.

Each of these methods of feedback poses unique challenges. E-mail is difficult largely because it's a text-based medium as well as because company representatives typically get so much e-mail that a single one is easy to dismiss or forget about. Blog comments are difficult because they don't publicly provide you with an individual's contact information, while blog posts are difficult because they are happening in a public space (although nothing says you can't e-mail the blogger to sort through the details). This means that it can require some research to find information about the blogger, and sometimes it means that directly contacting the individual isn't possible.

HAVING THE RIGHT MINDSET

At the beginning of this book, we looked at how to develop a blogging mindset, which focused on developing respect for customers, valuing the conversation that happens in the blogosphere, wanting to contribute, and being meaningful in how you do so. This is an important mindset for success in the blogosphere.

Similarly, mindset is an important ingredient for success in dealing with negative comments. This mindset focuses on respect, but also on valuing the feedback for its potential for change both in your company and in the customer, valuing fast and effective responses to that feedback, and understanding that the customer has made a sacrifice of time in merely responding to you. Unless you are the only business in town that sells your particular type of product or service, customers have a choice and can do business elsewhere. Unless you can create positive experiences, fix negative ones, and *always* treat your customers respectfully, you might find them voting for their favorite business with their feet.

AGAIN, RESPECT

I've talked about respect a great deal in this book—respecting your company enough to consider adding value to it by listening to customers, respecting customers enough to value them and their contributions, respecting blogging enough to listen at least but hopefully to blog yourself, and now respecting negative feedback.

> For customers, negative feedback is simply a reflection of the fact that they do not believe they have been treated fairly.

For most people, negative feedback is a personal affront to the quality of their work, their ability to produce results, and even their ethics. However, for customers, negative feedback is simply a reflection of the fact that they do not believe they have been treated *fairly*.

Our mothers may have told us that life isn't fair, but that doesn't mean people don't measure your business based on how fair it is: prices must be fair, issues must be handled fairly, wait times must be appropriate, quality of products must be of a level equal to the price, and a fair amount of parking must be available at your store.

Unfair treatment really offends people—your prices are 20 percent higher that those of others and the quality is the same, a customer feels mistreated by a rude associate, or the hotel room doesn't have enough towels and requests for more go unmet. People *expect* fair treatment, and they react quite strongly when it doesn't happen. As a result, you'll notice that most of the negative e-mail, blog comments, or blog posts you see during your searches of blogs will have a general undertone of the individual being *personally offended* that a situation has occurred. As a result, your ability to assuage their concerns, admit where your business failed them, and be conciliatory is paramount in turning the negative experience into a positive one. The more respect you have for your customer, his or her situation, and the mistakes your business may have made to allow the situation to happen, the greater your chances for stopping the slide into negativity and possibly even turning it around.

FAST RESPONSES

In the traditional world of customer service, a 24-hour response is considered optimal. That premise assumes, though, that customers aren't expecting a faster response. Now that you've learned to *value* conversations as dynamic and fluid relationship-builders and positive experience-makers, it should be obvious that while a 24-hour response is better than a 48-hour one, or a seven-day one, the timeframe isn't very conversational.

True conversational e-mail responses means a response time of under an hour. For most businesses, that's difficult to achieve. I once owned a service-based company, and one of our promises was that we'd respond in *under* an hour, 24 hours a day, 7 days a week.

That was difficult. But nothing builds loyalty, positive experiences, and relationships like conversational styles. Our company suffered a massive hardware failure, so much so that we couldn't provide services for nearly two weeks, and in spite of that, less than 1 percent of our customers left us for another service.

Fast, effective, and personal responses rooted in conversation build the kind of loyalty that most businesses can't even imagine. That said, if 24-hour responses are the best you can do, then *excel* at those 24-hour responses. However, if you have the resources, passion, and people necessary to respond more quickly, the returns are exponentially higher the closer you get to a true conversation with your customers.

In the blog world, fast and conversational are even more important, as people are *used* to fast communications. A blog entry is posted, and typically responses to that post appear in minutes; the author of the post then responds again in minutes, and a conversation ensues. If you aren't part of that conversation, or if you're absent for most of it, you simply aren't making the type of impact you could make if you were participating.

Posting only one response a day is about as effective as trying to participate in a conversation at a party by writing down your responses on a piece of paper and passing it around. It's disjointed and ineffective. The best way to participate in an active conversation is to be actively listening. This takes time. But it also creates relationships, value, and positive experiences that simply aren't possible if you respond only once a day.

Tom Peters, a respected management consultant, writes a blog (www.tompeters.com), shown in Figure 9-1, that often experiences 20 to 50 comments at a time, eagerly discussing the principles he's blogging about, sharing wisdom, and *learning from each other*. This is the type of conversation that brings great success to a blogger and his or her company.

Figure 9-1   Tom Peters's blog is a great example of empowering people not only to learn from you, but to learn from each other through mass discussions on your blog.

EFFECTIVE RESPONSES

Several factors are involved in formulating an effective response, whether it's in an e-mail or a blog posting. Most of these focus on fixing the problem and making customers happy. Everything you write in your responses *has* to be from one of these two perspectives— anything else is not only ineffective, it's just as likely to be filed under the "cover your backside" category as "just doing your job," neither of which is helping your customers.

An effective response has three main parts:

- **Acknowledge the issue**   Even if you aren't prepared to admit any wrongdoing, at least admit that the customer had a hard time. It's better, however, to admit to wrongdoing, because a customer already knows he or she has been treated badly, and admitting it will make the customer feel a lot better. Sidestepping won't do that, and it may even make the customer more upset.

- **Provide a fix**   Whatever can be done to fix the problem should be covered. At this point, it may be too early to offer a solution, as you may not have all the context you need to do so. At the very least, offer a way for the person to get in contact with you (if you aren't already in a one-to-one conversation, such as when you're commenting on a blog post).
- **Follow-up**   Good follow-up puts the shine on a great solution, because it shows that you care. Everyone feels special with a follow-up, largely because a business doesn't *have* to follow-up, so you know that the businessperson has taken time out of his or her busy day to make sure that the situation is still okay.

All of that said, many businesses do a few things wrong, even the smart ones. Once again, if any part of your response is not designed to fix the problem or make the customer happy, you need to evaluate exactly why it's there. Here are some examples of how to ensure successful responses:

- *Empower anyone who talks directly to customers to solve problems.* Customers shouldn't need to talk to multiple people to get one problem fixed.
- *Don't send form letters or responses.* Form letters do save time, but they don't actually do anything for the customer. Every response you generate needs to provide value to the customer; otherwise, you're not helping the customer or your business.
- *Put real people on the phone to talk with customers.* There is nothing like a real person answering the phone on the first ring, especially if that person is able to solve a customer's problem. This creates a *massive* positive experience.

VALUING YOUR CUSTOMER

No matter what form of communications occurs with your blog-based customers, you need to value the conversation you're having with them and with the blogosphere, and you need to value each customer as a person. It's far too easy to think of people as numbers, potential sales, and recurring customers. Truth is, customers are simply human.

Customers like to hear "I'm sorry," "Thank you," "I'll do my best to get this fixed for you," and "Does this help at all?" They don't like to hear "Sorry, but that's our policy," "There's nothing

TEXT IS AN AWFUL MEDIUM

One of the greatest challenges with responding to e-mails from blog readers, responding to bloggers, and responding to comments on blogs is that all of these methods of communication are *text based*. So much of real communication comes from tone of voice and body language that it's incredibly easy to misunderstand someone based purely on cultural things, such as where a comma is placed, usage of certain words, or sentence structure.

During my more than 10 years on the Internet, I've gotten into numerous disputes in e-mail, blog comments, and forums purely because I assumed the writer meant one thing, when really they meant something else entirely.

Text is an awful method for communication in the modern world. So when you get a message, make sure you aren't looking for the worst interpretation—look for the best one instead. Not only will it make your response more pleasant, but that pleasantness will likely make the person on the other end feel more valued.

further I can do," and "You'll need to talk to customer service about that."

Whether you run your business or you simply help make it work, whether your company is a Fortune 500 or your own little corner of heaven, you *always* have a choice about how you treat customers. You can create a negative experience or a positive experience, and whether you help a customer to become a saboteur or an evangelist, or something in between, is up to you. Remember that sometimes you're a customer, too, and you need to treat customers with the same value and respect you expect when issues come up with the companies you deal with, as they so often do.

REVIEWING NEGATIVE COMMENTS

You're starting on a new trend, you're opening up a new gateway to communication, and you're starting to engage directly with your customers. You *will* at some point receive negative comments. Be prepared for this reaction. If you aren't evoking both negative and positive responses, you're being mediocre, and mediocre doesn't cut it.

STANDING UP FOR YOUR CUSTOMERS

As Joe Flood illustrates in the short story that appears in this book, if you're talking about your customers or clients, you may well get flack on your blog about them, which can be an uncomfortable place to be in.

Responding to negative comments about someone else's company requires a tactic different from that used to respond to comments about yours—primarily because you can't actually fix the situation or make the customer happy. All you can do is acknowledge the comment, stand up for your customer (or not, depending on the situation), and be honest.

This is a communications issue: You need to pass on the feedback to your customer, perhaps even encourage him or her to blog and maybe even post a response. If the charge is serious, and true, it may cause you to re-evaluate your business relationship. In that case, consider blogging that information as well—not as a warning to future customers, but as a message to your readers and your customers that you care about how they are treated.

At the end of the day, responding to claims against a client or customer's company boils down to communication, discretion, and doing your best to stand by *your* values. You also need to value not only your relationships with your customers but also your partners. Don't dump partners and customers every time something bad is said about them. Use wisdom and respect to create positive experiences all around.

THE PROCESS

A distinct, and successful, process is necessary for responding to negative feedback—whether it's in a blog-related e-mail, on a blog post, or in a blog comment. Here's the seven-step lowdown:

1. *Find the value.* First and foremost, you need to find the value in a negative comment. If a comment says "Your product is junk!" finding value may be incredibly difficult, if downright impossible. However, most comments will be grounded in some form of truth or experience that you *can* fix, and you should be able to counter with something that makes the customer happy. Look for the value in the comment, even if it's buried deep.

2. *Find the problem.* Having found the value of the comment, determine exactly what is the problem. Is it a temporary lapse in process? Poor service? Was the customer mistreated or abused? Determining the actual problem and the cause of that problem is necessary before you can begin to solve it, fix the issue, and make the customer happy.

3. *Find the person.* When responding to issues, it's too easy to forget that real people are involved—both the customer who had the negative experience and possibly even the people internally at your company who may have had a hand in it. Remembering that people caused the issue, and people suffered, will make your response more real, human, and caring.

4. *Find the solution.* Whether the problem was a lapse in product quality that has already been fixed or an internal process that will take weeks or months to fix, the solution to the overall problem and to the customer's specific issue needs to be discovered and addressed.

5. *Fix the problem.* Where possible, implement the fix to your internal processes or training, or whatever caused the issue. Where a fix isn't possible, acknowledge that you're working on it. For the customer, fix whatever happened. If it's a deficient product, replace it. If poor employee training or a lapse in process was the cause, apologize and make it right.

6. *Make the person happy.* Once again, real people here. Be empathetic, and, when it comes time to respond, do so in a way that makes the person believe that you've not only fixed the problem, but that you *care.*

7. *Respond.* Now respond to the comment, keeping all of these steps in mind. I won't give you some weak form-letter response to follow, because that wouldn't be real. But if you

actually followed all of the previous steps, you shouldn't have any problem fixing the issue, making the customer smile, and improving things internally so that these types of issues shouldn't crop up again.

The goal of responding is to create a space for positive experiences. The first response may, in fact, not be the last. Maybe your

THINGS TO REMEMBER WHEN RESPONDING

Beyond making use of the tips and tricks discussed in this chapter, you can ask yourself a number of questions when you receive a new e-mail, find a blog post, or read a negative comment:

- Is this reader part of my target market?
- Are other readers saying something similar?
- Do these suggestions make intrinsic sense?
- Do they fit with my business's values, promises, and future?

People care enough about your business to tell you what they think. And if they're making suggestions on how to improve your business, they care enough to help your business grow. Several companies I work with actually offer both employees and customers a share of any profits or savings that result from ideas they generate. And why not? What better way to build a relationship based on value, respect, and communication than to value and respect your customers enough to say thank you with something of value to them?

first response will be to apologize and ask for more details so that you can fix the issue, or maybe the initial customer response was detailed enough that you can go through the entire process and fix the problem. Either way, dealing with real people can be difficult, and it requires a process that adapts to people's individual needs.

Your business depends on your ability to create positive experiences, and dealing with customers who have had negative experiences is one of the most powerful tools at your disposal. Use that tool well, and you'll start creating customer evangelists, but misuse it and you're more likely to create saboteurs.

KEYS TO DEALING WITH NEGATIVITY

Dealing with negativity is ultimately about balancing the personal needs of the individuals involved in the situation with the actual needs of your company. You can't, for example, solve a customer's angst by giving him or her a new car. It might make them happy, but it won't help your business survive if you give a car to every unhappy customer. Nor can you go to the other extreme and so protect your business that you don't actually fix the problem *or* make customers happy. Effectively dealing with negativity is all about walking the fine line between real customer *service* and real business principles.

That said, you can never really let any negative comment, e-mail, or blog post slip by. The one you don't respond to may end up being the biggest scandal of your business life. You need to be aware of what is being said and be able to respond effectively, even if you aren't able to fix the customer's issue to the degree that might be ideal in a perfect world.

As such, here are more tips, tricks, and thoughts on how to deal with negative comments effectively.

Don't Answer Instinctively

Before you answer any type of negative feedback, stop, look at the comment, and go through the process defined earlier in the chapter (if only quickly) so that you have the right perspective when responding. Some comments need responses quickly, but taking 5 minutes to refocus yourself on the right priorities will turn a *fast* response into a *fast and effective* one.

Evaluate Every Comment on Its Merits

As part of finding the value, ensure that you look at each comment as its own distinct feedback. Did the customer have a negative experience? Was your business at least partially to blame? Is there a way to fix the situation?

Don't Personalize

For too many of us, the instinctive answer to criticism is defensive in nature. This is the wrong type of reaction, as it simply reinforces the customer's innate belief that you won't do anything to fix the problem.

Answer

Any time anyone offers you feedback, it includes an underlying question. Sometimes this will be "Can you help me?" or "Do you care?" while other times it will be "Do you realize this product doesn't actually work for me?" or "Are you going to fix this?" Make sure that any response you give is the answer to that underlying question.

Be Aware of Possible Outcomes

Before you click Send or Post, be aware that each response you provide is going to do one of two things: create a positive experience and properly represent the company so that your customer hears the truth, or create a negative experience that makes the issue a personal *battle* between the customer and the company.

Passion Is Good

Most people who respond to events via blog or e-mail possess some degree of *passion* about the experience. It may be complaints about your product or your company in general, a mistake that's happened, or even a personal treatment. Either way, they *do* have passion, and passion is a good thing. Respond effectively, and that passion could be working for you. Respond poorly, and it will only work against you.

Expect Negative Feedback

Get used to it: negative feedback will happen. If you make the best product in the world, some people still won't like it. Even the best fashion designers and chefs in the world don't please all the people all the time. Even the most sought-after automobiles have their fans and their detractors. No matter how *good* your product, company, or service, you will receive negative feedback. Don't be shocked when it happens.

People's Expectations Are a Paradox

On the one hand, all customers hope for a near-immediate response on the Internet. At the same time, due to their experiences, they have an expectation that responses will not only be poor, but they will be late and completely unrelated to the frustration they experienced. A fast experience is a good thing, because it exceeds a customer's expectations, but you are delivering *exactly* what they expect when you respond quickly and impersonally. Your response needs to make the person feel *human, valued*, and *respected.*

All Feedback Is an Opportunity

Whether it's an e-mail, a comment, or a blog post, every bit of feedback is an opportunity for you to create a relationship. If you respond quickly, properly, and in a friendly fashion, it proves that your company (and you, by association) is about real people making real products for real customers.

The First Response Isn't the Last

Your first response needs to be as good as it can be. However, a great first response should lead to a second response, in which a customer (when treated properly the first time) will be willing to engage in a constructive dialogue. If you've identified the problem, run the solution by your customer to determine whether he or she believes it will help now and in the future. Your customers *are* your best product designers, because they buy your product.

People Transfer Blame

Whether or not it's your fault, people transfer blame for *all* past poor customer service onto you and your company. As a result, simply responding in a "good enough" fashion isn't good enough. Your response needs to be so extraordinary that the person knows he or she is dealing with a company that respects its customers.

Responding Takes Skill

Most responses will come in one of two flavors: a problem that has happened or an opinion being expressed. The potential for dialogue and relationship in dealing with a problem typically only goes as far as the solution to the problem, unless you really decide to get the customer involved in your business. With an opinion, though, you can acknowledge and respond to it, but begin a dialogue with the individual. An opinion expressed is a customer asking to be involved in your company. The best responses, no matter whether they're to an opinion or to a problem, get your customers to feel a sense of ownership and participation in your business.

Poor English Isn't Bad

Most businesses are accustomed to receiving feedback in only one language. On the Internet, though, you may receive feedback from people who do not speak English as their first language. In fact, thanks to online translation services, you may get feedback from someone who doesn't speak English at all. Although translation services are helpful, the translation often makes the feedback appear as though it's coming from a child using a dictionary to sound important.

For example, using AltaVista's translation service (http://world .altavista.com), the English phrase "I don't appreciate your lack of quality control. I'd really appreciate it if you fixed this business issue" translated to Dutch and back to English generates this mangled masterpiece: "I do not appreciate your lack of quality control. I'd appreciate it really as you this company question confirmed." Do not assume that simply because the quality of language is poor that someone's experience and ability to recognize an issue is also poor.

WRAPPING IT UP

All feedback is good feedback—even negative feedback. It's far better to have an unhappy customer than to have no customers at all, so deal with every response as an opportunity to create a positive experience. This chapter should have given you not only the perspective necessary to deal with negative feedback effectively, but also the tools necessary to do so. It really all comes down to one little word, though: respect. If you can respect your customers enough to value *all* of their feedback, you'll do well even on the worst days.

In the next chapter, we'll look at how to apply blogging to your company, set up *smart* goals for your blog, measure your blog's effectiveness, and make *sure* your blog succeeds.

10

HOW TO SUCCEED IN BLOGGING

By this point in the book, you should have a clear perspective on what a blog is as well as how to blog. You should also be aware of how to track blogs and how to respond to comments, and you should be comfortable developing a blogging strategy. This leaves you asking that most pressing of questions: "How do I succeed?"

Most of the questions I receive via e-mail, when I'm speaking at conferences, or when I'm talking to clients concern one thing: how to succeed in blogging. Some questions are about how to build traffic, others are about how to build relationships, and others ask how to increase overall visibility. Granted, blogs do these things naturally, but once you get a little bit of traffic, a little bit of relationship, and a little bit of visibility, you quite naturally want *more*.

The word *success* in relation to blogging is an odd one in my opinion, because success in blogging isn't like success in business, which is measured by money; success in entertainment, which is measured by fame; or even success in life, which can involve a number of things. Succeeding in your blog simply means you've reached your goals.

For your company, success may be defined purely by the fact that you can now post company news more easily. For other companies, success may be based on specific increases to sales that are tracked through whatever means necessary. Still others will measure their success in blogging in more pragmatic terms: number of relationships, connections, customer evangelists, and positive experiences.

This chapter tackles some fundamental questions about success that people and businesses who blog might ask.

TEN TIPS FOR SUCCESSFUL BLOGGING

Most successful bloggers can offer some tips for successful blogging. Some people develop methods based on experience. Others simply offer what they've been told—like *post often, link often, and be yourself* (once identified as the three cardinal rules for successful blogging). What follows are *my* ten tips for achieving a popular and successful blog within your industry, whatever it may be.

Be Real

Knowing yourself and your audience are extremely important aspects of successful blogging. Too many bloggers start out trying to blog about *everything* that interests them and, in doing so, quickly burn out, largely because there is simply *too much* to blog about when you blog about everything. Identify who you are as a blogger, what you'll be blogging about, and who your audience will be; these are key to a successful blog.

Be Passionate

Passion breeds passion. If you aren't enjoying what you're blogging about, it's difficult to be passionate, so blog about things you truly enjoy. Find a voice that you enjoy writing in and stick with it.

The passion that comes from writing a blog and connecting with dozens, hundreds, or thousands of readers is contagious.

Write Often

Writing often isn't just good for the blog, it's an absolute requirement for success. Anything less than once a day (during weekdays) is abandoning the potential of your blog. Updating your blog is often rooted in two major facets of blogging: search engine "juice" and the fact that readers love new and fresh content. Search engines love fresh content and will revisit your site more often the more it's updated. The result is that your blog will get searched regularly and will carry more weight with the search engines once they trust your ever-changing content.

Link Lots

Links are called the "currency of the blogosphere." Most bloggers link for one of two reasons: either they are interested in the subject matter or they respect the blogger to whom they are linking. Links carry an inherent value, so providing links shows your readers and users what interests you—and the higher the quality of bloggers to whom you link, the more respect readers and other bloggers will have for you and your blog. Combine that with the ability for bloggers to find out who links to them via services such as Technorati and PubSub, and you can see how a link can be a great way to show who you know and to let people know that you exist. Many of the top bloggers I know have confessed that the way they most often find new blogs is after those blogs link to them.

Leave Comments on Other Blogs

Creating a community of interest is key to blogging successfully at the business or personal level. For most businesses, the community will be a mixture of existing bloggers, news sources, and influential people in the industry, combined with employees, partners, suppliers, and customers. Your community of interest is the community in which *you are interested* as well as the community that is *interested in you.* By commenting on blogs in your community of interest, you are letting existing bloggers, and their readers, know that your blog might be of interest to them. One of the most common ways that people find new blogs is through links in comments—get involved, and you'll reap the traffic rewards and build relationships with other bloggers and their readers.

Have Fun

Blogging is meant to be fun. Yes, it's serious business that will radically change the way your business is presented online while also changing the way your customers view and relate to you, but it's also about having fun. Try new things and link to fun and interesting sites.

Push the Envelope

One of the challenges with blogging is that it's new. Try something unusual, and if you do the "wrong" thing, it *will* get you some attention (bad or good). Any new communications tool that remains stagnant ultimately dies, so don't be afraid to make changes and ask questions. Entirely new types of cutting-edge communication, such as podcasting and video blogging, were created when someone asked, "Why does blogging have to be just text?" Ask your own "why" questions and see if you can come up with exciting ways to use blogs.

Ping

Pinging is something your blog software does to tell several services that you've posted something new. This quick note, or *ping,* is used to produce lists of the most recently updated blogs to let Technorati and PubSub know to come by and see what you've posted and generally to make sure the blogosphere stays *connected*.

If you ping only one service, make it Ping-O-Matic (www .pingomatic.com). This neat, and free, little tool by the creators of WordPress (www.wordpress.org) allows you to ping Ping-O-Matic, which then pings all of the most important services for you, instead of you having to do it. This cuts down on your effort, but it also means you don't need to worry about whether you're pinging the right places. Ping-O-Matic takes care of it for you.

Use Feeds

Whether you choose to use full-text feeds or provide some of the text, make sure you are providing feeds. I'm a big fan of full-text feeds, because they create less of a boundary for your customers to read your ideas. Feeds make it easy for people to read your content on their own schedules—while traveling on an airplane, via audio as they're driving home, or generally however and whenever they want to hear what you have to say. Feeds are all about lowering the barriers to getting at quality information, so do whatever you can to make sure you aren't putting up any artificial barriers.

Create Meaningful Titles

Titles are absolutely essential to blogging successfully: good titles mean search engines find you and send you more traffic; attractive and useful titles entice readers to read your stuff, and this translates into more links. Every blog post title should give readers a reason to want to read the entire post. If you own a fashion company, for example, "Exquisite shoes" is probably a bad title, while "Ferragamo designs exquisite shoes!" is far more descriptive.

RUBEL'S TEN COMMANDMENTS
OF BLOGGING

In June 2005, Steve Rubel, a prominent public relations blogger, wrote these "10 Commandments" for PR professionals (see www.micropersuasion.com/2005/06/10_commandments .html), but they are also great starting points for achieving true success in the world of blogging:

1. *Thou shall listen*. Utilize every avenue available to you to listen actively to what your public has to say and feed it back to the right parties.
2. *Remember that all creatures great and small are holy*. It doesn't matter if it's *The New York Times* calling on you or an individual blogger, both have power. Take them all seriously.
3. *Honor thy customer*. Create programs that celebrate customers and they will celebrate you.
4. *Thou shall not be fake*. Keep it real; don't hide behind characters and phony IDs.
5. *Covet thy customers*. Don't sue your fans. You will alienate them.
6. *Thou shall be open and engaging*. Involve your customers in the PR process. Invite them to help you develop winning ideas and become your spokespeople.
7. *Thou shall embrace blogging*. It's not a fad, it's here to stay. Be part of it.
8. *Thou shall banish corporate speak*. People want to hear from you in a human voice. Don't hide behind corporate speak. It will soon sound like ye olde English.

9. *Thou shall tell the truth.* If you don't tell the truth, it will come out anyway.
10. *Thou shall thinketh in 360 degrees.* Ask not what you can do for your customer, but also what your customer can do for you.

BUILDING TRAFFIC

Because a blog is a website, and because websites have tangible metrics such as the number of visitors per day, number of pages those visitors visited, and where those visitors came from, one of the standard measures for growth and success in any blog is traffic—that is, the number of visitors who come to your blog, generally measured daily and monthly.

While traffic may not be the best overall metric, it isn't a bad one to track. Plus, it's always nice to see those traffic graphs going up month by month.

However, traffic doesn't matter all that much, because if you're building a valuable conversation, it doesn't really matter if it's with 2 people or 200. Also, the *number* of visitors doesn't matter as much as the *quality* of those visits, how influential visitors are, and how much they contribute to the conversation and to your company. All that said, more traffic typically *does* mean more conversation, more influential visitors, and more contributors. So while traffic may not be the best overall metric, it isn't a bad one to track. Plus, it's always nice to see those traffic graphs going up month by month.

Traffic on blogs generally comes from one of three places:

- Links from other websites, specifically blogs
- Search engines
- Traditional marketing efforts

CONVERSATION BREEDS TRAFFIC

Blogs are linking machines, and bloggers love to link. Depending on the readership of a blog, a single link to your site from another blog may mean five more people or 5000 more people will visit your site. Those who follow links on other blogs will typically be one of three types: another blogger, a new reader, or a "drive-by" visitor.

It is good to have other bloggers come to your site, because that gives you higher odds of securing yet another link. Blog-driven traffic tends to be exponential in nature. If one blogger sends five visitors your way and one of those is a blogger who links to you and sends ten other bloggers your way, and three of those are bloggers who link to you and send six more visitors your way.... Well, suffice to say that even a link from a minor blog can result in hundreds, if not thousands, of new visitors to your blog.

The second type of visitor to your blog is a new reader. These are also valuable readers, largely because once you've secured a reader, you have an opportunity to turn him or her into a customer, an evangelist, and a contributor to your company. New readers are a little bit like shareholders in a company: they *want* to hear what you have to say and they *want* you to do well.

The final class of visitor is the drive-by. These visitors hold little inherent value (about as much as someone who sees your ad in a newspaper or hears it on the radio), but a series of impressions may eventually lead them to recognize your company and brand and become either a customer or a reader. Don't dismiss the value of drive-by visitors.

Ultimately, a link on a blog—any blog—is very, very good. The biggest reason for this is that typically visitors who come from other blogs are coming because they're interested in what you've said in the past, which opens a huge door for them to be interested in what you're saying now. One of the keys to designing a blog properly is to provide visitors who see only one page (the one they arrive at from a search engine or from another blog) to find the newest content, the most valuable content, and related content. This will help you turn drive-by visitors into readers.

SEARCH ENGINE OPTIMIZATION

For most bloggers, traffic they receive is split somewhere around 30 percent from other blogs, 30 percent from search engines, and 40 percent from their regular readers. As a result, appealing to search engines is incredibly important, because it can mean you gain (or lose) massive amounts of potential readers, customers, and contributors. The practice of making your site as search engine friendly as possible is known as *search engine optimization* (SEO for short). This is a bit of a dark art, but if all you do is the following three things in your blog, you'll hit most of the high points of SEO:

- *Have "good" blog post addresses.* Search engines love blogs for which each post has its own page. Most blog packages like WordPress, Movable Type, TypePad, and Expression Engine do this for you. They like it even more when those addresses are meaningful. So www.myblog.com/about-our-business .html is more meaningful than www.myblog.com/5313 .html, because the first URL contains recognizable words (separated by dashes). Search engines find your page more easily when the page address describes what's on the page, and most blog packages allow you to do this with some minor configuration.
- *Link back to your blog home page and main home page.* Most search engines today use a Google-style of page ranking: more links to a page means more importance for that page. So linking to your blog home page and your main home

page as part of the template for your blog could mean hundreds or thousands of distinct links (the more you post, the more links there will be). Some blog systems will create these links for you "automagically," while others will require you or the person who maintains your website to make the links part of the blog setup. Providing users with a way to get around your site and your blog is critical.

- *Use good page titles.* Most search engines display the title of the page as part of the search results. If the title for your page is just your company name, people who find your page via search engines may not know it contains the answer to their question (even though it's in the list of results). Great titles include two things: your blog or company name as well as the title for the post. If you've constructed meaningful post titles, new visitors will know not only *what* they're going to see when they arrive, but also *who* they'll find when they get there.

MAKE THE MOST OF A VISIT

Once visitors find your site, it's your job to make it easy for them to find information, ask questions, and ultimately build relationships with you. (Hint: having an *actual* e-mail address on every page is much, much better for new visitors than having to go to Contact Us, clicking on E-mail, and then filling in a form.) You can make it easier on your new search engine visitors (and all first-time visitors) to make the choice to begin a relationship in three ways:

- *Include an "About the Author" page.* If this is your official company blog, include information about your company (short and sweet is good, you can always link to your main "About Us" page on your website). Make sure that each blog author is a person, has a name, and includes basic information about him or herself. Large companies with dozens of employees blogging on their main blog tend to link the profile back to the individual contributor's blog or link back to the first post the contributor made. Either way, the goal is to provide new visitors an idea of who the author is and who the company is in such a way that they want to find out more.

- *Provide relevant links.* While most blogs' templates are the same for the main blog page or an individual post page, I'm a big fan of having some different bits of information on the pages for individual posts. If nothing else, include a small welcome message that tells visitors where they have arrived and how they can find similar information (for example, see Jason Kottke's blog, shown in Figure 10-1). You may also

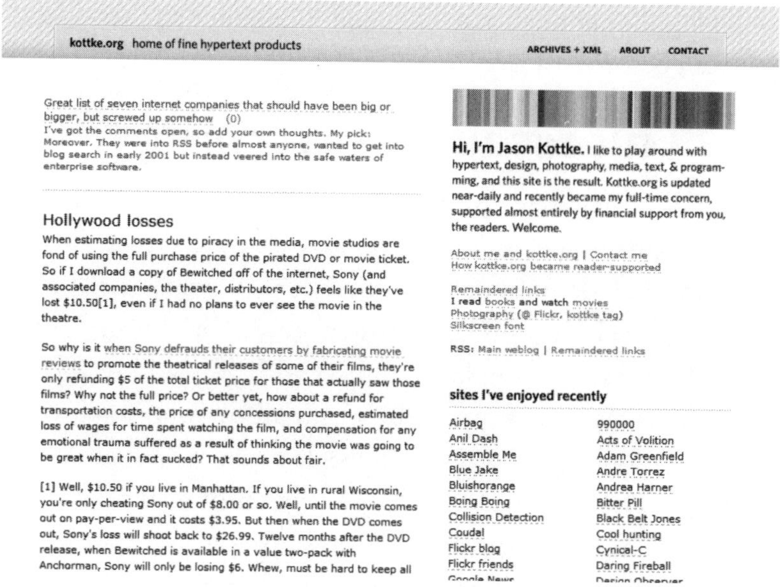

Figure 10-1   Jason Kottke (www.kottke.org) uses a contextual area on the side of his blog to tell new visitors where they've arrived.

want to show your most recent posts, categories list, links to other blogs, and other information. Provide *relevant* links and *context* so that new visitors can explore your blog if they like the content.

- *Turn visitors into readers.* Providing first-time visitors with a way to subscribe to your blog (either via e-mail or feeds) is key, as it allows them to establish a quick relationship on their terms. You may want to include a page that explains how to subscribe, or you can include a "syndicate this site" link, with the orange XML icon that many blogs use to show that a site is subscribable. You can also provide alternative ways for users of specific feed readers to subscribe to your blog. NewsGator, Bloglines, FeedDemon, and most other feed readers include these buttons, which make it easy for users to subscribe to your feeds using those services. Empower your readers to make a choice to subscribe to your blog. Lower the barriers as much as possible so that visitors can become readers.

IT'S THE MARKETING, STUPID

Another way that new visitors will arrive at your blog is via traditional marketing methods. If you have a personal blog at your company, include it on your business card. If your official blog is valuable, include it on your business card. Your business card should be a way for people to connect with you, and including "blog: www.mycompany.com/blog" on all of your employees' business cards is a great way to get people to check out your blog.

You can also advertise your blog using traditional marketing techniques. If your blog is the best way for people to establish a relationship with you (other than meeting you in person), be proud of your blog and tell the world about it.

Anywhere that you post your website address should also include your blog address. Similarly, you should advertise your blog prominently on your website. If nothing else, it should be part of the main navigation, and it should be one of the most important elements of that navigation (don't put it way down by "Contact us").

Advertising your blog in this way will bring in drive-by visitors. But if they're potential clients, a well-written blog will not only provide them with yet another positive experience (hopefully their first contact with them was positive, right?), but it will show them that you are authoritative, passionate, and you know your industry. If partners, suppliers, or customers see your blog in your traditional advertising, they have another way to build a relationship with you and your company and will likely open the door for further conversations, which could range from "So, how's that blog working for you?" to "Isn't that blogging thing a fad?"

TIPS FOR BUILDING TRAFFIC

Provide a reason for people to come back to your blog, for bloggers to link to you, and for people to tell others about a great new post on your blog. You can build traffic in many different ways. Although traffic isn't the only measure of success you should have on your blog, more people reading your blog means more people interacting, commenting, contributing, and generally being aware of your company—which is the goal of most business blogs in the first place.

Following are tips for building traffic to your blog.

Provide Comment Notification

Many people who read your blog will comment. Thanks to feeds, they can stay up to date on your newest post. If I'm interested in your post asking for opinions on how to fix one of your products and I leave you a few ideas, I'd be *very* interested to know your response. However, there is currently no blog-based way (such as feeds) for me to stay up to date easily on whether you (or anyone) have responded to my post.

You may want to allow readers to receive an e-mail notifying them when someone replies to a post to which they've responded. This notification of a new comment (hence, *comment notification*) should be optional (in case a user doesn't want to receive these types of e-mails), but for those who choose to use it, it's a great way to keep the conversation going.

When people know a conversation is happening about something of interest, they'll often contribute even more. Thanks to comment notifications, posts that normally would have had only two or three responses may suddenly get 20 or 30 responses as your readers engage in a discussion on your blog. In fact, the day I added comment notifications to my blog, traffic jumped by 20 percent.

Conduct Interviews

Interviewing important people in your company is a great way to let your readers know who works at the company, that smart people work there, and that ultimately the company employs real people with real passions. For example, Microsoft's Channel 9 (http://channel9.msdn.com) was created expressly to give readers a view into the lives of people working inside the company. Your interviews may not be video based, and they needn't appear frequently, but adding interviews (especially with real people who work on real products) is a great way to help your readers relate to your company. As an added bonus, bloggers love linking to interesting interviews.

Ask Questions

The absolute best way to get someone to participate in a real-world conversation is to ask a question—and blogs are no different.

Asking your readers "What do you think?" and "How would you have handled this?" doesn't show (as some may fear) that you don't know what you're talking about. On the contrary, it shows that you know that even the smartest people in the world sometimes need to bounce ideas off others—and your blog readers are the best people for this, since they want you to succeed. Bloggers love to say "*Company x* is looking for some ideas on their newest product, so go tell them what you think." And people love to offer opinions.

State Your Opinion

The second best way to get someone to participate in a real-world conversation is to state an opinion. Stating an opinion gives people three options: they can agree, disagree, or propose a different opinion. The more conversation you can get happening on your blog, the more people will return and the more people will link to it.

Take and Answer Reader Questions

Regularly respond to reader comments, questions, or e-mails as a post. You may do this by saying "Ask a question" (as Microsoft recruiter Gretchen Ledgard does with her suggestion kitty, as illustrated here), by asking a reader who e-mails you a question if you can use that question on your blog or by taking a question a reader posed in a comment. This answers readers' questions and does it publicly. Open-ended "What would you like to know?" questions are also great ways to solicit this type of feedback—and they are also the types of posts to which bloggers enjoy linking.

Submit a topic to the suggestion kitty ! Careful ... she bites!

BUILDING RELATIONSHIPS
WITH BLOGGERS

Blogging is built upon a foundation of relationships. From the earliest bloggers through today's modern bloggers, relationships are a key reason people love to blog (and they are also one of the reasons bloggers love blogging conferences so much). Establishing relationships with bloggers can be a valuable part of your blog strategy for a number of reasons, including the following:

- *Allows blogger to be an expert on your company.* Many of the best blogging companies work with people who serve as blog "groupies" or blog fans. These bloggers watch what that company does and regularly report on the interesting tidbits. Many have inside contacts at the company, do interviews with staff members on their blog or podcast, and generally get and stay involved. Neville Hobson (www.nevon.com) covers GM's blogs, for example, and his insight was valuable as I was putting together information in Chapter 4. Having these blog experts work with your company is powerful because they will not only frequently link to you, but they'll compare other companies who blog to how well you blog, and then blog about the differences. You can read your blog experts' and blog fans' blogs to find out how you can better use your blog.

- *Offers feedback on how well you are blogging.* Having bloggers read your blog, and establishing relationships with bloggers, means that they have no problem helping you out with your blogging—like a musician teaching you a new chord on the guitar or a new melody on the piano. As you begin establishing relationships with bloggers, feel free to ask questions, because giving and receiving is part of every successful relationship.

- *Builds positive experiences with a blogger who has a public profile.* Most bloggers aren't publicly recognizable, but that doesn't mean that individual bloggers don't have a measurable amount of influence. As you build positive experiences by building relationships with these bloggers, they will happily use that influence to help your company. Most bloggers believe that any company who is willing to ask for help and to establish real relationships is worth talking about.

STEPS FOR BUILDING RELATIONSHIPS

While no single process can be used to build relationships with bloggers, as with other types of relationships, most blogging relationships follow a *natural* progression:

1. *Read the blog.* For most non-business bloggers, a blog is a great way to get to know someone. Reading the blog or subscribing to the feed will give you occasional, if not regular, insight into who the blogger is, what he or she likes, and his or her personality and passions. This foundational framework of understanding already puts you miles ahead of when you are first introduced to someone in real life, and provides a great framework for conversation going forward.
2. *Comment on the blog.* After you've read a blog for awhile, the natural next step is to comment on the occasional entry. You don't need to comment on every entry, but leaving a note or an opinion on half a dozen posts over a couple of weeks should be enough so that the blogger at least recognizes your name, and he or she will likely click through to read your blog.
3. *Link to the blog.* Since links are a measure of respect, one of the best ways to show a blogger respect is by linking to his

or her blog. Once is good but several times is even better, as it means you are actively reading the blog instead of just finding one item of interest.

4. *E-mail the blogger.* After learning about the blogger, reading his or her blog, and participating in it, followed by linking, you've established enough of a basic relationship to e-mail the blogger. This isn't to say that you couldn't begin a great relationship with a blogger by sending e-mail, as most bloggers love e-mail as much as they love a link. But building a foundation of respect and conversation means that when you do begin using e-mail, the first message won't be something like, "Uh, hey, you don't know me but...." You can simply extend the conversation you've been having in comments in posts into e-mail, and then grow it from there.

5. *Talk to the blogger.* If it isn't obvious by now, bloggers *love* to talk. Blogging is an extension of the blogger's desire to participate in conversations, especially with interesting and engaging people (like you). So don't be shy about asking for a phone call to talk things over, and don't be afraid to try other real-time methods such as Skype. (See "What the Skype?" for more information on this software application.)

6. *Meet the blogger.* The absolute best way to build a relationship with a blogger is to meet the blogger face to face. Most every blogging conference sells out because bloggers love to talk with other bloggers. In fact, hosting a blogging conference for your industry may be a great way to get to know bloggers who are interested in your business. Blogging conferences are rarely just about blogging; they're about the socializing—the drinks, the chats, the dinners, and the parties. Consider attending a blogging conference either to learn more about blogging or meet interesting bloggers from around the world.

WHAT THE SKYPE?

Skype (www.skype.com) is an instant-messaging application, similar to Windows Messenger or Yahoo! Messenger, with a twist: it's also a phone. Using Skype, you can place free calls anywhere in the world to other Skype users (more than 100 million of them). This free little application also lets you call the regular phone network (for a nominal fee), receive calls from that network (for a minor monthly fee), and have a voicemail system (for a small fee). Most bloggers love Skype because of its simple design and because it lets them make phone calls, send instant messages, and send files—all things bloggers love to do. Consider using Skype as an alternative to telephoning a blogger, as Skype can be less intimidating since it's more socially oriented.

Some of these tips may not be practical for you, and if bloggers actually initiate relationships by sending you e-mails or posting about your company, you're already there. The goal of establishing a relationship should be so that both you and the blogger find value, so whatever gets you to that point is a good thing.

In addition, you can, of course, include other steps, such as asking for help, interviewing the blogger, being on his or her podcast, or interacting in dozens of other ways. You know you're establishing a real relationship when you begin caring less about how the relationship affects your business and more about the person on the other end.

PITCHING TO BLOGGERS

Pitching bloggers is in many ways similar to pitching journalists, but it's also completely different. Pitching to journalists is called *media relations*, which is one of the reasons that I affectionately call pitching to bloggers *blogger relations.* Both are powerful sources that help you spread the word about your company, so when you are looking for them to mention you specifically, you want to make sure you're being as effective as possible in making the pitch.

Public relations and marketing professionals first started waking up to blogs in 2004, and, as such, the principles and tactics that are being tried to maximize blogger relations are fairly diverse—it's all so new that nobody's sure how to do it best.

In early 2005, as I was starting to get daily pitches from PR professionals, I wrote a post on this subject offering the following top three things to know about pitching bloggers:

- *Make it personal.* My blog provides more than enough information for anyone to know my interests and to provide a cursory understanding of who I am. Any pitch to a blogger should at least *sound* like it was written to the individual. (Hint: it's even better if it *is* individually written.)
- *Make it applicable.* Don't send me pitches for industries in which I'm not interested. Not only is my blog clearly labeled as a business and technology blog, but it's also immediately obvious to anyone who reads it that those are my passions. Don't pitch me on new innovations to panty liners (which I've received) or gardening (also received).
- *Make it short and sweet.* Generally, the shorter and more concise a pitch to a blogger, the better. There's no real point to sending the press release and hoping it will have an impact. Tell me why I should be interested in your news in 50 words or less, and then provide a link to more information. If you can't tell me why this new thing is interesting to me in 50 words, you probably can't do it in 500.

Steve Rubel noted the following (located at www.micropersuasion .com/2005/02/how_not_to_pitc.html) in response to my post:

The only thing I would add here to what Jeremy wrote is leverage exclusivity. Plant a powerful idea with an influential blogger and then ride the Long Tail (www.webpronews.com/news/ebusinessnews/wpn-45-20041117HowToPitchIntoTheLongTailNewsCurve.html).

Note: Rubel has written extensively on the subject of pitching. See "How to Pitch Into the Long Tail News Curve," at www.micropersuasion .com/2004/11/how_to_pitch_in.html; and "Abandoning Email in Favor of RSS," at www.micropersuasion.com/2004/07/dan_gillmor_ to_.html.

CRAFTING EFFECTIVE BLOGGER RELATIONSHIPS

Nick Wreden, author of *ProfitBrand: How to Increase the Profitability, Accountability and Sustainability of Brands*, noted seven keys to crafting an effective blogger relations strategy.[1] His post from February 2005 is excerpted here (with permission):

- *Never pitch, personalize.* A longstanding tenet of effective PR has been to read the publication and, ideally, the reporter's work. That has been like preaching abstinence to teen-agers: great in theory, but not very applicable to the real world. No PR person could be expected to read all publications pertaining to a company or an industry, much less of a reporter's work. But a blog has everything a blogger has written, complemented by relevant links. There is absolutely no excuse for not knowing what a blogger's passions and idiosyncrasies are before you converse about—not pitch—a concept.

- *Respect a blogger's time and intelligence.* Start emails with an informative subject line. "Press release" is grounds for immediate deletion. Make emails short and concise. Avoid attachments. Especially avoid PowerPoint attachments. If anyone can show me a corporate PowerPoint presentation worth the bandwidth it takes up, I will personally clean your cat's litterbox for a month. Do not send HTML email, which has dangerous potential. Do not kowtow; remember it's a conversation. No more "read your great post" or other pick-up lines. Do not send an email to a blogger until your website is in order, with the information and a contact easy to find and read.

- *"A blog is not about you, it's about me."* Never, ever use the words, "I think your readers would be interested in this story." To a large extent, bloggers are more interested in a point of view or the power of an idea than they are "readers." While the thought of a worldwide audience is certainly an ego rush, many bloggers would continue blogging for an audience of one. Think less about what I can do for you and more about what you can do for me [and for your readers]. Can you get immediate access to a top exec? Provide a customer to talk? What about metrics?

- *Quality, not quantity.* Here's a new rule for agencies. Never send out more than one or two communications to blogs a day. Use the remaining time to research the industry and relevant issues, study the blogger's hot buttons and craft a finely tuned email. Make the email seem like it's coming from a knowledgeable best friend, not a direct mail house.

- *Feed the food chain.* In the distant days when I had a PR agency, clients would ask, "How do I make the cover of *BusinessWeek*?" First step: Make the cover of your industry publication, and inevitably coverage in better-known publications will follow. Already, almost every industry has its blogging superstars, the go-to bloggers for both insight and buzz. Instead of stuffing their inbox, start by conversing with the bloggers who are likely being read by the superstar. That's not hard; just read blogrolls of the superstars. Not everyone has blogrolls, but for those who do, it can provide insight into who they value, as well as providing great reading material.

- *It's no longer about the media.* Many PR professionals focus on the prominent journalists and influencers who have blogs. That is understandable. But remember that customers, prospects, suppliers, industry associations and others who can influence your brand also have blogs. Converse intelligently with them as well. It needs to be recognized that pitching influential bloggers is just another method of getting in front of their face, something they are dealing with on a growing level every day, online and off. Respect and consideration is key: the last thing you want to do is become yet another "junk mail" sender—it's far better to invest the time to establish a real relationship.

- *Keep learning.* According to a blog monitoring organization, the number of blogs worth tracking has grown from 1.5 million to 7.5 million in less than six months. This emerging field is changing so fast that even these tips will have to be revised in a year. Keep up by reading at least the blogs of two experienced and thoughtful professionals: Tom Murphy and Steve Rubel.

Tip: A great source for all kinds of blog-related information is the NewPRWiki (www.thenewpr.com/wiki). Originally designed to contain PR-specific info, it now contains a wealth of business blogging information, including a large roundup of information on how to pitch bloggers, available at www.thenewpr.com/wiki/pmwiki.php/Resources/ PitchingBlogs.

ADVERTISING ON YOUR BLOG

The topic of advertising on your blog is a sticky one, primarily because blogs are about conversations, and most advertising is really about transmitting instead of engaging with your readers via conversations.

One of the best ways to advertise anything in blogs is not to advertise it at all.

That said, sometimes you'll want your blog readers to be aware of things happening in your company, and using effective advertising techniques is definitely one way to do that.

Following are some thoughts for advertising on your blog, if you are inclined to advertise there. Remember that all blog ads ultimately need to be grounded in respect. If you can both respect your audience while bringing *value* to your company, your blog-based advertising will be a success.

- *Don't distract from the content.* In the world of online advertising, you can use a variety of techniques to get users to click ads; most of these involve getting increasingly in users' faces by overlaying ads on top of the main content, having a page of ads users have to see before they can see the content, and using other tricks of the trade. On your blog, your content is your only means of gaining trust, building relationships, and relating to your customers. Don't let your ads hide your blog. Most customers who have a relationship with you via your blog will *want* to know interesting new things about your business, so figure out ways to tell them without overpowering your content.

- *Why not write a post about it?* Instead of placing a fancy ad for a new product or something you want to highlight, consider writing a post about it. This provides room for discussion and lets you tell your readers why you're passionate about what you're advertising. This technique will not only result in more people clicking an ad link (because you've given them a reason to), but it will also fuel discussion and increase trust. Users like to be told why you like a new product or service.

- *Don't use ads in your feeds.* Many executives at some point realize that lots of people are reading their feeds. In fact, if your blog is like most blogs, more people will read your feeds than go to your website. Resist any temptations to force people to go to your site or to put advertising in your feeds. Remember that traffic isn't the inherent value in your blog, it's the conversations that build relationships and trust. Doing anything to compromise that is a bad idea.

- *Place the ad well.* If you put an ad on your blog, place it in a location where people who are "looking around" your blog will find it. This can be in the top section of your blog, along the side, or even at the bottom below all the content. As long as it doesn't interrupt the content, a number of options for placement are possible.

- *Give people a reason to click the ad link.* If you put an ad on your blog, give people a reason to click it. Don't use standard advertising techniques like "Fantastic new product!" and "This will change your life!" Respect your readers enough to tell them the truth in your advertising. Consider offering blog-specific promotions, having contests for the best feedback on the product or ad, or offering other activities around the product or ad. People enjoy being part of your company, so leverage that in your advertising.

- *Give customers ownership.* I've talked about Microsoft's Channel 9 site several times in this book. In early 2005, Channel 9 ran a contest for Microsoft's annual developer conference. Anyone could enter, and anyone could win an all-expense paid trip to the conference (worth roughly $2500) if they blogged about the conference and displayed a little graphic promoting the conference. This allowed the readers and participators at Channel 9 not only to enter a cool contest, but to carry the message beyond the original blog. Giving your customers ownership of advertising and allowing them to carry that advertising is a powerful way not only to get buy-in, but also to create a community around an event, product, or service.

- *Don't advertise.* One of the best ways to advertise anything in blogs is *not* to advertise it at all. Bloggers love finding secrets, telling others about those secrets, and posting about secrets. This technique of "hiding" a new product or another announcement in content is extremely effective. It's a little bit like reverse-psychology: you don't tell bloggers what you really want them to do. For example, if you were operating a clothing company and blogged about some of your favorite fabrics, you might note as an aside that you're using the fabrics in your new product line—which you aren't talking about.

- *Be passionate.* Many blogs are inherently advertising and marketing tools: you create them because you want to increase your visibility, build relationships, drive sales, increase your interactivity with customers, and for all kinds of other reasons. This is one reason why simply having a blog and not in any way leveraging it to advertise is such a powerful method of actually advertising. A large number of bloggers have put their companies on the map simply by being incredibly smart on their blogs. Joel Spolsky's blog (www .joelonsoftware.com/) is just about the only means of advertising his company, Fog Creek Software (www.fogcreek .com) uses; Joel's passion and intelligence is all the advertising Fog Creek really needs.

- *Have a cause.* Another great way to advertise is to get involved in a cause or a charity drive. Many of our clients have successfully promoted blog-based fundraisers for charities to kick off new products they're launching. Bloggers, in general, love to link to interesting charity events happening on other blogs.

- *Interview the person behind the ad.* Instead of simply announcing a new product, you can get readers interested in the product by having a blog or podcast interview with the person in charge. It's the equivalent to director's commentary on a DVD and a great way to see into the mind, and the passion, of the person who brought whatever it is you're advertising from an idea to reality.

BUILDING A BLOG COMMUNITY

All businesses, whether they like it or not, operate in communities. In some businesses, these are called *industries*; in others, they're called *vertical markets*. But all businesses also operate in a more intangible community: the community of ideas centered around their business. Your community of ideas is made up of your company, your employees, your partners, your suppliers, your customers, and any industry analysts, reporters, or bloggers who are interested. This community of ideas includes all the people who have any interest in your company, and it likely encompasses a sizeable number of people, even if yours is a small one-person business.

A healthy community of ideas and interests builds itself up: it means two clients who may have supply and demand opportunities (a new business who needs business cards and a printing company, for example) learn about each other and work together. Your blog is one of the best ways to unite that community around your company. Having a blog written either specifically for this

BLOGGING CONFERENCES: THE FAST-TRACK TO BUILDING RELATIONSHIPS

Blogging conferences are to bloggers what going out for a drinks on a Friday night is for many people: a way to connect. Blogging conferences are held every month (or every week) all over the world, and they are generally attended by 200 to 300 bloggers and people in various industries. These conferences are primarily about three things:

- Meeting people who blog or want to learn how to blog
- Listening to talks, generally while blogging about them
- Meeting people who blog or want to learn how to blog

For most bloggers, the conference itself is really beside the point. Blogging conferences are about solidifying relationships, catching up on gossip, meeting new people, and talking to company reps who are present. Higher profile bloggers will also conduct press interviews, podcasts from the conference floor, panel sessions, and open-ended discussion sessions (these come in various flavors).

group or at least with this group in mind allows you to tap into the potential that is created when companies, individuals, the media, bloggers, customers, and government work together to come up with great ideas—and it allows it all to happen on your blog.

WHAT COMMUNITY LOOKS LIKE

A community of ideas or community of interest blog is a fairly new phenomenon and one that few companies are using (yet); however, it's an incredibly powerful tool.

The community spreads news about what's happening in the community. If you own a sign-making company, your community may comprise a large variety of businesses, most of which might be in a fairly specific geographic area. It may also involve suppliers of the materials you use, readers of your blogs, employees, and any government officials who work with you. It may involve competitors (if you have a relationship with them). A healthy community blog will list interesting things happening in all of these factions: from a new shish-kabob restaurant, to new government issues that affect businesses like yours and those of your community, to a new type of product that either you or other businesses in your community would find interesting. By spreading news about what's going on and what's applicable, everyone stays in the loop, and everyone's business benefits.

Community advertises new opportunities. A healthy community blog will post new job opportunities in the businesses involved, post new contracts that are available, post links to new government grants that may be applicable, and generally keep everyone informed as to opportunities that may be of interest. Obviously, this doesn't have to be to the detriment of your business, but if some information will help everyone, it's worth posting.

Community offers challenges. I know of a business that was burglarized, and the insurance company refused to cover the damages or the lost goods. This news was posted on a community site, and several businesses stepped in to offer help; the business that was robbed repaid the favors in new business and a variety of other ways. In another community, one of the owners of a two-man printing shop was diagnosed with cancer. When this news was posted to the community, several people offered part-time staff (to be paid by the printing shop, of course) who could help one or two days a week. This isn't about generosity so much as about realizing that a large and healthy community helps all businesses involved.

Community shares important information or tips. Whatever information is relevant to the community industry, the geographic location, or a school of thought should be posted to the community blog. Perhaps a new conference is of interest, or a major department store is coming to town that people may want to support. Sharing this information makes everyone's business stronger and more able to compete.

In many ways, community is like an advanced contacts systems online—like LinkedIn (www.linkedin.com)—where everyone tries to be available to help everyone else. As the old saying goes, "A rising tide raises all ships." By hosting this community of ideas or community of interest, you not only get to be identified as the business that's doing the actual sharing, but you get to establish stronger relationships with all of these businesses as you maintain contact, share ideas, and ultimately build everyone's business to a greater degree than would have happened without you and without the new community blog.

WRAPPING IT UP

Ultimately, whether you buy into my overall vision for blogging or not, blogging is still valuable for your business in that it *does* increase your visibility (when done well), and it *does* allow you to experiment with all kinds of interesting customer interactions. What you choose to do with your blog is ultimately up to you, and how you succeed with your blog will be decided by how committed to it you and your business are.

In the next, and final, chapter of this book, we look at the future of blogging and how blogging is challenging various business paradigms. I've talked about many such paradigms throughout this book—such as transmitting versus engaging, treating your customers as participants instead of wallets, and so forth. In the next chapter we look at how blogging will ultimately evolve as it collides with these and other paradigms.

My hope is that this book has provided you with food for thought, the information and examples necessary to develop a blogging strategy, and the excitement needed to take a leap into something as new and sometimes scary as blogging can be. Chapter 11 is meant to provide you with some forward-thinking information to make that leap just a little bit easier.

11

THE FUTURE OF BUSINESS BLOGGING

The blog was an unqualified success. By posting examples of how a good sign could impact business, Arnold had inspired a wave of sign-buying in the town. Businesses were now competing to see who could have the best sign. Even the new developments along the interstate were getting in on the act. A falafel shop had placed an order for a big stand-alone sign for the front of the store.

Zylon had appreciated the tactful way Arnold had defended the company in the "u suck" incident. Zylon was a good corporate citizen as far as Arnold was concerned, and he was glad to say so. It had been a learning experience all around. Until the nasty comments on the blog, the leadership at Zylon hadn't been aware of the poor relationship the company had with the community, and the CEO vowed to address it. He had started his own blog to explain the Zylon side of the story and to reach out to the town. Zylon had even started an internal blog to improve efficiency and to make employees feel like valued partners.

"I understand the web. I even understand blogs," Arnold explained proudly to June, whose hair was now a pale shade of peach.

"Don't rest on your laurels yet," June said with a smile. "We're just getting started."

—Part 4 of "Blog," a short story by Joe Flood

Much of this book has focused on what blogging is and can be. I would be remiss in not telling you where I, and many in the industry, believe blogging is going. After all, it won't remain stagnant—as new companies engage in the blogosphere, new communities begin to form, and new methods of pushing the envelope emerge, a considerable amount of change, tension, and growth will ensue.

It's been said that the measure of a man is how quickly he accepts change. I believe the same is true for blogging. Blogging started out as a way for people to communicate; to update each other on important, relevant issues; and to establish relationships. From the earliest days of blogging, the purity of relationships was valued above everything else. Similarly, most bloggers believe that they are agents of change, helping the world come to appreciate blogging.

However, these agents of change don't realize that by involving more people, the very thing they love *will* change.

As change is inevitable, this chapter is dedicated to providing some insight and best guesses into what those changes will be and how they will play out. I can't render judgment on whether certain approaches are good or bad. Ultimately, it requires risk-takers and people ready to push the envelope for us all to see what blogging can and will become.

While hundreds of small and large changes to blogging are certain to occur during the years, I'll touch on three specific trends as this book nears its close:

- The shifting focus from accuracy and relationships to communication and relationships
- The growing trend of businesses wanting to build "real" relationships with customers
- The principles of "awareness publishing" and how companies can relate one-to-one with customers on a global scale

TRENDS FOR THE FUTURE

Authenticity, relationship, and honesty—you'll remember these three themes since they've been included as a consistent part of this book. Bloggers, who are a representation of your audience, value these themes above all else, primarily because bloggers value relationships above everything else, and they rightly believe that any relationship that isn't authentic and honest probably isn't worth having.

This focus on realness and authentic relationships is one of the reasons blogging grew so quickly. As people tired of the mainstream media's perspective, they could get an authentic report on events, people who wanted real financial advice without any spin could get a real opinion, and voyeuristic people who wanted to peer into someone else's life could do just that—all by using blogs. In the beginning of blogging, nearly everything was *real*.

As your company enters into blogging, you *must* be aware of how important these values are to your audience, and as these values shift slightly, you need to be aware that peoples' reactions will change. Some companies that haven't been aware of these values have tried a number of things to appeal to blog readers, ultimately ending in fairly disastrous "lessons learned."

First, *character blogs* were written by novelists trying to create "real" people online. One of the largest of these was "Plain Layne," a sexually active, deeply troubled young woman. She had a following of tens of thousands of people all around the world—that is, until it became known that every story, every picture, and every painful memory that readers had followed and offered help with were fakes.

Next came companies who started "blogs" that were entirely and completely fake. Not only was no real person behind them, but their sole purpose was to get people to believe in an ad campaign. McDonald's, for example, engaged in this type of activity with a blog about a French fry that looked like Abraham Lincoln and was sold on eBay (see www.museumofhoaxes.com/hoax/weblog/comments/2450/).

And, as always happens in our capitalist society, the change from a relationship-driven community to one that still valued relationships but also wanted to make money slowly crept in. First it was ads on individual pages; then companies paid bloggers to blog about them; then companies sponsored entire blogs.

Each of these changes shocked the blogging world but also brought about a more natural balance. Yes, sometimes bloggers will tell stories. And, yes, some bloggers want to make money. Overall, most bloggers eventually accepted these facts, as long as bloggers and companies *disclosed* that this is what they were doing. The word *disclosure* became so important that not disclosing whether you were receiving corporate money or not disclosing a relationship with companies you were blogging about was a shot against your authenticity and your character.

All of these trends will continue to collide in the future. Companies *will* want to pour money into blogging. Bloggers *will* want to make money off of blogging. Fake blogs, character blogs, and inauthentic blogs *will* appear. But these will not prosper unless the writer behind them is authentic. Authenticity will continue to drive serious blogging for many years to come, which is a good thing for your business, because it allows you to *relate* to your customers directly—something that smart businesses crave.

I believe that several minor trends will collide with interesting results in the future:

- Accuracy versus timeliness
- Relationships versus readers
- Purity versus income

In the past, reporting things in an accurate fashion was highly prized by bloggers who reported events. They knew that even if it took an extra half hour to do so, verifying the facts was an important part of what they were doing. In many ways, they were acting as micro-journalists—or as citizen journalists. However, some individuals and groups have realized that others out there are doing similar things on blogs; as a result, some bloggers have become more like mass media in general in that they not only strive to publish something before the mainstream media (which is surprisingly easy to do), but also to publish it *before other bloggers*. This is sometimes at the expense of accuracy. I see this trend continuing for some time, at least until bloggers decide to take a stand for the truth instead of blogging for attention.

The pressure on increasingly popular bloggers is immense. Most bloggers start out with just friends and acquaintances reading their new blogs. Then readers who don't know them find their blogs, and a community of hundreds or even thousands of readers can develop. When a blogger has that kind of reader base, what follows is pressure to write about certain topics in certain ways and to do all of this on a very frequent basis. The challenge for bloggers who enter this stage is to continue to value *relationships* ahead of *readers*. However, the lure of readers, fame, and fortune can be strong, and quite a few bloggers have either given up or even stabbed their friends in the back seeking out that fame or fortune. I expect this type of behavior to continue. Like it or not, blogging fame can distort your view of reality to the point where the reason you started blogging in the first place becomes less important than the things you can get by blogging.

On a similar vein, I believe the purity of blogging will start to be called into question, specifically by those who started blogging the earliest. Many of these early, and very vocal, bloggers will see the increasing presence of media and corporations in the world of blogging as a bad thing. This is ironic, considering they once claimed it would become vital to those same corporations. However, many newer bloggers will eschew this purity in favor of income, reputation, and visibility. Not that they will necessarily be any less interested in authenticity, honesty, and other themes, but they will be looking for something that gives *them* benefits and not benefits just to the entire blogosphere.

Overall, expect the blogosphere and bloggers in general to become more professional, more money and visibility focused, and, in spite of that, to continue to resist change. (Sounds very much like the open-source movement!)

ACCURACY VS. TIMELINESS

One of the hallmarks of blogging is its *accuracy*—not necessarily in the traditional mainstream media type of accuracy, but accuracy as to what the blogger is experiencing. When bloggers write reports, they do so largely from an experiential and emotional point of view. They state their opinions, show off other opinions, link to a variety of sites, and somehow come together with writing that is real, honest, and accurate—at least to the blogger who wrote the post.

This focus on accuracy is one of the reasons that bloggers and blog readers don't enjoy hearing what they call "marketing speak," which is effectively the canned, hyped-up type of talk that goes into press releases and that emphasizes the "new" and "innovative" and "world-changing" nature of some new product a company is touting. Bloggers, and to a growing extent the general public, would rather hear *why* your company is doing something, *why* it excites you, and what *you* believe it will do for customers.

Blogging is also an *incredibly* time-sensitive activity. In the mainstream press world, it's a big deal if you are behind on a story by a few hours (in TV), or a day (in newspaper), or a week (in a magazine). In blogging, you lose the advantage if you're off by *minutes*. For bloggers whose traffic, reputation, and style is built on their ability to find news first, minutes matter.

As a result, I've seen occasions in which these two paradigms collide: nobody can be the fastest *and* the most accurate—one or the other needs to be the priority. As you begin to explore blogging further, you will undoubtedly encounter this phenomenon and you'll likely wrestle with the desire to write something *first* instead of writing it *right*.

THE VALUE OF FAST

Generally speaking, the blogger who finds and posts something first gets recognized as such by receiving the most incoming links on the subject. People look at the original post more than any other, primarily because that's assumed to be the one that has the most information.

The value of getting information out quickly is a double-edged sword, though, because it's difficult to include every perspective, to verify information, and to form a full opinion if you have only seconds or minutes in which to write the post. These posts will often be framed in a "I just came across this . . ." or "This is just a rumor at this point . . ." style of post.

That said, unlike mainstream media, blogs can be *edited* live, so many bloggers begin adding context, accuracy, opinion, other perspectives, and such *well after* their original post appeared. Nevertheless, this value on fast over right does play havoc with the first readers to a post who don't necessarily get all the accurate information on the story.

Gawker Media (www.gawker.com; see Figure 11-1) is an interesting blog network, in that it is highly focused on the "fast" side of blogging: lots of rumors, lots of unconfirmed stories, and lots of sensationalism appear on this blog. Gawker is based on the concept of fast reporting, possibly with more in-depth reporting being provided later (if there's anything new of interest). In many ways, it's similar to a tabloid, and we all know how much tabloids improve the value of the mainstream press.

As you begin blogging, you will often encounter the choice of whether to report *everything* or to report *something*. Whichever choice you make, be aware that you *are* making a choice, and that

Figure 11-1   Gawker Media focuses largely on the "tabloid" side of news: rumors, leaks, and interesting celebrity news.

you are (in many ways) setting a precedent; so make sure it's the precedent you want to set.

Ultimately, the choice of valuing fast or right needs to be considered as you're developing your blogging strategy and blogger relations strategies. True niche blogs have the ability to be first and foremost, since breaking stories will often be sent their way before being offered to the mainstream media.

THE VALUE OF RIGHT

In blogging terms, *right* is about two things: the *facts* and the *context.* Facts are facts; context is your opinion or the opinion of others, what the situation at hand means to your company and industry, and anything that might matter to your readers. Compiling a full contextual post often means considering topics from a variety of angles. In the beginning of blogging, context was purely about the individual and what he or she thought and how things applied to him or her, but with a business, you need to provide more depth: readers want to know your opinion, what it means to the company, *and* what it means to the industry.

That said, you can provide context in three ways:

- **Opinion**   By providing your or your business's opinion on a matter, you offer readers your beliefs about what the situation or event or news means. Is it important? Will it change the industry? Is it merely a "good to know" piece of information? Your opinion is key to positioning the situation in your customers' minds.

- **Perspective**   Perspective is all about stepping back and asking "What does this mean?" as well as "Are we looking at this the right way?" One of my earliest bits of business reporting regarded the Canadian Bre-X gold scandal in the late 1990s, wherein a Bre-X geologist's fake report indicated that a huge gold deposit was found in the jungles of Borneo. At the time the scandal made the mainstream news, everyone was talking about what it meant to investors and to the gold industry, while I was seeking to lend a different perspective—what it meant for trust in Canadian business, and how could such a situation be averted in the future. Perspective is really about taking what is being said elsewhere and asking *different questions* to provide a different kind of value.

- **Meaning**   Whenever a scandal happens in politics, one of the involved parties' first responses is "This isn't important." While this typically means the scandal *is* important, it's also a great example of assigning meaning to a situation. For example, rightly or wrongly, US President George W. Bush wrapped national security, terrorism, and patriotism into one big ball that can't be undone; whenever anyone tries to challenge one of these, he insists that they must be challenging American democracy and freedom. Hopefully, when you provide meaning, it won't be in such black-and-white terms; providing the answers to "why?" and "what does this mean?" questions is one of your key responsibilities when blogging to your customers.

Blogging is a fantastic platform for communicating with your customers and for getting their feedback. Make sure you write your posts in such a way that both of these can happen, and recognize that going forward with the two paradigms of *right* and *fast* will collide, largely with unexpected results.

THE PARADIGMS AT PLAY

Blogs were founded on the value of *right*. For most blogs, this was about individuals being *authentic*, and therefore true to themselves—but even the earliest blogs sometimes pointed out new stuff as interesting, without necessarily reporting all the facts.

In fact, the earliest blogs really didn't put a lot of value on factual accuracy, at least at the community level. Blog authors obviously weren't trying to deceive anyone, and they weren't reporting untruths, but few people questioned what other bloggers wrote.

This collision of paradigms between fast and right is a natural by-product of blogging growing up: as time passes and more questions are asked, people become more cynical and skeptical and start to ask more questions (valuing *right*)—plus, people are looking to get traffic, reputation, and advertising dollars (valuing *fast*). Fundamentally, the paradigm shift is the result of a movement away from the value of a single person's truthful (to themselves, at least) account, opinion, and perspective, as well as a complete valuing of relationships and people, and a shift toward truth, security, and *integrity* (which, without authenticity, is an interesting thing to desire).

For your business, this shifting paradigm means that bloggers will have *different* expectations of you, depending on their perspectives. Some will expect you to comment right away on a new scandal, product, or development, while others will be content waiting for a few hours or a couple of days while you get your facts together. (That isn't to say that waiting is *always* the best thing to do.) Ultimately, values will collide in unusual ways, so that saying "valuing right is always best for your company" in the future is a difficult call to make.

Be aware of these shifting paradigms and reader and blogger expectations, and take advantage of them. For example, if your company is facing a major scandal, why not *acknowledge* it on your blog, updating your readers as events happen internally? Here is an example snapshot of how one of my clients handled a recent scandal using a blog:

Day 1

10:00: Posted acknowledgement to blog.

1:00: Posted about filing of lawsuit on blog.

3:00: Posted (from a trusted source) a denial, promising more details tomorrow after he'd had a chance to go over exactly where the company was at.

Day 2

9:00: Posted detailed overview of what led up to the lawsuit.

11:00: Posted an interview with the individual inside the company who had mishandled the situation (this was not a criminal lawsuit and ended up being a minor civil one).

2:00: Posted an apology to customers, the customer who had been mishandled, and the industry at large.

Day 3

Remained a source of objective news on the subject.

This client ultimately tried to balance fast *and* right. Because this was a lawsuit issue, the company obviously consulted with lawyers at each step of the way, but my clients really, really wanted to maintain a sense of being the *first and best* place to get information on what had happened, why it had happened, what was going on inside the company, and where this experience was taking the company.

A lawsuit is an extreme example, but a good one: if you have to make a choice, you can choose to do *both* fast and right by making it clear to readers that you'll be posting more information as you can. Making a time promise is also a good idea, if you can keep it.

RIDING THE TRENDS

It is difficult to say exactly how and when these trends will collide, but the first precursors to that collision are beginning to appear. In many ways, these types of trends are to be expected—any time something goes from niche to mainstream growing pains and shifting values always ensue. Thankfully for your business, you can take advantage both of the current focus on authenticity and relationships as well as dedicating resources into the coming trends of timeliness and depth of reporting. There isn't any reason you can't ride both of the trends, which will ultimately give you a deeper and more meaningful message in the conversation.

RELATIONSHIPS VS. READERS

When blogging began, relationships were a huge focus. This hasn't changed much over the years, as bloggers still love to get together, find new blogs, talk to new people, interact with new companies, and generally be social butterflies. However, things have begun to change as the value of the blog becomes less about the actual blogger and more about how many people read the blog.

Some attempts to counteract this trend have been made by blogging's originators, who try to focus on *who* is reading a blog rather than *how many* are reading it, figuring that having 10 "influential" people reading your blog is exponentially more powerful than 1000 "non-influential" folks. However, for most blogs, this argument simply doesn't hold up, as most blogs *don't* have even 10 influential people reading them. This trend has become more and more visible, as high-profile bloggers begin posting their traffic levels publicly and the blogosphere begins to be separated into two distinct groups: those who *have* (traffic, that is), and those who *have not*.

Realistically and historically, a mild bit of the class system has crept into the blogosphere. *A-List* bloggers are the most popular people in any given niche. These people were, almost without exception, the first to start blogging in that niche. Those who started later enjoyed nowhere near the popularity of the A-List bloggers.

This class system, though frequently mentioned in the blogging realm, generally didn't matter much, since even the A-List bloggers valued relationships (even if it was generally with other A-List bloggers). Eventually, *B-List* bloggers—those who were making waves but weren't really popular enough to be on the real A-List—and even the *C-List*—those who had traffic, but weren't making waves and were not extremely popular—were mentioned.

In mid-2005, a site showed up claiming to have compiled the definitive lists of A to C Lists; Blogebrity is shown in Figure 11-2 (www.blogebrity.com). This site was actually meant as satire, but the lists are still posted and remain the closest to any documented blogger class system.

Despite the popularity contest, relationships still do matter to bloggers, and even though the trend toward measuring the importance of a blogger by his or her traffic will likely increase (as people

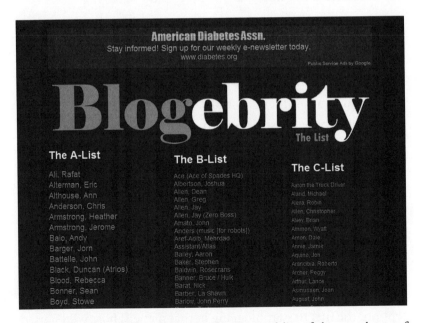

Figure 11-2 Blogebrity produced a documented list of the top classes of bloggers.

like to measure how important they are), there will continue to be measures taken to "preserve" the blogosphere. Some of this will focus on reminding bloggers and readers what blogging really stands for, and some will focus on defining your own "personal A-List" of people who matter to you.

These trends are important for businesses not because a business needs to get sucked into either of these debates, but because these subcultures of people (those who value traffic, and those who value relationship) *will* visit your blog and will look for signs of whether you measure up in their eyes.

MEASURING YOUR BUSINESS BLOG'S SUCCESS

The pressure to measure a blog's success by external standards (such as links, Technorati ranking, PubSub ranking, traffic, comments, and list ranking) is high, and it is also incredibly natural. We humans tend to look for ways to compare ourselves to others, either to make us feel better by beating the other guy or to stop us from feeling bad because we're not *as bad* as the other guy. This tendency is natural in blogging, too, but your business must fight it.

Developing a blogging strategy that focuses on your metrics for success is important. If the only way you measure success is by traffic and other external measures, you could easily shut down your blog in spite of the importance of the relationships you build, the communication that happens, and the real value to your business that blogging brings.

Part of that set of metrics will almost certainly be external measures, and that's fine, because it's good to know your reach, your audience, how many pages people are seeing each visit, and other statistics. It's all valuable *marketing* information. However, you also need to figure out ways to measure the value blogging is bringing to your business via other factors: How many customers did blogging let you help? How much buzz did the blog create? Did comments from customers bring more clarity to how a product should work (or why it doesn't)? These are all important pieces of the successful blog puzzle. Simply measuring success by traffic is like measuring the success of a baseball team only by how many pitches get thrown: it's good to know, but it doesn't help you determine whether you should stay in the game.

Projecting Your Importance

The challenge for business blogs is that some readers will care about how "important" the business is and more specifically how important the blog is. This may happen not in obvious ways, but subversively. By defining your success publicly, defining how well you're doing publicly, and projecting that you *value blogging*, you can project your importance and meet this challenge.

Show that you value your readers and that you value blogging, perhaps by papering a wall in your office with postcards and e-mails sent by readers, and then regularly taking pictures of that wall and posting them on the blog. Or tell the world about things posted on your blog, and then point the world to your blog. Or sponsor contests. Ultimately, readers need to know that you value your blog not for the traffic it brings or for how visible it is externally, but for how it affects them—the readers.

Pleasing Everyone

As you go forward in your blogging, you will encounter internal and external challenges. You will also encounter wildly different expectations from your readers, customers, and partners. Some will think you've lost it for starting a blog or for posting certain information to the blog, while others will think you're great for doing the same things.

We all know that there's no way to please everyone, and this is the biggest reason for defining your own success instead of letting the blogosphere, analysts, or even your blog's readers define it for you. As long as you have created and can continually refer back to your blogging strategy, you'll know whether or not you're succeeding.

Just as you should be cautious when entering blogging, to make sure you're doing it for the right reasons, so, too, should you be cautious as you're blogging: don't let anyone else define your success; otherwise, you'll let them also define your failures.

PURITY VS. INCOME

Many of the paradigms and trends we've discussed in this chapter are about "old values" versus "new opportunities," and the arguments of purity versus income are no different. Until 2004, seeing any kind of ads on blogs was an anomaly, and the blogger who allowed ads was generally regarded with some level of disdain. When Google launched its AdSense program, which let even the smallest blog publishers earn money from their websites, blogs started to include more advertising.

During the 2004 US presidential elections, advertising became prominent on many types of blogs, as both political parties and all kinds of action groups tried to saturate the blogosphere with opinion, "facts," and diatribes. Since then, advertising on blogs has become fairly commonplace. Some blogs have understated ads that barely cover the costs of running the blogs, while other blogs are proudly for-profit endeavors. Some bloggers, such as Darren Rowse (www.problogger.net), even make a living purely by their blogging efforts, and entire networks of for-profit blogs such as Weblogs, Inc. (www.weblogsinc.com) and Gawker Media (www .gawker.com) have shown up. Even blog-specific ad networks, such as Blogads (www.blogads.com), AdBrite (www.adbrite.com), and Pheedo (www.pheedo.com), are increasing in number.

Advertising has become an accepted practice on blogs, but that doesn't mean everyone's happy about it.

In 2005, a crisis occurred in blogging regarding the use of ads in blog feeds. While ads in blog feeds was probably a natural evolutionary step for blog-based advertising, it still riled many original bloggers to the point where Dave Winer, one of blogging's founders, got sponsorship for a talk he made at a conference just to show how silly he believed ads in feeds were. Still, bloggers and blog publishers went ahead with the ad feed program. Readers didn't end up clicking many ads, though, so many publishers eventually removed them entirely, but not before a certain cadre of bloggers got upset enough to kick up a minor fuss.

The argument for purity is largely that any attempt to advertise products on a blog will diminish the blogger's ability to speak honestly—after all, if you're being paid by some company to talk about it, are you *really* likely to be objective and honest? Also, not all blogs talk about ads that appear on the site. Blog ads can be much like magazine ads—a relevant company asks to post an ad and the publisher includes it for a fee. By giving the blogger final say-so over which ads are posted, though, the issue of being objective is moot. The ads become as authentic as the blog content. Of course, many people say they just ignore the blog ads anyway.

WORKING IT FOR YOUR BUSINESS

This collision of ideals will probably never be truly resolved: people who refuse to believe bloggers or businesses should make money are unlikely to change that stance, and people who believe that making money from something you spend a heck of a lot of time doing is natural are unlikely to concede.

However, this trend is important to note for your business blog, because it could shape your customers' expectations of how you deal with the public, how and why you blog, and what benefit you're receiving. If the vast majority of readers begin wanting a more "pure" blog, they may tell you that your business shouldn't receive a direct financial benefit from blogging either.

Preparedness is key. Public opinion constantly changes, and being prepared and flexible will make your response that much more valuable and measured.

AWARENESS PUBLISHING

Blogs empower people to be able to write their own thoughts quickly and easily online as a "personal publishing" forum. Blogs are equally powerful for companies, though, as we've explored throughout this book. Business blogging isn't really about personal publishing at all—it's a different kind of publishing power: I call it "awareness publishing."

Using the blog, companies small and large are in charge of generating awareness and visibility and attracting attention. Before blogs, communication occurred through the media, public relations, and marketing. With blogs, businesses and business leaders can talk directly to customers and build relationships in entirely new ways, with great results.

Awareness publishing, and business blogging, are important because they put companies in control. Company blogs create a new degree of interactivity with customers that had rarely been experienced before blogging, especially since most interaction occurs on a small scale with a few dozen or a few hundred of your customers. Now, though, you can interact with anyone—your customers as well as hundreds or thousands of potential new customers—all at the same time, and you can allow them to respond to you directly.

In addition, your audience can be in control. One reason blogs work so well is because people get to respond in the comments area of the blog. Comments create a great two-way conversation, allowing your blog to interact with clients instead of just being a way to push your ideas onto your clients. As a result, customers are empowered to choose to read and participate in your blog and are therefore empowered to begin a relationship with you, which would have been much more difficult in other circumstances. In other media, communication is about your business *selling* something to the customer, while blogs are really about *communication*, with no strings attached.

Awareness publishing also helps spread the message. As good as your message may be, and as good as communication on your blog will surely become, your business needs to reach beyond the four walls that surround your physical offices into the larger world. Blogs spread the message in a variety of ways, with tracking tools such as Technorati to bloggers' tendency to generously link to interesting tidbits, and this gives your message a greater ability to spread naturally and quickly throughout your community.

NEW AWARENESS

The concepts of awareness publishing aren't just about raising your company's visibility; they're also about raising awareness in areas for which your customers and readers may not otherwise be able to access. Blogs provide a way for you to shed light on what your company is *really* doing, and what your company is *really* about. It doesn't need to come in the form of announcements or press releases; instead, it should be in the conversational tone of the blog. If a customer asks about your civic-mindedness, for example, you can let him or her know that you honestly care about the community so much so that you've decided to sponsor a local park, and that you're donating employee time to help with a local wetlands issue.

Blogs shouldn't be used as a pulpit for this type of thing, but they do offer a way to engage your audience in areas of which they may not otherwise be aware. Use this capacity wisely: You don't need to brag about your company's philanthropic events or other deeds. Remember that real conversations are based on respect, and that your feedback is most wanted and most valuable when it's *asked* for. So while your wetlands project may be great for the community, boasting about your community-mindedness is not necessarily the best way to respond to someone who posts a message like "You stink!"

BENEFITS OF AWARENESS PUBLISHING

When I envisioned this book, the concepts of awareness publishing were incredibly important to me. Problem was, they were largely concepts until my editor began pushing me for the *real* benefits. As we brainstormed on these benefits, it became clear that blogging was about more than just raising your business's awareness and visibility.

Gaining Awareness

As discussed several times in this book, the measure of your brand and your business's advertising effectiveness is really about how much mindshare you have with your customers. Conversations are great ways to increase mindshare, and your blog provides a great mechanism for at least kick-starting those conversations.

Getting Feedback

The more people are aware of you and your company, the more they talk about you and your company. By providing a place for people to talk to you, and each other, about their joys and frustrations, you not only create a community of people who get to hear directly from you, but you get to participate in some great feedback sessions.

Presenting Your Side of the Story

Several high-profile executives, such as Dallas Mavericks owner Marc Cuban and Sun Microsystems' Jonathan Schwartz, have turned to blogging as a way to express the *real* "whys" behind a story. Too often with the mainstream press, the truth of the story can get lost in the reporter's "angle." Blogs provide a fantastic way for you not only to say exactly what you mean to say, in context, but also to provide answers to why your business is doing what it's doing in an open and honest way.

Creating Opportunities for Dialogue

Much of blogging is about dialogue. A lot of talk happens in the blogosphere, but one of the great benefits of blogging is that it can kick off person-to-person conversations. Text is great for getting introduced, but nothing beats a phone call, a lunch date, or a round of golf or tennis for really getting to know someone. Blogs are great for introducing yourself, establishing relationships, and kick-starting conversations that create new opportunities.

WHERE BLOGGING IS HEADED

So where is blogging going? We looked at some of the trends that will begin converging (or diverging) earlier in this chapter, but our final area of discussion in this book will be about where blogging is going and what's going to take it there.

I've done hundreds of interviews in magazines, newspapers, and radio shows about blogging. I'm frequently asked this question: "Where is blogging headed in the next five or ten years?"

Blogging is just so new that it's hard to say exactly where it will be by, say, 2010. Typically, when asked, I've offered one of three responses:

- *Blogs will disappear.* Blogs will become so ubiquitous that they'll be forgotten as a buzzword. Everyone will have a blog, it will be a natural extension of every website, and it will be natural for people to post comments on all kinds of content, including news articles and movie trailers.

- *Blogs will change everything.* This one is sometimes used just to precipitate discussion, but I'll sometimes say "Blogs will completely redefine everything businesses do" to start a real conversation on the merits of blogging. The fact is, blogs could easily change many of the facets of how people react to, and expect to interact with, businesses from corner stores to major corporations. Blogs are the embodiment of the consumer's ability to discern, and the business's ability to listen: together, these two forces could easily change how all businesses interact and converse with customers.

- *Blogs are a communications medium and will never die.* Early in the process of writing this book, I had a mild epiphany: blogs are a communications medium. I realized that *no* communications medium that reached the mainstream has died—not the fax, not the telegraph, not the letter, not the phone. OK, so some *have* died—we rarely use carrier pigeons or smoke signals anymore—but the point remains: once something is mainstream, it takes years, even decades, for it to change, even if something better comes along.

Blogs will change. Lots of companies will have blogs. Blogs are revolutionary. But no matter what happens, blogs will be a communications medium for many years to come. As long as you keep

BLOGS REPLACE WEBSITES

One of the main schools of thought relative to where blogs are going is that they may eventually completely replace most typical corporate websites. Instead of having an "About Us" page that stays the same, companies will have an "About Us" category on their blogs that gets updated at least once a month with new company-related information. Instead of having an "About the CEO" page, the CEO will have his or her own blog.

At their core, blogs are simply websites that empower communication. Why wouldn't a company want to empower communication across its entire website?

communicating with your customers using your blog, and even if blogs go out of style and you keep using them and communicating with them, they can still bring value to your company; there may *never* be a reason to stop using blogs.

WRAPPING IT UP

Each of the trends in this chapter is important; however, exactly how these collisions will play out and what the changes in blogging will mean to your business are uncertain. Does it even matter if a blogger makes money off his or her blog, as long as the blogger stays authentic? Can a blogger not find a way to be both fast *and* accurate? Can traffic matter to a business, as long as relationships still matter?

All of these questions will be answered with time. Your business needs to keep its finger on the pulse of blogging; you need to know why you are blogging, why you're succeeding, and how best to use this exciting medium, publishing platform, and communications tool to your advantage. Some of that will be internal to your company and some of it will be external to the world. Either way, though, you need to find out how you can use blogging to help you and your business.

This glimpse into the future of blogging brings this book to a close. I've included an appendix with a sample blogging policy, as well as a glossary of blogging terms, should you need them. Hopefully this book has provided you with insight into how blogging can best be used. If you have questions, please see the book's blog (www.blogmarketingbook.com) or my blog (www.ensight.org), or send me an e-mail (jeremy@ensight.org).

Good luck in your blogging endeavors!

APPENDIX

SAMPLE BLOGGING POLICY

Throughout this book, I've mentioned the importance of creating blogging policies to guide you as you blog. Blogging policies can be complicated strategies that consider both legal and cultural issues, and, unfortunately, no "one-size fits all" blogging policy works for every business. For example, some companies will encourage employees to blog, while restricting posting information about financial topics, while other companies won't want employees to blog externally about work-related topics whatsoever. Regardless of the details, you do need to communicate with your employees regarding the boundaries of what is acceptable in blogging at and for your company. Some companies, such as IBM, ask their employees to write their own blogging policies, which the company then reviews and approves, if appropriate.

This appendix looks specifically at the blogging policy of the Thomas Nelson publishing company.

Thomas Nelson's policy takes the bold step of not only allowing employees to blog, but encouraging them to do so, and the company provides a central location where employees can go to read employee blog posts so that non-bloggers can stay up to date without the need for a feed reader. This community-centric blogging policy is a great example providing advice (start with a service, write as yourself, and be nice) and boundaries (what you say is your own responsibility, keep secrets, and respect copyrights). Overall, it is one of the best blogging policies I've ever seen—it's simple, it's clear, and it *communicates.*

THOMAS NELSON BLOGGING GUIDELINES

At Thomas Nelson, we want to encourage you to blog about our company, our products, and your work. Our goal is three-fold:

- To raise the visibility of our company,
- To make a contribution to our industry, and
- To give the public a look at what goes on within a real live publishing company.

Therefore, we have established a "blog aggregator page" that is linked to the ThomasNelson.com Web site. "House Work," the name of this page, contains links to employee blogs, along with the first few sentences from the most recent entry. The page is automatically updated whenever a blogger creates a new post. This way readers can quickly scan new entries, click on those that interest them, and then read the entry on the blogger's site. This makes it convenient for people who are interested in reading employee blogs. It also helps publicize individual blogs and generates traffic for everyone.

In order to give some direction to employees who wish to blog, we have established a "Blog Oversight Committee" or "BOC." This is a group of fellow-employee bloggers who are committed to promoting blogging within our company and making sure that the Company's interests are served.

If you would like to have us link to your blog, you must submit it to the BOC. Before doing so, you should design your blog and write at least one entry. Once you have done this, send an e-mail to Gave Wicks with a link to your blog. The BOC will then review your blog and notify you whether or not it meets the criteria.

In order to participate in this program, you must abide by the following guidelines. (Please keep in mind that review by the BOC and participation in this program does not absolve you of responsibility for everything you post.)

1. Start with a blogging service. We do not host employee blogs. We think it adds more credibility if the Company does not officially sponsor them. Therefore, please use one of the many third-party blog hosting sites on the Internet. Some of these are free, such as Blogger.com, LiveJournal.com, Blog-City.com, Xanga.com, and MSN Spaces. Others charge a nominal fee. Examples include TypePad.com, SquareSpace.com, BlogIdentity.com, and Bubbler.com. If you use one of the latter, any expense is your responsibility.

2. Write as yourself. In other words, please use your real name. We don't want people writing anonymously or under a pseudonym. Your name should be prominently displayed on your blog's title or subtitle. This will add credibility with your readers and promote accountability within our company.

3. Own your content. Employee blog sites are not Company communications. Therefore, your blog entries legally belong to you. They represent your thoughts and opinions. We think it is important that you remind your readers of this fact by including the following disclaimer on your site: "The posts on this blog are provided 'as is' with no warranties and confer no rights. The opinions expressed on this site

are my own and do not necessarily represent those of my employer." You assume full responsibility and liability for all actions arising from your posts. We also encourage you to put a copyright notice on your site in your name (e.g., "© 2005, John Smith").

4. Write relevant. Write often. Whether you know it or not, you are an expert. You have a unique perspective on our company based on your talents, skills, and current responsibilities. People want to hear about that perspective. Also, in order to develop a consistent readership, you should try to write on a regular basis. For some, this will be daily; for others, it may be weekly. The important thing is consistent posting. New content is what keeps readers coming back. You may also write on company time, provided it doesn't become excessive and doesn't interfere with your job assignments and responsibilities.

5. Advertise—if you wish. While there is no requirement to run ads on your blog, you are free to do this if you wish. Some of the free blog services run ads as a way to offset their costs. If you use such a service, you won't have a choice. On the other hand, if you pay for your service, you can avoid advertising altogether or participate in a service like Google's AdSense or Amazon's Associate Program. These types of programs will pay you based on "page views," "click-throughs," or purchases made on participating Web sites. You might want to ask the BOC or fellow bloggers for suggestions. The only thing we ask is that, to the extent you have control, you run ads or recommend products that are congruent with our core values as a Company.

6. Be nice. Avoid attacking other individuals or companies. This includes fellow employees, authors, customers, vendors, competitors, or shareholders. You are welcome to disagree

with the Company's leaders, provided your tone is respectful. If in doubt, we suggest that you "sleep on it" and then submit your entry to the BOC before posting it on your blog.

7. Keep secrets. Do not disclose sensitive, proprietary, confidential, or financial information about the Company, other than what is publicly available in our SEC filings and corporate press releases. This includes revenues, profits, forecasts, and other financial information related to specific authors, brands, products, product lines, customers, operating units, etc. Again, if in doubt, check with the BOC before posting this type of information.

8. Respect copyrights. For your protection, do not post any material that is copyrighted unless (a) you are the copyright owner, (b) you have written permission of the copyright owner to post the copyrighted material on your blog, or (c) you are sure that the use of any copyrighted material is permitted by the legal doctrine of "fair use." (Please note: this is your responsibility. The Company cannot provide you with legal advice regarding this.)

9. Obey the law. This goes without saying, but by way of reminder, do not post any material that is obscene, defamatory, profane, libelous, threatening, harassing, abusive, hateful, embarrassing to another person or entity, or violates the privacy rights of another. Also, do not post material that contains viruses, Trojan horses, worms, or any other computer code that is intended to damage, interfere with, or surreptitiously intercept or expropriate any system, data, or information.

10. Remember the Handbook. As a condition of your employment, you agreed to abide by the rules of the Thomas Nelson Company Handbook. This also applies to your blogging activities. We suggest you take time to review the section entitled, "Employee Responsibilities" (pp. 36–39).

If you do not abide by the above guidelines, we reserve the right to stop linking to your blog.

Note: More examples of blogging policies can be viewed at www .blogmarketingbook.com

GLOSSARY

The following is a glossary of commonly used blogging terms and their meanings.

biz blogs Also known as *business blogs*, these blogs are written by business people about business topics and day-to-day operations to impart wisdom from within a company, offer education, and provide industry information.

blog/weblog *Blog* is a contraction of *weblog*, and is a series of individual comments, called *posts*, that generally appear in reverse chronological order. A blog is a means of communication and, as such, most often includes comments available for each post, though they are not required. See *internal blog; post*.

Web analyst Steven Streight defines a blog in a more abstract sense:[1]

> A communications, connectivity, and interactivity platform that enables users with no HTML skills to quickly and easily publish web content for a global audience, thus the democratization of web content publishing, the revolutionary rise of universal access to internet content. In short, a blog is

like a "thin website"—all of the power of a full website, without having to know all of the technical details.

blogger   A person who owns or writes in a weblog.

blogosphere   Blogging extends beyond individual blogs to a larger community of people who blog and their blog sites, all called the blogosphere. Blogs are a publishing mechanism. What separates blogs from other media is the communicative and connective nature of the larger blog community—that is, the blogosphere.

blogroll   A list of links that generally appears along the side of a blog page that can be clicked to link to other blogs that the author(s) respect and/or like. Also, a blog link management system such as www.blogrolling.com. See also *sidebar*.

comment   Comments are submitted by users on individual blog posts, thus extending the author's thought through the community of readers. Comments usually appear at the bottom of a post, with the oldest comments listed first so that readers can read the post and then read the ensuing discussion in chronological order.

comment spam   *Spam* is defined as unsolicited e-mail of a commercial nature; comment spam is unwanted comments that attempt to drive users to another site. Comment spam is typified by being completely off-topic and is often created by a program that automatically sends comments to thousands of blogs with hundreds of comments each. Numerous anti-comment spam systems are in place, most of which rely on specific keywords that the spam originators use, which have to do with gambling, various drugs, and a variety of illicit activities.

commenter An individual who leaves a comment on a blog.

feed The XML-based system that allows a reader to be updated automatically when a new post is created on a blog, typically by using some kind of feed reader application. See *feed reader.*

feed reader As you can access e-mail via web-based e-mail and via your desktop e-mail client, feeds can be read either via a web-based feed reader or a desktop feed reader. Both types of feed readers work equally well. Some feed readers can be added to other programs such as Microsoft Outlook, Internet Explorer, Mozilla FireFox, and a variety of other popular applications.

HTML Hypertext Markup Language, the language in which web pages are created. HTML allows for formatting changes, such as making text bold or italicized, changing font styles, and so on. An advantage of blogs is that they generally do not require that the blogger know HTML to create pages, although many blog tools allow the use of HTML for people who want more control over their post's appearance.

internal blog While external business blogs are often created for communication or marketing purposes, internal blogs are generally dedicated to increasing the effectiveness of communication within a company and among individuals, teams, and departments. Also known as *K-logs* (Knowledge logs), typical uses include knowledge management, project management, and project awareness.

permalink Because of the number of individual posts most blogs create, it would be impractical to include all of them on one page. As a result, archives exist for nearly all blogs. To make it practical to link to individual blog posts, permalinks were created. A permalink is a link to a specific posting that remains valid even after the post is no longer on the blog's front page. A permalink gives the blogger a way to help the reader easily determine what the blogger is talking about.

ping   Pinging allows you to notify other sites that your blog has been updated. Ping-O-Matic (www.pingomatic.com) is a useful service that broadcasts the news that your site has been updated to all of the most important blog updating services, including Technorati.

podcast   Just as blogging allows individuals to publish for themselves and their audience, podcasting allows individuals to create online broadcasts for themselves and their audience. Podcasting is the technique of creating a show as an MP3 file, and then updating a feed with the location of the show. A special feed reader then automatically downloads the show to a music device. Podcasts are provided by amateurs around the world and can be fed directly to your portable music player. The beauty of podcasting is in the convenience: no more missing an important show because you aren't near a radio. Listeners are in control of when they listen to the program.

post   A single entry of content of any length, which could be graphics and text on a blog.

referrer   As in real life, where you can be referred to a doctor, a *referrer* is the person who sent you to a specific blog. It can be important to know who is sending you traffic so that you are aware of who is talking about you. Services such as Technorati, PubSub, and BlogPulse can also track this information for you.

RSS, RDF, Atom   RSS (Really Simple Syndication), RDF (Resource Description Framework), and Atom are standards that make up the overall scheme of feeds. While the differences between these are important for software developers, for people who use feed readers, the differences are negligible. Atom is the newest and leading format, with RSS and RDF being the original formats in which feeds were created. Dave Winer, one of the earliest bloggers, is generally credited with popularizing, if not creating, RSS as well as feed systems for podcasting.

sidebar   One or more columns along either, or both, sides of a blog. These columns may contain the blogroll, a list of links, contact information, lists of recently updated posts, books the blogger is reading, and other information pertinent to the blogger or the topic of the blog.

trackback/pingback   A trackback or pingback is the technique of sending a ping to another site to let a blogger know that you are linking to his or her site. Trackbacks are one of the mechanisms for the virtual links that form between blogs, as they allow conversations to be seamlessly distributed between blogs. If Johnny posts information on his blog, and Timmy writes about it, Timmy can trackback to Johnny's blog so that both Johnny and Johnny's readers know that Timmy has posted on the subject as well.

URL/URI   Uniform Resource Locator/Uniform Resource Identifier. The specific web address of a web page, which can include both the domain name (such as http://blogmarketingbook .com) or a specific file or web page on a website (such as http:// blogmarketingbook.com/category/blogging-for-your-business/).

wiki A collaborative online environment that allows readers to add content to a subject. Typical wiki uses include encyclopedias, product documentation, and help systems. While not directly related to blogs, the concept of social interaction is strong in wikis, as well. Companies who embrace blogs often eventually begin using wikis for internal projects.

XML Extensible Markup Language. A web language used for a variety of tasks. The various feed standards (RSS, RDF, and Atom) are all XML-based standards that feed readers understand and translate into a human-readable format.

ENDNOTES

Chapter 1

1 From Duncan Riley, *The Blog Herald*: "Blog Count for July: 70 Million Blogs," July 19, 2005, www.blogherald .com/2005/07/19/blog-count-for-july-70-million-blogs/.

2 See "Blogs Will Change Your Business," by Stephen Baker and Heather Green, at www.businessweek.com/magazine/content/ 05_18/b3931001_mz001.htm.

3 Mark Cuban's response to the question "Why are you blogging?" from the I Want Media website, September 6, 2004, www.iwantmedia.com/onequestion.html.

Chapter 4

1 Neville Hobson, "The GM FastLane Blog," September 2, 2005, www.tle.us.com/weblogs/nevon2wp/new-media-focus/the-gm-fastlane-blog/.

Chapter 10

1 Nick Wreden, "7 Habits of Highly Effective PR, FusionBrand," February 24, 2005, http://fusionbrand.blogs.com/fusionbrand/2005/02/nbsp_nbspnbsp_n.html.

Glossary

1 Steven Streight quote taken from a *Wall Street Journal* article and included in "Still in the Dark About Blogs," Vaspers the Grate website, May 26, 2005, http://vaspersthegrate.blogspot.com/2005/05/wall-street-journal-still-in-dark.html.

INDEX

ABOUT THE AUTHOR

Jeremy Wright is an internationally recognized authority on blogging who focuses on how businesses can best use blogs to broaden their financial and customer horizons. Wright has worked with companies ranging from Microsoft and eBay to *Business Week* and CanWest Global, as well as dozens of small businesses, to determine how blogs can best work for them. He has also written hundreds of articles on this topic for dozens of publications, and he has spoken at numerous blogging conferences. His blog, Ensight .org, is read by more than 250,000 people every month.

About the Technical Editor

Yvonne DiVita is a successful writer and blogger who has been widely quoted and interviewed regarding business blogging. She has been blogging for business since 2003 and uses her own blog as a critical marketing tool. Yvonne runs a blog on writing and publishing at http://windsormedia.blogs.com/aha and maintains a blog to support her focus on marketing to women online at http://windsormedia.blogs.com/lipsticking.